T0375435

Lecture Notes in Computer Science 15470

Founding Editors

Gerhard Goos
Juris Hartmanis

The series Lecture Notes in Computer Science (LNCS), including its subseries Lecture Notes in Artificial Intelligence (LNAI) and Lecture Notes in Bioinformatics (LNBI), has established itself as a medium for the publication of new developments in computer science and information technology research, teaching, and education.

LNCS enjoys close cooperation with the computer science R & D community, the series counts many renowned academics among its volume editors and paper authors, and collaborates with prestigious societies. Its mission is to serve this international community by providing an invaluable service, mainly focused on the publication of conference and workshop proceedings and postproceedings. LNCS commenced publication in 1973.

Yan Jia · Zhaoquan Gu · Aiping Li · Binxing Fang
Editors

MDATA Cognitive Model: Theory and Applications

 Springer

Editors
Yan Jia
National University of Defense Technology
Changsha, China

Aiping Li
National University of Defense Technology
Changsha, China

Zhaoquan Gu
Harbin Institute of Technology
Shenzhen, China

Binxing Fang
Guangzhou University
Guangzhou, China

ISSN 0302-9743   ISSN 1611-3349 (electronic)
Lecture Notes in Computer Science
ISBN 978-981-96-3527-6   ISBN 978-981-96-3528-3 (eBook)
https://doi.org/10.1007/978-981-96-3528-3

This Springer imprint is published by the registered company Springer Nature Singapore Pte Ltd.
The registered company address is: 152 Beach Road, #21-01/04 Gateway East, Singapore 189721, Singapore

If disposing of this product, please recycle the paper.

Foreword

"The MDATA cognitive model provides a comprehensive and systematic knowledge framework that is invaluable in navigating the complexities of the cybersecurity landscape by breaking through the challenges of representing, managing, acquiring, and applying spatiotemporal knowledge.

By leveraging advanced knowledge representation methods, the MDATA model integrates multi-source, heterogeneous data to provide a unified view of cybersecurity events, capturing the intricate relationships and temporal dynamics that traditional methods often overlook. Its automated knowledge acquisition methods extract key entities, relationships, and spatial-temporal attributes from unstructured data, continuously enriching cybersecurity knowledge and enabling adaptive responses to evolving cyber threats.

The model's reasoning capabilities are particularly transformative, enabling it to deduce potential attack strategies by analyzing known cyber events in the cyber range. This predictive analysis, combined with its ability to correlate cross-domain attacks, empowers organizations to identify and mitigate sophisticated threats with greater accuracy. By addressing issues such as false positives and false negatives, the MDATA model significantly improves the precision of detecting cyber security threats. Additionally, its distributed fog-computing architecture further enhances its capabilities by enabling collaborative, real-time computation across large-scale datasets. This architecture ensures low-latency processing and scalability, making the model suitable for organizations of all sizes.

In essence, the MDATA cognitive model redefines the standards for understanding cybersecurity knowledge by providing a robust, adaptive, and efficient framework for cyber threat detection and analysis. Its ability to manage spatiotemporal knowledge comprehensively not only enhances real-time assessment and response but also establishes a new paradigm for proactive and intelligent cybersecurity management."

Philip S. Yu (University of Illinois Chicago, IL, USA)

"Cybersecurity events detection and analysis have been recognized as a global challenge. The MDATA model, the first cognitive model in the cyberspace security field, emerges as a pioneering solution to this complicated problem, offering an innovative approach that streamlines the process of cybersecurity event detection and analysis.

The MDATA model's core innovation lies in its ability to transform raw cybersecurity data into structured and actionable intelligence. Through the knowledge representation methods, the model encodes entities, relationships, and spatio-temporal attributes in a way that captures the intricate interplay of cybersecurity events. These structured representations simplify cybersecurity events analysis, making it possible to detect hidden patterns, anomalies, and evolving attack strategies with high efficiency.

To achieve high-performance capabilities, the MDATA model integrates machine learning, graph computing, and big data analytics, enabling it to process information across multiple dimensions simultaneously. For example, temporal evolutions of cybersecurity threats, multi-step cyber attacks, and cyber attack organizations can be efficiently analyzed by associating the multiple dimensions of data. The MDATA model also has strong adaptability as it evolves continuously based on newly discovered cybersecurity knowledge and reasoning results. This self-learning capability enables the model to adapt to new attack methods and stay ahead in a constantly changing cyber threat environment.

As cybersecurity events continue to grow and cyberspace is becoming increasing complex, the MDATA model provides a new paradigm for studying cyberspace security. The combination of cognitive intelligence, real-time processing, and scalable architecture makes the model the cornerstone for understanding and analyzing modern cybersecurity."

Ioannis Manolopoulos (Member of Academia Europaea; Aristotle University of Thessaloniki, Greece)

"Understanding and utilizing cybersecurity knowledge is an important foundation for analyzing cyberspace attacks. The MDATA model breaks through the representation problem of spatiotemporal knowledge on the basis of knowledge graphs, supports comprehensive acquisition and management of cybersecurity knowledge, and supports its online evolution in many applications.

Building on traditional representation methods of knowledge graphs, the model introduces efficient ways to represent temporal information and spatial information of cybersecurity events, where they play a vital role in analyzing complicated cyber attacks. This intuitive representation enables not only better knowledge reasoning and knowledge extension, but also seamless integration of spatiotemporal data into computable intelligence. In addition, it has a strong capability to manage large-scale and dynamic data such as cybersecurity events by introducing spatiotemporal indexing to optimize the organization, retrieval, and analysis of cybersecurity knowledge. Moreover, it integrates the associations among the semantics, temporal, and spatial dimensions, which significantly enhances the computational efficiency and the depth of knowledge representation. Hence, it enables real-time cyber attack detection and assessment, especially for complicated multi-step cyber attacks.

Beyond its technical advancements, the MDATA model establishes a strong theoretical foundation for next-generation cybersecurity systems. Its innovations in spatiotemporal knowledge representation and management mark a significant leap forward, paving the way for more intelligent, adaptive, and efficient cybersecurity defenses in the future."

David Bassir
ENS- University of Paris-Saclay, France

Preface

Cyberspace security is an important part of national security strategy. Under the traction of national cyberspace security's major demands, the editorial team has long been engaged in theoretical and technological research and engineering system construction in the field of cyberspace security, and has developed the situational awareness system "YHSAS", the public opinion analyzing system "Eagle Strike YHSAS", "Eagle Strike" and "Eagle Eye" public opinion analysis systems, "Sky Arrow" open-source intelligence analysis system, and Pengcheng Cyber Range, etc., which have been successfully applied in the state departments of net information, public security and safety, and have greatly enhanced China's cybersecurity protection capability. The development of the above important engineering systems requires theoretical and technological research to solve the problem of accurately investigating and judging cyberspace security incidents, i.e., comprehensively, accurately, and in real-time detecting or discovering cyberspace security incidents, as well as comprehensively analyzing their means, paths, trends, and hazard assessments.

A cyberspace security incident is a security event that occurs in cyberspace, including attacks in cyber systems at the system level, public opinion events, open-source intelligence events, etc. at the content level, and application-specific security such as cyber fraud and cyber theft at the application level. Cyberspace security events have three main characteristics: giant scale, evolution, and correlation. Among them, giant scale refers to the large number and scale of cyberspace security events and the huge scale of cyberspace data involved; evolution refers to the continuous evolution of cyberspace security events with the development of new technologies; and correlation refers to the complex correlation behaviors of cyberspace security events in multiple dimensions, such as time and space. There are three aspects of comprehensive, accurate, and real-time demand for research and judgment of cyberspace security events, in which comprehensive refers to the need to cover all known cyber-attacks, all public opinion events and open-source intelligence, etc., and not to omit to check any security event; accurate refers to the discovery of security events that really exist and are not false alarms and misreporting; real-time refers to the ability to quickly detect and dispose of security events, and even reach the second level in response to cyber-attacks and other security events, so as to realize the security events against cyber attacks and other security events. Due to the three major characteristics of cyberspace security events, namely, huge scale, evolution, and correlation, the comprehensive, accurate, and real-time investigation and judgment of security events is a correlation computation problem with exponential growth in computational complexity, and a worldwide problem that cannot be computed in real time.

Drawing on the process and experience of human cognition of security events, the editorial team proposes the MDATA cognitive model, which simulates the three major steps of human cognition, namely knowledge acquisition, knowledge representation, and knowledge utilization. From the dimensions of human cognitive methods in time, space, and their interconnections, and based on the pre-acquisition and effective management of cybersecurity knowledge, it reduces the computational complexity of the research and judgment of cybersecurity events to a subgraph based on the large graph. computation, thus solving the comprehensive and accurate, the challenge of studying cybersecurity incidents in real time.

The MDATA cognitive model consists of three sub-models: knowledge representation and management refers to the effective representation and management of cybersecurity knowledge; knowledge acquisition refers to the automatic acquisition of cybersecurity knowledge for multimodal network big data; and knowledge utilization refers to the research and judgment of security events based on the cybersecurity knowledge, etc. The working mechanism of the MDATA cognitive model is that the three sub-models constantly work together with feedback and modification; it is an activated model and is the first cognitive model in the field of cybersecurity. Based on the MDATA cognitive model, it can cope with the three characteristics of cyberspace security: huge scale, evolution, and correlation, and can support the demand for comprehensive, accurate, and real-time research and judgment of cybersecurity events. In order to let readers understand how the MDATA cognitive model can support the research and judgment of cyber security events, this book will introduce the theoretical system of the MDATA cognitive model in the first four chapters, and then describe the application of the MDATA cognitive model in the fields of cyber attack detection, public opinion analysis, and open-source intelligence analysis in the last four chapters.

Chapter 1 Overview of MDATA Cognitive Modeling is authored by Jia Yan, Gu Zhaoquan, and Fang Binxing. The chapter focuses on the background and needs of cyberspace security event research and judgment, analyzes the three characteristics of cyberspace security events: giant scale, evolution, and correlation, and the three major needs of research and judgment of security events: comprehensive, accurate, and real-time. At the same time, it analyzes the human cognitive processing of events from the perspective of several existing cognitive models, and introduces the components and working mechanism of the MDATA multidimensional associative cognitive model.

Chapter 2 MDATA Knowledge Representation and Management is authored by Jia Yan, Song Xiangyu, and Li Jianxin. The chapter focuses on the MDATA Knowledge Representation and Management sub-model, summarizes the needs of knowledge representation and management in cybersecurity event research and judgment based on the analysis of common knowledge representation and management methods, and then introduces in detail a variety of knowledge representation and knowledge management methods suitable for the field of cyberspace security.

Chapter 3 MDATA Knowledge Acquisition is authored by Jia Yan and Li Aiping. The chapter focuses on the MDATA knowledge acquisition sub-model, and, based on the introduction of traditional knowledge extraction and deduction methods, analyzes the difficulties and challenges faced by the application of traditional knowledge extraction and deduction methods in the field of cybersecurity, and then describes in detail the automatic knowledge extraction and knowledge deduction methods oriented to the cognitive model of MDATA.

Chapter 4 MDATA Knowledge Utilization is authored by Jia Yan and Yang Jianye. The chapter focuses on the MDATA knowledge utilization sub-model, introduces how to map MDATA knowledge utilization to sub-graph computation based on the big graph, analyzes the difficulties and challenges of knowledge utilization in cyber security incident investigation and judgment based on the introduction of existing graph computation methods such as sub-graph matching and reachable path computation, and then introduces in detail a variety of knowledge utilization methods oriented to the MDATA model.

Chapter 5 Application of MDATA Cognitive Modeling in Cyber Attack Research and Judgment is authored by Gu Zhaoquan and Jia Yan. This chapter focuses on how to use the MDATA cognitive model for cyber attack investigation and judgment. On the basis of analyzing the existing technologies for detecting and judging cyberattacks, we summarize the difficulties and challenges faced by cyberattack research and judgment, and then introduce a new model based on the MDATA cognitive modeling of cyberattack research and judgment techniques and effects, and finally, we introduce the system architecture, functions, and typical applications of the developed YHSAS system.

Chapter 6 MDATA Cognitive Modeling for Open-Source Intelligence Analysis is authored by Bin Zhou, Binxing Fang, and Ye Wang. The chapter focuses on how to use MDATA cognitive modeling for open-source intelligence analysis. On the basis of analyzing the existing open-source intelligence analysis technology, it summarizes the difficulties and challenges faced by current open-source intelligence analysis by taking scientific and technological intelligence as an example, then introduces the open-source intelligence analysis technology based on the MDATA cognitive model and its effect, and finally introduces the system architecture, functions, and typical applications of the developed "Sky Arrow" open-source intelligence analysis system.

Chapter 7 MDATA Cognitive Modeling in Public Opinion Analysis is authored by Guandong Xu and Binxing Fang. The chapter focuses on how to use MDATA cognitive modeling for public opinion analysis. Based on the background of public opinion analysis and related technologies, the chapter summarizes the difficulties and challenges of public opinion analysis, then introduces the technology and effect of subject, object, and network structure association analysis based on the MDATA cognitive model, and finally introduces the system architecture, functions, and typical applications of the developed "Eagle Strike" public opinion big data monitoring system.

Chapter 8 Application of MDATA Cognitive Modeling in Network Security Measurement is authored by Weihong Han and Yan Jia. The chapter focuses on how to apply MDATA cognitive modeling to the security assessment of network systems throughout their life cycle. Based on the introduction of existing network security assessment policies and methods, it summarizes the difficulties and challenges faced by network security assessment at present, then introduces the technology and effect of full-life-cycle security assessment of information systems based on the MDATA cognitive model, and finally describes the method and effect of the assessment through a real case based on Pengcheng network range.

The book was co-authored by Jia Yan, Gu Zhaoquan, Li Aiping, and Fang Binxing. Teachers and students from the teams of Pengcheng Laboratory, Harbin Institute of Technology (Shenzhen), Guangzhou University, and National University of Defense Technology also participated in collecting and organizing materials during the writing of this book, including Jianxin Li, Xiangyu Song, Jiawei Zhang, Wenying Feng, Xiao

Jing, Cuiyun Gao, Wen Xia, Shiyi Li, Le Wang, Shudong Li, and Denghui Zhang, for which we would like to express our sincere thanks. In addition, we would like to thank the editors Zou Wenbo and Zhang Xiaofen of the People's Posts and Telecommunications Publishing House, who have done a lot of hard work for the publication of this book.

The MDATA cognitive model has been applied in many directions of cyberspace security, such as cyber attack research and judgment, open-source intelligence analysis, and cyber public opinion analysis, etc. However, the field of cyberspace security is complex and involves many more specific applications and scenarios, which this book has not been able to cover one by one. Meanwhile, different scholars still have their own opinions and systems on how to analyze cybersecurity events. Therefore, it is difficult for this book to cover the research ideas of all academic schools, and this book only throws out bricks to attract jade, hoping to give scholars engaged in cyberspace security research a new way of thinking. I hope the readers will understand the omissions.

Jia Yan
Gu Zhaoquan
Li Aiping
Fang Binxing

Contents

Overview of Cognitive Models

Yan Jia[1]($\boxtimes$), Zhaoquan Gu[2,3], and Binxing Fang[3,4]

[1] National University of Defense Technology, Changsha 410073, China
jiayanjy@vip.sina.com
[2] Harbin Institute of Technology (Shenzhen), Shenzhen 518055, China
guzhaoquan@hit.edu.cn
[3] Pengcheng Laboratory, Shenzhen 518066, China
fangbx@cae.cn
[4] Guangzhou University, Guangzhou 510066, China

Cybersecurity is a crucial component of national security strategy, receiving significant attention from countries worldwide. Cyberspace data is a typical example of big data, characterized by its diverse sources, various types, and large volume. Security incidents in cyberspace exhibit three main characteristics: large scale, evolvability, and correlativity. Addressing these characteristics to comprehensively, accurately, and in real-time assess cybersecurity incidents is a global challenge. Drawing on the human cognitive process for understanding cybersecurity incidents and based on a comprehensive analysis of existing cognitive models, this chapter introduces a new cognitive model in the cybersecurity field—the MDATA cognitive model. Additionally, it details the composition and operational principles of the MDATA cognitive model.

The structure of this chapter is as follows. Section 1 introduces the background of cybersecurity, analyzing the needs and challenges in assessing cybersecurity incidents through their characteristics. Section 2 examines the human cognitive process of cybersecurity incidents from the perspective of cognitive models, introducing several classic cognitive models and evaluating their strengths and weaknesses. Section 3 presents the MDATA cognitive model, the first model tailored for the cybersecurity field, with a focus on its components and operational principles. Section 4 provides a summary of the chapter's content.

1 Background of Cybersecurity

With the rapid development of information technologies such as the Internet, the Internet of Things (IoT), and mobile Internet, cyberspace has become an integral part of political, economic, cultural, social, and military domains. The data associated with cyberspace exhibits typical big data characteristics: in terms of scale, the data is vast, grows rapidly, and is diverse in type and source. In terms of content, the value and authenticity of the data need significant improvement. These characteristics pose greater challenges to cybersecurity. When assessing cybersecurity incidents, it is necessary to consider various factors such as the nature, origin, and impact of the events. Analyzing cyberspace data helps to determine the incident's occurrence time, attack methods, targets, and attackers' identities, which is crucial for implementing effective countermeasures.

© The Author(s), under exclusive license to Springer Nature Singapore Pte Ltd. 2025
Y. Jia et al. (Eds.): MDATA Cognitive Model: Theory and Applications, LNCS 15470, pp. 1–23, 2025.
https://doi.org/10.1007/978-981-96-3528-3_1

1.1 Cybersecurity Incidents

Cyberspace is an artificial "activity" space where humans interact through "cyber roles" using "information and communication technology systems" to exchange "broad signals" [1]. "Cyber roles" refer to the entities that generate and transmit signals, while "information and communication technology systems" encompass the Internet, the Internet of Things (IoT), and various networked information devices. As information technology advances, cyberspace has become a unique and highly valuable medium for communication, interaction, information dissemination, and processing.

Cybersecurity incidents are defined as security events occurring within cyberspace, encompassing events at the system layer, content layer, and application layer. At the system layer, these incidents involve attacks on network systems, such as penetration attacks targeting network infrastructures. At the content layer, incidents include online public opinion events and open-source intelligence events. At the application layer, incidents involve specific applications, such as online fraud and data theft. These security incidents can compromise the integrity, availability, and confidentiality of cyberspace, causing economic losses, social instability, and pervasive impacts.

For instance, in ransomware incidents, attackers exploit system vulnerabilities like the "EternalBlue" to infect computers and servers, encrypt and access user data to extort Bitcoin ransoms from victims, leading to significant economic losses. The 2022 Cyber Threat Report [2] by SonicWall indicates that there were 236.1 million ransomware attacks in the first half of 2022 alone, exemplifying a significant threat to cybersecurity.

On March 17, 2018, Facebook, a leading social media company, faced a significant data breach incident when personal information of 50 million users was leaked to Cambridge Analytica. This incident led to a 7% drop in Facebook's stock price, reducing its market value by $37 billion. The company's CEO, Mark Zuckerberg, exacerbated the situation by selling stock and avoiding addressing the issue publicly, further eroding trust in Facebook's data protection capabilities. Consequently, U.S. and EU authorities demanded an investigation and new data-sharing policies from Facebook, gradually mitigating the incident. This case illustrates how online public opinion, a typical example of content layer security incidents, can arise from complex factors and requires addressing the root causes to be effectively managed.

Open-source intelligence (OSINT) is a prominent example of cybersecurity content, illustrated by Greenspan's military materials prediction during the 1950 Korean War. To forecast the U.S. military's need for metal raw materials during war preparations, Greenspan analyzed information on the U.S. Air Force's size and equipment from military news releases and government announcements. He estimated the demand for different fighter jet models and calculated the U.S. government's total requirement for raw materials. Ultimately, his predictions closely matched the figures in the U.S. government's classified documents at the time. Investors, relying on Greenspan's insights, bought metal materials early and made significant profits. This case highlights how Greenspan used open-source military reports and integrated other information sources to infer the scale of military equipment and predict metal demands, benefiting investors.

The above cases demonstrate the substantial impact of cybersecurity incidents, leading to economic losses, disrupting social stability, and even causing serious consequences. By accurately assessing these incidents, we can quickly detect them and effectively prevent further malicious attacks on cyberspace.

1.2 Three Main Characteristics of Cybersecurity Incidents

Cybersecurity incidents are characterized by three main features: large scale, evolvability, and correlativity.

"Large scale" refers to the vast number of incidents and the extensive scope of data involved in cybersecurity. For example, online public opinion events illustrate this feature well. According to the "Digital 2023: Global Overview Report" [3] by Datareportal, Meltwater, and We Are Social, there are 4.76 billion social media users globally, amounting to 60% of the world's population. The International Data Corporation (IDC) reports [4] that global data generation will grow from 33 ZB in 2018 to 175 ZB by 2025, equating to approximately 491 EB per day. Public opinion events occur constantly, with platforms like the Civiw Intelligence System processing over a billion real-time public opinion data entries daily [5], covering news media, social media, and major portal websites. This demonstrates the vast scale of public opinion events. Similarly, large scale in cyberattacks refers to billions of attacks, hundreds of thousands of vulnerabilities, and millions of resources, along with their complex combinations. According to the "China Internet Network Security Monitoring Data Analysis Report", the National Internet Emergency Response Center captured approximately 23.07 million malicious program samples in the first half of 2021, with an average daily spread of 5.82 million. By the end of 2022, the National Vulnerability Database reported a total of 199,465 vulnerabilities. Furthermore, as of 2023, the Common Platform Enumeration (CPE) had cataloged over a million information technology resources [6]. The complex interplay of diverse attacks, assets, and vulnerabilities in cyberspace requires addressing its large-scale nature for accurate assessment.

"Evolvability" signifies that cybersecurity incidents continually evolve with technological advancements. Cybersecurity is inherently linked to the development of information technology. As the Internet, big data, and artificial intelligence (AI) evolve, cybersecurity techniques also progress rapidly. For instance, in 2007, terminal device cracking techniques emerged in the IoT field, soon exploited for eavesdropping attacks. In 2014, adversarial examples techniques appeared in AI, subsequently used for deepfake attacks that trick AI models. With attack methods growing more diverse and unpredictable, cybersecurity incidents are increasing in both number and complexity, making them harder to assess.

"Correlativity" in cybersecurity refers to the complex interconnections among various dimensions of cybersecurity incidents. Advanced Persistent Threat (APT) attacks, for example, exhibit strong correlations in attack methods, vulnerabilities, resources, and time and space. In the typical APT OceanLotus attack, attackers first exploit office software vulnerabilities to conduct spear-phishing attacks and install Trojan viruses on computers. The virus then infects database servers through routers, ultimately stealing and exfiltrating sensitive files. These steps are interconnected by temporal sequences, IP addresses, and other factors. Moreover, there are correlations between the systems and vulnerabilities targeted by attackers, as well as among different servers. Given the intricate nature of these connections, relying on single-dimensional data makes accurate assessment of cybersecurity incidents difficult.

1.3 Requirements and Challenges in Evaluating Cybersecurity Incidents

The three main characteristics of cybersecurity incidents—large scale, evolvability, and correlativity—pose significant challenges for accurate assessment, primarily in terms of comprehensiveness, accuracy, and real-time analysis.

Comprehensiveness ensures that the assessment of cybersecurity incidents covers all known cyberattack behaviors, all relevant online public opinion events, and open-source intelligence, without missing any attacks or sensitive events. The diversity, severity, and high correlation of cyberattacks necessitate a comprehensive approach to avoid omissions and ensure complete detection of attacks on network systems.

Accuracy means that identified cybersecurity incidents are real and not fabricated. For cyberattack assessments, accuracy requires that detected attacks are not false positives but actual cyberattacks. Accurate assessment is crucial for analyzing the current security status of network systems. Many security devices generate alerts in a monotonous form, leading to a high volume of false positives, complicating the accurate detection of attacks. For online public opinion or open-source intelligence events, particularly high-profile and sensitive topics, inaccurate assessments can lead to mishandling and damage to an organization's[1] reputation. The large volume and rapid updating of cyberspace data present significant challenges for accurately identifying these events.

Real-time detection requires the ability to quickly identify and promptly address cybersecurity incidents. For cyberattacks, this means rapidly detecting and issuing warnings, and sometimes even repairing network systems to prevent further attacks. For online public opinion events, it is essential to issue warnings before the events escalate, preventing their spread and minimizing their impact.

Accurate assessment of cybersecurity incidents entails comprehensive, accurate, and real-time detection and analysis of the methods, paths, trends, and impacts of these incidents. For instance, assessing cyberattacks involves not only detecting the attacks but also analyzing related attack techniques and tactics, development trends, and potential impacts. To provide timely warnings and rapid responses to cybersecurity incidents, minimizing their impact on organizations, it is essential that the assessment of such incidents meets the requirements of comprehensiveness, accuracy, and real-time capability.

The large scale, evolvability, and correlativity of cybersecurity incidents make achieving comprehensive, accurate, and real-time detection highly challenging. The process of assessing cybersecurity incidents can be viewed as a cognitive process. Therefore, we draw on the human cognitive process for understanding cybersecurity incidents, using cognitive modeling to achieve accurate assessment of these incidents.

---

[1] In this book, "organization" refers to government agencies, corporations, and other institutions.

2 The Concept and Evolution of Cognitive Models

2.1 The Concept of Cognitive Model

American psychologist George Miller [7] proposed that cognition refers to the process of individual acquisition, processing, organization, storage and use of information, including perception, attention, memory, thinking, language, etc. George Lakoff [8], an American cognitive scientist, proposed that cognition refers to the process of individuals' perception, understanding and expression of the outside world, including perception, emotion, sense, intention, attention, memory, reasoning, judgment, decision-making and other aspects. In the cybersecurity field, we believe that cybersecurity events refer to the comprehensive acquisition of cyberspace security knowledge based on data in cyberspace, the efficient representation and management of knowledge, and the use of the obtained cyberspace security knowledge to fully understand the process of the cybersecurity event.

American computer scientists Herbert Simon and Allen Newell [9] proposed that the cognitive process is the process of processing and conversion of external information, so that this information. It has meaning and value, and can be stored and applied to future behaviors and decisions. Peng Yili and others [10] proposed that the cognitive process refers to the human brain through feeling, perception, memory, thinking, imagination and other forms reflect the nature of objective objects and the process of the relation between objects. In the cybersecurity field, we believe that the cognitive process refers to the representation, transformation, and management of information about cybersecurity events in the cyberspace, through the collection, analysis, and curation of data in the cyberspace. This is done to identify, understand, detect, and assess the scale, impact, and threats of cybersecurity events.

Anderson et al. [11] proposed that a cognitive model is a description of a particular cognitive capability, which includes how input information is encoded, processed, and stored, as well as how outputs are generated. The definition of a cognitive model on Wikipedia is that it approximates the cognitive processes of animals (primarily humans), through which people can understand the cognitive process and make predictions based on it.

Currently, there is no unified definition of cognitive models. We believe that a cognitive model is a computational modeling of the cognitive process, which is a knowledge-oriented model and its application process.

2.2 The Evolution of Cognitive Models

Classic cognitive models can be divided into two categories: one is to simulate the structure of the human brain, and the other is to simulate the human learning process. In recent years, there have also been cognitive models proposed for specific domains. We will introduce these cognitive models and analyze their advantages and disadvantages for the assessment of cybersecurity events.

2.2.1 Cognitive Model that Simulates the Structure of the Human Brain

The human understanding of the brain can be traced back to ancient Greece. Prior to that, while many physiologists had analyzed the structure of the brain, it was not until the 5th century that people gradually recognized the brain's importance. With the lifting of the taboo on human dissection, the emergence of comparative anatomy and cranioscopy, as well as the appearance of devices such as the microscope and electroencephalography, many philosophers, medical professionals, anatomists, and ethicists joined the research on the brain. The research on the brain's structure flourished, leading to significant advancements in our understanding of the brain.

Michelangelo was a great Renaissance artist. In the early 16th century, Michelangelo created the painting "The Creation of Adam", which demonstrated a profound observation and understanding of human anatomy. This work depicts the scene of God creating the progenitor Adam, with God reaching out to touch Adam with his finger, transmitting the spark of life. The painting's background portrays the side profile of the brain, promoting reflections on the brain's structure and inspiring subsequent scientists to delve deeper into brain research, which has had a profound impact on our understanding of cognition, perception, and behavior.

The 20th century was a critical period for the research on the structure and function of the brain. In 1906, Ramón y Cajal proposed the neuron doctrine, revealing the process of information processing in the brain. In this doctrine, sensory input information is transmitted through synapses to neurons, and processed through the neural networks formed by the interconnections between neurons, enabling the brain to perform various cognitive tasks. The neuron doctrine is an indispensable foundation for establishing cognitive models. Furthermore, it provides a biological basis for the development of cognitive models, as scientists can draw inspiration from the structure and function of the nervous system to design computational models and apply them to cognitive model research.

To this day, the research on the brain's structure has made significant progress, from electroencephalography to functional magnetic resonance imaging, and to research at the molecular and cellular levels, providing scientists with new perspectives for studying the brain's structure and function. The scientific research on the brain's structure and function not only helps people understand the mechanisms of cognitive functions, such as cognition, thinking, consciousness, and language, but also enables scientists to better understand the fundamental principles of intelligence, thereby greatly promoting the development of cognitive models that simulate the brain's structure.

Cognitive models that simulate the structure of the human brain are a method developed jointly by AI scientists and cognitive scientists. The goal is to simulate the real brain functions as accurately as possible within limited resources and time, in order to help people understand and solve complex problems in cognitive behavior. Figure 1 shows the development timeline of cognitive models that simulate the structure of the human brain. Commonly seen cognitive models today include the Executive-Process/Interactive-Control (EPIC) model, the Adaptive Control of Thought-Rational (ACT-R) model, and the Hierarchical Temporal Memory (HTM) model, among others.

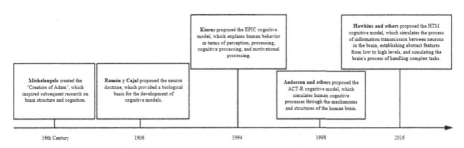

Fig. 1. The evolution of the cognitive model that simulates the structure of the human brain

(1) EPIC cognitive model

The EPIC cognitive model was first proposed by Kieras and Meyer [12]. This cognitive model explains actual user behavior in real-world environments from the perspective of parallel processing of multiple tasks. The perceptual processing system can receive and process information from the environment, and this system is referred to as the "processor" in the EPIC cognitive model. The system architecture of the EPIC cognitive model shown in Fig. 2 includes components such as the auditory processor, visual processor, and speech processing processor.

The cognitive processing system is composed of working memory, long-term memory (production memory), and a production rule interpreter. The working memory stores various information elements, while the production memory can serve as part of the long-term memory to store the results of completed tasks or product information. The information transmitted by the cognitive processing system needs to be transformed into specific action characteristics. If these action characteristics meet the pre-set conditions for the response actions, the brain will receive the command and prompt the user to perform the corresponding actual action.

The EPIC cognitive model has an efficient cognitive architecture that can better simulate human thought and cognitive processes. In the cybersecurity field, the EPIC cognitive model is commonly used to analyze and simulate security incidents. However, the model has deficiencies in dealing with real-time issues and complex problems. Firstly, the forms and changes of cyberattacks are constantly evolving, making it difficult for the EPIC cognitive model to adapt and make effective adjustments. Secondly, due to the large amount of symbolic processing and reasoning involved, the EPIC cognitive model often results in significant latency. These shortcomings greatly limit the application of this model in the cybersecurity field.

The factors involved in cybersecurity are numerous, beyond just simulating cognitive processes. Technical, legal, and policy factors also need to be considered. This requires a more intelligent and powerful cognitive model that can better improve people's ability to handle cybersecurity incidents.

(2) ACT-R cognitive model

The ACT-R cognitive model was proposed by Anderson et al. [13] aiming to simulate human cognitive processes by emulating the mechanisms of the human brain in extracting and manipulating information from memory. This cognitive model includes modules for goal, vision, action, and declarative knowledge, all of which

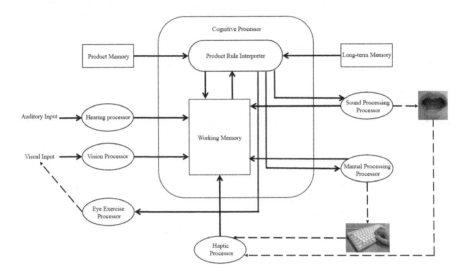

Fig. 2. EPIC system architecture of cognitive model

are coordinated by the system. In the system architecture of the ACT-R cognitive model shown in Fig. 3 [15], the target module and the visual module are responsible for representing complex information and visual experiences respectively. The action module mainly consists of two sub-modules - the driver and the executor. The driver generates action plans based on the current situation and rules, while the executor translates the action plans into specific actions. The declarative knowledge module is used to organize and manage knowledge, helping the cognitive model to analyze and process complex information, and provide results based on rules and representations.

The ACT-R cognitive model is based on the cognitive mechanisms and structure of the human brain, and can provide powerful explanations of cognitive processes. In the cybersecurity field, the ACT-R cognitive model provides an effective tool to precisely simulate human behavior. However, the ACT-R cognitive model still has limitations in terms of comprehensiveness and accuracy. Firstly, the ACT-R cognitive model primarily focuses on the high-level abstraction of cognitive processes, but is unable to simulate the content of perception, memory, and emotion. For example, when describing a phishing attack, the ACT-R cognitive model cannot accurately capture the emotional reactions and behaviors of a user upon receiving a phishing email. Secondly, the analysis and prediction of the ACT-R cognitive model are based on the assumptions and parameter settings of the model, which may differ to some extent from actual conditions, thereby affecting the accuracy of the processing results. The ACT-R cognitive model struggles to encompass the complex and diverse factors in the cybersecurity domain, and thus cannot effectively provide comprehensive analysis and prediction of cybersecurity incidents.

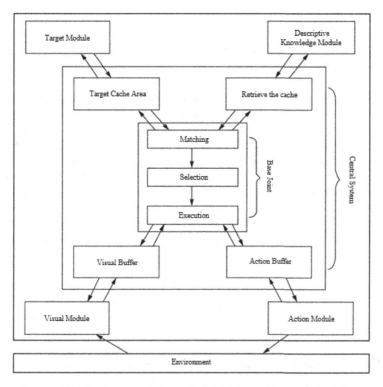

Fig. 3. System architecture of ACT-R cognitive model

(3) HTM cognitive model

The HTM cognitive model, proposed by Hawkins et al. [14] is a bioinspired neural network with a hierarchical structure that can simulate the information transfer patterns between brain neurons. Specifically, the HTM cognitive model divides the input signals into role processing units, ignore processing units, and meta-cognitive processing units. The role processing units receive input signals from the external environment and perform preliminary processing and encoding to enable the model's comprehensibility. The ignore processing units focus on meaningful inputs, primarily used to filter out repetitive information or noise. The meta-cognitive processing units transform the abstract features from the previous layer into the current layer's abstract features. In this way, the HTM model establishes a hierarchy of abstract feature layers from low to high, simulating the human brain's functions in cognitive tasks such as perception, filtering, learning, and prediction.

The hierarchical structure of the HTM cognitive model allows it to establish different levels of abstraction from low to high, making the model more flexible and effective in handling complex tasks, such as anomaly pattern recognition, trend forecasting, and data analysis. However, the cybersecurity domain has extremely high requirements for accuracy and real-time performance, which the HTM cognitive model may struggle to meet. Firstly, the HTM cognitive model requires a large and reliable dataset for training and prediction, but the dataset in the cybersecurity domain is often small in scale and difficult to obtain, which inevitably leads to insufficient training and weak predictive capabilities of the model. For example, when dealing with complex cyberattacks, the HTM cognitive model may experience false positives and false negatives, significantly affecting the model's accuracy. Secondly, the cybersecurity domain requires rapid identification and response to attacks, but the HTM cognitive model requires a large amount of computational resources and time for training, which may result in insufficient real-time performance. In summary, the application of the HTM cognitive model in the cybersecurity domain still faces some challenges, requiring further improvements and refinements.

Cognitive models that simulate the structure of the human brain can help us develop better AI solutions, enabling intelligent technologies to be applied more effectively in areas such as natural language processing, information retrieval, and image processing, providing efficient services for people. However, due to the complexity of the brain's structure and the interactions between its various parts, cognitive models based on brain structure have difficulty in precisely simulating the brain's structure and function, and are unable to adapt quickly to environmental changes or new tasks. When applied to the cybersecurity domain, cognitive models based on brain structure struggle to have the same flexibility and adaptability as the human brain, and are unable to adequately meet the real-time and complex requirements of the field.

2.2.2 Cognitive Model that Simulates the Human Learning Process

Cognitive models that simulate the human learning process typically abstract the learning process of the human brain into a mathematical model, thereby simulating human cognition of the real world. These models establish a learning framework based on experience and feedback, based on the way humans learn new knowledge. For example, computers can automatically discover and extract features relevant to a task by observing large datasets that have already been correctly labeled, and thereby learn how to complete these tasks correctly. Furthermore, these types of models can also perform data clustering or classification, effectively solving various problems by identifying new patterns through the similarities and differences between data points. Figure 4 illustrates the development trajectory of cognitive models that simulate the human learning process. Classic cognitive models simulating the human learning process include the State, Operator, And Result (SOAR) and Instance-Based Learning Theory (IBLT).

Fig. 4. The development trajectory of cognitive models that simulate the human learning process

(1) SOAR cognitive model

The SOAR cognitive model was proposed by Laird et al. [16] in 1987. The model includes three core elements: state, operator, and result. The state refers to all the known information in the knowledge structure, the operator refers to the steps or methods for executing tasks or operations, and the result refers to the impact or outcome of the operator's execution. The SOAR cognitive model uses state, operator, and result to simulate human thought processes, enabling machines to solve problems and make decisions like humans. As shown in the system structure of the SOAR cognitive model in Fig. 5, SOAR includes a production memory and a working memory. The production memory is information encoded according to production rules, and the (symbol-based) working memory is a temporary storage area for storing and processing symbolic representation information. The content of the working memory comes from other modules and can be modified and updated through the decision-making process to support task execution and completion.

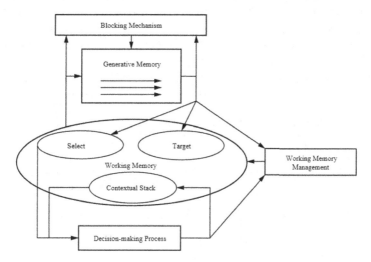

Fig. 5. The system organization of SOAR cognitive model

The SOAR cognitive model is mainly used to solve complex reasoning and decision-making problems, and can flexibly handle different types of tasks. In the cybersecurity field, the SOAR cognitive model can integrate multiple security tools and systems to help security analysts quickly identify, analyze, and respond to threats, thereby improving network defense capabilities. However, the cybersecurity field has very high requirements for accuracy and real-time performance, which the SOAR cognitive model still struggles to meet. This is mainly reflected in two aspects: 1) The SOAR cognitive model requires a large amount of knowledge and rules for modeling and reasoning, but the attack methods and techniques in the cybersecurity field change rapidly, and the SOAR cognitive model is difficult to update and adapt in a timely manner, resulting in a decrease in model accuracy; 2) The SOAR cognitive model requires complete security data (such as data with spatial-temporal characteristics) and a large amount of computing resources for long-term reasoning and decision-making, while the cybersecurity field requires rapid identification and response to attacks, making it difficult for the SOAR cognitive model to ensure network security in real-time. In summary, the SOAR cognitive model needs further improvement to be better applied in the cybersecurity field.

(2) IBLT cognitive model

The IBLT cognitive model was proposed by Gonzalez et al. [17] The model requires learners to group all the instances they encounter during the thought process, using individual instances as the basis for categorization, in order to achieve a deeper understanding. By applying this specific instance memorization process to specific behaviors, it is possible to effectively separate different values, allowing learners to make appropriate choices based on specific situations. As shown in the decision-making process of the IBLT cognitive model in Fig. 6, the model learns and refines instances through accumulation during the dynamic decision-making process, where an instance is defined as a triple of situation-decision-utility (SDU). When there is a need to interact with a dynamic task to make decisions, the user will identify the situation based on tasks similar to past instances, adjust the judgment strategy from a heuristic-based method to an instance-based method, and refine the accumulated knowledge based on the actual feedback of the actions.

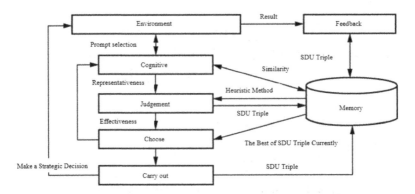

Fig. 6. The decision-making process of the IBLT cognitive model

The IBLT cognitive model can retrieve similar past instances from existing memories through a cognitive judgment mechanism, fully consider multiple factors in the decision-making process, and combine the utility function to better handle complex problems. However, in the cybersecurity field, this model is difficult to meet the requirements of comprehensiveness and real-time performance. First, attackers may adopt various attack methods and techniques to carry out attacks, while the IBLT cognitive model mainly focuses on the quantification and representation of information, making it difficult to consider multiple attack methods and techniques simultaneously, leading to its lack of comprehensiveness. Second, when dealing with large-scale data, the IBLT cognitive model requires longer computation time, which leads to its lack of real-time performance. For example, attackers may use distributed denial-of-service (DDoS) attacks to overwhelm network traffic, and this type of attack requires real-time response and processing, while the IBLT cognitive model cannot perform timely reasoning and decision-making. In summary, the IBLT cognitive model focuses on analyzing and studying the decision-making process and decision-making results, and cannot effectively predict and prevent cybersecurity attacks.

In addition to the above two classic cognitive models, there is a cognitive model that can simulate the human learning process, namely the 3M cognitive model.

(3) 3M cognitive model

In general, human cognition of the objective world can be simplified into answering three questions: "what is it", "why", and "how". "What is it" relates to the essence and functional characteristics of things, used to distinguish the inherent properties of the thing from other things, such as understanding the thing through its form, attributes, features, and properties that are directly related to the essence of the thing. "Why" is to explore the causes of the occurrence of things, that is, to believe that any event has a causal relation, and only by correctly understanding the causes of the thing's occurrence can one truly understand the thing. "How" is the human understanding of the specific process of the thing's occurrence, with obvious temporal characteristics.

The 3M cognitive model aims to explore and study the thinking mechanism of the human brain by answering the above three questions. In the cybersecurity field, this model can help security analysts understand the characteristics of various attacks and formulate effective response strategies, thereby improving the professional level of security analysts, but it is difficult to comprehensively and accurately handle network space security incidents. For example, some attackers may use vulnerabilities or malicious code to carry out attacks, and this type of attack method may not be fully described by the 3M cognitive model. In addition, the attack methods and attack strategies of attackers are diverse, and the 3M cognitive model cannot be updated in a timely manner, which leads to its lack of accuracy. In summary, the 3M cognitive model has great limitations in comprehensiveness and accuracy, which leads to its deficiencies in effectively detecting malicious attack behaviors.

2.2.3 Cognitive Models for Typical Fields

The cognitive model was originally proposed by psychologists to study human learning, thinking and decision-making behavior. With the development of computer technology, cognitive models have been widely used in different fields to help people understand and master business processes more deeply, so as to better serve application needs.

The four-dimensional real-time control system (4D/RCS) cognitive model is a framework based on the cognitive process [18], and it is also a cognitive model oriented towards the unmanned driving field. Specifically, the 4D/RCS cognitive model combines four elements - data, description, recognition, and meaning - to realize a multimodal perception and reasoning framework, which can complete tasks such as target identification, behavior analysis, and decision-making in different environments.

Although the cognitive models oriented towards the fields of unmanned driving and network space security are both highly evolving fields, the problems and challenges they face are quite different. For example, in the unmanned driving field, sensors can provide a large amount of relatively high-quality data to assist decision-making, while in the cybersecurity field, attackers can mislead defenders by forging or tampering with data, thereby affecting the accuracy of decision-making results. Furthermore, attackers will change their attack methods at any time, and defenders need to respond to such dynamic spatial-temporal changes, so the 4D/RCS cognitive model oriented towards the unmanned driving field is difficult to apply directly to the cybersecurity field.

Although the existing cognitive models have their own characteristics, in the cybersecurity field, these models all have some problems, such as insufficient real-time performance, lack of accuracy, and inadequate comprehensiveness, and therefore cannot comprehensively, accurately, and in a timely manner analyze network space security incidents. The cybersecurity field requires a more suitable cognitive model to specifically solve these problems.

3   MDATA Cognitive Model

3.1   Definition of MDATA Cognitive Model

The MDATA cognitive model meets the comprehensive, accurate, and real-time requirements for assessing cybersecurity incidents. It starts from the three dimensions that align with human cognition: time, space, and spatiotemporal association. Based on the three steps of human knowledge cognition—knowledge acquisition, knowledge representation and management, and knowledge utilization—it achieves comprehensive, accurate, and real-time assessment of cybersecurity incidents. This effectively addresses the challenges caused by the three main attributes of cybersecurity incidents. The MDATA cognitive model is a novel cognitive model centered on knowledge, integrating cognitive methods and processes, and it is also the first cognitive model in the cybersecurity field.

The MDATA cognitive model is suitable for the cybersecurity field. Given the diverse data sources and varied forms of knowledge representation (KR) in this field, the MDATA cognitive model first standardizes the representation and management of knowledge to eliminate cognitive differences caused by inconsistent knowledge representation. It then associates and integrates cyberspace data from different sources, dimensions, and forms, using artificial intelligence, big data, and other technologies to extract and automatically deduce knowledge, laying the foundation for a comprehensive understanding of cybersecurity incidents. Finally, it conducts intelligent analysis of cybersecurity incidents, combining knowledge from the cybersecurity field to conduct a comprehensive analysis and assessment of the generation patterns, impact range, and development trends of cybersecurity incidents, thereby achieving an understanding and accurate assessment of cybersecurity incidents.

3.2   Components of the MDATA Cognitive Model

The MDATA cognitive model comprises three main components: knowledge representation and management, knowledge acquisition, and knowledge utilization. Knowledge representation and management display knowledge in a reasonable manner, supporting knowledge utilization. Knowledge acquisition extracts knowledge from vast amounts of data (cyberspace data), providing a foundation for knowledge representation and management. Knowledge utilization further promotes the deduction and completion of knowledge, providing updated data for knowledge acquisition. The system framework of the MDATA cognitive model is shown in Fig. 7.

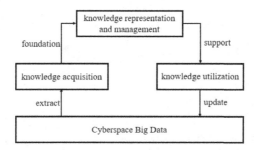

Fig. 7. System Framework of the MDATA Cognitive Model

3.2.1 Knowledge Representation and Management

Knowledge representation involves converting complex, high-level human -understandable language into simple, machine-understandable low-level forms, making it easier for computers to process. In the MDATA cognitive model, knowledge representation refers to representing cybersecurity knowledge from the dimensions of semantics, time, space, and spatiotemporal association. This improves the computer's processing efficiency and knowledge representation capability, enabling better understanding and handling of complex knowledge, and more effective support for knowledge utilization. Currently, there is substantial research on knowledge representation. However, due to the diverse sources, rapid updates, and dynamic spatiotemporal associations of cybersecurity knowledge, existing methods are insufficient to effectively support efficient representation and utilization of cybersecurity knowledge.

To address the effective representation of cybersecurity knowledge, the MDATA cognitive model proposes graphical, dynamic quintuple, and vector-based knowledge representation methods. By overlaying spatiotemporal attributes on entity relations, it introduces properties like time vectors and space scalars, achieving high-fidelity representation of complex dynamic knowledge. This effectively addresses the three main characteristics of cybersecurity incidents: large scale, evolution, and association. Additionally, the MDATA cognitive model uses spatiotemporal indexing to achieve comprehensive coverage and efficient management of large-scale cyberattack incidents.

The graphical knowledge representation method of the MDATA cognitive model is shown in Fig. 8. In Fig. 8, each entity is overlaid with time (T) and space (S) attributes, effectively representing the spatiotemporal characteristics of cybersecurity knowledge. Taking the OceanLotus attack report as an example, we demonstrate how the graphical knowledge representation method of the MDATA cognitive model expresses an attack incident.

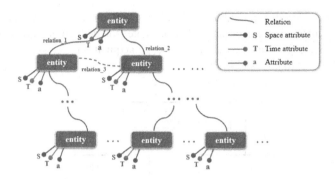

Fig. 8. Graphical Knowledge Representation in the MDATA Cognitive Model

[Case 1] Starting from October 19, 2019, a certain network system continuously received phishing emails. The administrator of the web server (IP address: 192.168.12.58) opened a phishing email, after which the attacker (IP address: 101.1.35.X) exploited the Microsoft.NET Framework URL Redirection Vulnerability (CVE-2011-3415) to redirect the administrator to a malicious URL (IP address: 101.1.35.X) for a phishing attack. On October 20 of the same year, the attacker exploited the Apache Web Server security vulnerability (CVE-2002-0840) on the malicious website to release a remote control Trojan and established a persistent connection with the web server via a backdoor on October 22. The attacker then remained dormant for about a year.

On November 1, 2020, the attacker exploited the Artifex Ghostscript vulnerability (CVE-2018-16509) to perform lateral movement within the intranet from the compromised web server and gained control of a file server (IP address: 192.168.12.143). Starting from November 2, the attacker began exfiltrating data from the file server using the established connection.

The MDATA cognitive model represents cybersecurity knowledge from the dimensions of assets, vulnerabilities, and attacks. For instance, in Case 1, the first step of the attack can be represented using the knowledge "the phishing attack exploited vulnerability CVE-2011-3415, which existed in the server with IP address 192.168.12.58." This is illustrated in Fig. 9. As shown, entities such as the phishing attack and server contain both time and space (IP address) attributes, effectively representing the dynamic nature of cybersecurity knowledge.

Additionally, the aforementioned knowledge can be represented using the MDATA cognitive model's quintuple format (which will be detailed later) as follows:

<Phishing attack, exploits, CVE-2011-3415, [2019-10-19, —], {101.1.35.X, 192.168.12.58}>

<CVE-2011-3415, exists in, server, —, 192.168.12.58>

In the quintuple, the time attribute indicates the time the attack occurred or the time the vulnerability existed on the server, while the space attribute provides information such as the attacker's IP address and the target IP address.

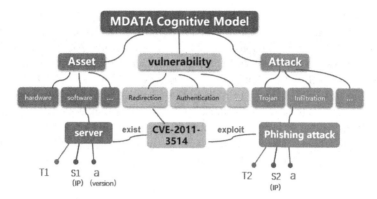

Fig. 9. Graphical Representation of Case 1 in the MDATA Cognitive Model

The MDATA cognitive model's vector knowledge representation method encodes entities and relations as computable vectors, supporting knowledge deduction through vector calculations.

Knowledge management (KM) involves organizing, categorizing, and storing knowledge to enhance its utilization, improve the rate of knowledge generation, and increase knowledge sharing. In KM, to better manage and retrieve knowledge, the MDATA cognitive model establishes attribute indices to help locate the storage positions of knowledge. Furthermore, the MDATA cognitive model proposes various time and space indexing methods for the storage management of cybersecurity knowledge, achieving efficient querying and improving query efficiency for cybersecurity knowledge. The detailed content of knowledge representation and management in the MDATA cognitive model will be discussed in Chapter 2 of this book.

3.2.2 Knowledge Acquisition

Knowledge acquisition refers to obtaining knowledge through various means (such as expert interviews, surveys, literature reviews, etc.) and transforming this knowledge into resources to support the organization in better leveraging these resources. In the MDATA cognitive model, knowledge acquisition involves obtaining spatiotemporal cybersecurity knowledge from multi-dimensional, multi-source, and multi-modal cyberspace data. In the cybersecurity field, the data is vast, comes from diverse sources, updates rapidly, and exists in various formats, with most data being semi-structured or unstructured. Therefore, knowledge acquisition is crucial in the cybersecurity domain, supporting the representation and processing of cybersecurity knowledge.

The MDATA cognitive model includes a set of inductive and deductive operators for acquiring cybersecurity knowledge. Inductive operators primarily acquire knowledge from vast amounts of cyberspace data, including entity extraction, relation/attribute extraction, and time/space attribute extraction. Deductive operators mainly infer unknown knowledge based on known knowledge, including methods such as rule-based reasoning, maximum likelihood concept reasoning, and spatiotemporal information-based relation inference.

For example, in Case 1, using inductive operators, the MDATA cognitive model can extract cybersecurity knowledge from texts such as "Starting from October 19, 2019, a certain network system continuously received phishing emails. After the administrator of the web server (IP address: 192.168.12.58) opened a phishing email, the attacker (IP address: 101.1.35.X) exploited the Microsoft.NET Framework URL Redirection Vulnerability (CVE-2011-3415) to redirect the administrator to a malicious URL (IP address: 101.1.35.X) for a phishing attack" and "The attacker exploited the Apache Web Server security vulnerability (CVE-2002-0840) on the malicious website to release a remote control Trojan." The resulting cybersecurity knowledge in quintuple form is as follows, and the illustration is shown in Fig. 10.

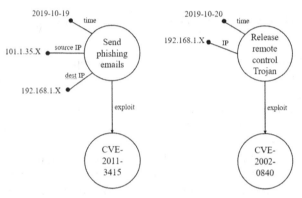

Fig. 10. Graphical Representation of Cyberspace Security Knowledge Acquired by Inductive Operators

Knowledge 1: <Send phishing emails, exploits, CVE-2011-3415, [2019-10-19], [101.1.35.X, 192.168.12.58]>.

Knowledge 2: <Release remote control Trojan, exploits, CVE-2002-0840, 2019-10-20, [192.168.1.X]>.

Deductive operators can infer potential cybersecurity knowledge. For example, by analyzing IP addresses, it can be observed that the destination IP address for "sending phishing emails" is the same as the IP address for "releasing a remote control Trojan," and the date of Knowledge 1 ("2019-10-19") is earlier than the date of Knowledge 2 ("2019-10-20"). This suggests that "sending phishing emails" is a precursor step to "releasing a remote control Trojan," as shown in Fig. 11. In Fig. 11, the dashed arrows indicate knowledge inferred through deduction: sending phishing emails → releasing a remote control Trojan. Chapter 3 of this book will provide a detailed explanation of knowledge acquisition in the MDATA cognitive model.

3.2.3   Knowledge Utilization

Knowledge utilization refers to analyzing and extracting knowledge contained in the model through computer programs (algorithms) and applying it to various downstream fields to accomplish user-specified tasks and functions. For cybersecurity incidents,

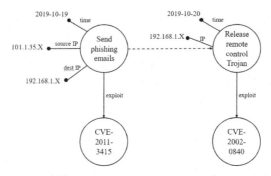

Fig. 11. Graphical Representation of Cyberspace Security Knowledge Acquired by Deductive Operators

knowledge utilization in the MDATA cognitive model involves comprehensive, accurate, and real-time assessment of cyberattacks.

The MDATA cognitive model includes a series of knowledge utilization algorithms, such as subgraph matching, reachable path queries, and subgraph queries, which can achieve real-time detection of cybersecurity incidents. For example, in the OceanLotus attack case presented in Case 1, the MDATA cognitive model can use inductive and deductive operators to obtain a pattern diagram of the OceanLotus attack, as shown in Fig. 12, which illustrates the relations between the attack steps. This pattern diagram can serve as a query graph for the subgraph matching algorithm.

In the pattern diagram of the OceanLotus attack, a node represents a specific attack behavior, such as sending phishing emails or releasing a remote control Trojan, while an edge represents the relation between two attack behaviors. The MDATA cognitive model detects the actual OceanLotus attack process based on this pattern diagram as follows:

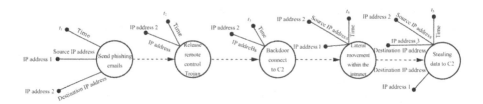

Fig. 12. Pattern Diagram of the OceanLotus Attack

First, extract the attack events from the collected cybersecurity data (e.g., log data, alert data).

Then, use deductive operators to infer the sequential relations between the attack events, dynamically composing a large data graph that includes the discovered attack events and their sequential relations.

Finally, use the pattern diagram of the OceanLotus attack (Fig. 12) as a query graph for subgraph matching to detect the OceanLotus attack within the data graph.

Similarly, the MDATA cognitive model can extract patterns of other complex attacks and use these pattern diagrams as query graphs to detect potential complex attacks in the data graph.

The volume of knowledge in the cybersecurity field is enormous, and the assessment of cybersecurity incidents requires real-time analysis. The complexity of knowledge utilization algorithms based on graph computation increases with the volume of knowledge. Therefore, improving computational efficiency is a key issue for knowledge utilization in the MDATA cognitive model. To address this issue, the MDATA cognitive model proposes a solution based on a fog-cloud computing architecture. This approach divides the large graph into multiple smaller graphs, with an architecture consisting of three layers: fog end, middle layer, and cloud end. The fog end quickly detects knowledge in the smaller graphs, the middle layer integrates the detection results, and the cloud end aggregates the results from multiple knowledge bodies and performs collaborative computation, thereby achieving the detection of complete complex attack chains[2].

The fog-cloud computing architecture can integrate and coordinate knowledge bases from different dimensions[3], providing comprehensive coverage of cybersecurity knowledge from a global perspective. The fog end can promptly acquire knowledge, thereby enhancing the real-time detection of cybersecurity incidents. Chapter 4 of this book will provide a detailed explanation of knowledge utilization in the MDATA cognitive model.

3.3 Principles of MDATA Cognitive Model

The working logic of the MDATA cognitive model is illustrated in Fig. 13. Based on collected cyberspace data, the MDATA cognitive model uses inductive operators to extract known cybersecurity knowledge. This knowledge is then efficiently represented and managed to form a cybersecurity knowledge base, leveraging various indices to enhance retrieval efficiency and support diverse graph computation algorithms and the fog-cloud computing architecture for knowledge utilization. The knowledge representation method of the MDATA cognitive model is both comprehensible and computable, enabling deductive operators to infer unknown cybersecurity knowledge, thereby refining and updating the existing knowledge base. The MDATA cognitive model is a dynamic model that continuously updates and perfects cybersecurity knowledge through knowledge representation and management, knowledge acquisition, knowledge utilization, feedback, and iteration.

---

[2] The knowledge entity is an intelligent software component. It can range from a simple, target-oriented knowledge extraction component on the front end to a large-scale knowledge cloud on the back end, such as a health knowledge entity, a weather forecast knowledge entity, or a general human knowledge entity.

[3] The knowledge base can be understood as a repository of knowledge entities within specific dimensions or scenarios. It can include a knowledge base for asset dimensions, a knowledge base for vulnerabilities or different corresponding vulnerabilities, and a knowledge base for threat dimensions involving attack behaviors. We can consider these as knowledge entities within a fog-cloud computing architecture.

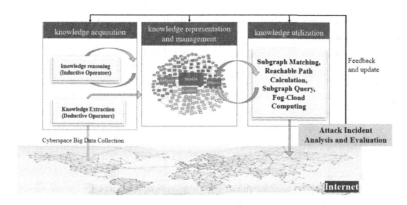

Fig. 13. Operational logic of the MDATA cognitive model

3.4   Innovations and Contributions of the MDATA Cognitive Model

The MDATA cognitive model is the first cognitive model in the cybersecurity field, addressing the need for comprehensive, accurate, and real-time assessment of cybersecurity incidents. Unlike existing cognitive models that simulate brain structure or human cognitive processes, the MDATA cognitive model is the first to focus on knowledge as its core.

The MDATA cognitive model effectively meets the three major characteristics of cybersecurity incidents: large-scale, evolutionary, and interconnected. By employing various inductive and deductive operators, the model extracts known cybersecurity knowledge and infers unknown knowledge. It also manages and represents large-scale cybersecurity knowledge across multiple layers, including the fog end, middle layer, and cloud end.

The MDATA cognitive model's knowledge representation constructs various attribute indexing methods (such as temporal, spatial, and spatiotemporal indices) to effectively represent cybersecurity knowledge with spatiotemporal evolutionary characteristics, thus accommodating the evolutionary nature of cybersecurity incidents.

Cybersecurity incidents are highly interconnected, such as the strong relations between cyberattacks and assets, vulnerabilities, and threat behaviors, as well as the close ties between cyber public opinion incidents and their themes, dissemination platforms, and event information. The MDATA cognitive model employs various knowledge utilization methods, including subgraph matching, reachable path queries, and subgraph queries, to enable the sharing and association of multidimensional cybersecurity knowledge, meeting the interconnected nature of cybersecurity incidents.

In addressing the challenges of comprehensive, accurate, and real-time assessment of cybersecurity incidents, the MDATA cognitive model functions as a dynamic model, capable of acquiring cybersecurity knowledge from various modalities of data, ensuring comprehensive coverage. For example, the cybersecurity knowledge base constructed using the MDATA cognitive model includes 1 billion nodes and 10 billion edges, covering known cyberattack behaviors, existing asset-vulnerability associations, and ensuring no detection omission of attack behaviors. Moreover, the MDATA cognitive model achieves accurate detection of cybersecurity incidents through various knowledge utilization methods, such as subgraph matching based on complex attack pattern diagrams, enabling accurate and complete detection of complex attack chains. The model also enhances knowledge retrieval efficiency through multiple indexing methods and achieves real-time detection of cybersecurity incidents using the fog-cloud computing architecture.

4 Summary

Cybersecurity incidents exhibit three main characteristics: large scale, evolution, and correlation. Accurately assessing these incidents comprehensively, accurately, and in real-time is a global challenge. This chapter introduces the first cognitive model in the cybersecurity field—the MDATA Cognitive Model. The MDATA Cognitive Model centers around knowledge and models the process of understanding cybersecurity incidents. It comprises three main components: knowledge representation and management, knowledge acquisition, and knowledge utilization. Through continuous feedback and evaluation, the model is refined to address the global challenge of accurately assessing cybersecurity incidents, effectively supporting the three main characteristics of these incidents.

References

1. Binxing, F.: On Cyberspace Sovereignty. Science Press, Beijing (2017)
2. SonicWall. 2022 SonicWall cyber threat report. (2022-10-27) [2023-06-25]
3. Kemp, S.: Digital 2023: global overview report. (2023-01-26) [2023-06-25]
4. Reinsel, D., Lifeng, W., Gantz, J.F., et al.: IDC: China Will Have the Largest Data Sphere by 2025 (2019-01) [2023-06-25]
5. Yifang. What Short Video Public Opinion Data Analysis Systems are Available? Recommendations for Video Public Opinion Monitoring and Analysis Platforms [EB/OL]. (2022-03-30) [2023-06-25]
6. Buttner, A., Ziring, N.: Common platform enumeration (CPE)—specification: version 2.1[EB/OL]. (2008-01-31) [2023-06-25]
7. Miller, G.: The magical number seven, plus or minus two: some limits on our capacity for processing information. Psychol. Rev. **63**(02), 81–97 (1956)
8. Lakoff, G.: Women, Fire, and Dangerous Things: What Categories Reveal about the Mind. University of Chicago Press, Chicago (2008)
9. Simon, H., Newell, A.: Heuristic problem solving: the next advance in operations research. Oper. Res. **06**, 1–10 (1958)
10. Yilian, P., Qinrong, M.: Dictionary of Logic: Revised Edition. Shanghai Lexicographical Publishing House, Shanghai (2010)
11. Anderson, J.R., Crawford, J.: Cognitive Psychology and Its Implications. W. H. Freeman and Company, San Francisco (1980)
12. Kieras, D.E., Meyer, D.E.: The EPIC Architecture for Modeling Human Information-Processing: A Brief Introduction. University of Michiga, Ann Arbor (1994)
13. Anderson, J.R., Lebiere, C.J.: The Atomic Components of Thought. Lawrence Erlbaum Associates Publishers, Hillsdale (1998)

14. Hawkins, J., Ahmad, S.: Why neurons have thousands of synapses, a theory of sequence memory in neocortex. Front. Neural Circuits **10**, 1–13 (2016)
15. Yan, J., Binxing, F.: Network Security Situation Awareness. Electronic Industry Press, Beijing (2020)
16. Laird, J.E., Newell, A., Rosenbloom, P.S.: SOAR: an architecture for general intelligence. Artif. Intell. **33**(01), 1–64 (1987)
17. Gonzalez, C., Lerch, J.F., Lebiere, C.: Instance-based learning in dynamic decision making. Cogn. Sci. **27**(04), 591–635 (2003)
18. Albus, J.S.: 4-D/RCS: a reference model architecture for intelligent unmanned ground vehicles. In: Proceedings of 2000 ICRA Millennium Conference, IEEE International Conference on Robotics and Automation, Symposia Proceedings, Piscataway, pp. 3260–3265. IEEE (2000)

MDATA Knowledge Representation and Management

Yan Jia[1]([✉]), Xiangyu Song[2,3], and Jianxin Li[2]

[1] National University of Defense Technology, Changsha 410073, China
jiayanjy@vip.sina.com
[2] Chang'an University, Xi'an 710064, China
{Xiangyu.song,jianxin.li}@chd.edu.cn
[3] Pengcheng Laboratory, Shenzhen 518066, China

Knowledge representation and management is one component of the MDATA model. Knowledge representation is mainly achieved by transforming human comprehensible language into computer processable form, thus improving knowledge representation capability and computer processing efficiency and realising automatic knowledge utilisation. Knowledge management improves the efficiency of knowledge utilisation through effective organisation, classification, storage and retrieval of knowledge. In the cybersecurity field, the MDATA knowledge representation model embeds important spatio-temporal information in the form of quintuples and conceptual graphs to achieve knowledge representation of cybersecurity events. In addition, the proposed MDATA knowledge storage management method based on spatio-temporal information retrieval is used to achieve real-time research and judgement of cybersecurity events.

Firstly, Sect. 1 introduces the research related to knowledge representation and knowledge management, as well as generic knowledge representation methods and their development history. Secondly, Sect. 2 analyzes and summarises the limitations and challenges of existing knowledge representation methods in the cybersecurity field in terms of the three main characteristics of cyberspace security events and the knowledge representation needs in the cybersecurity field. Then, in Sect. 3, MDATA knowledge representation methods, computational models, and knowledge management approaches suitable for cybersecurity are described in detail. Finally, Sect. 4 provides a short summary of the chapter.

1 Research Related to Knowledge Representation and Management

1.1 Basic Concepts of Knowledge Representation and Management

Knowledge Representation (KR) refers to the combination of symbols to describe facts about the objective world by means of rules, so that the factual information can be encoded as a combination of symbols that can be processed by computers sothat these combinations of symbols can be interpreted by some rules [1].

Knowledge Management (KM) refers to the identification and use of collective knowledge in an organization to help it compete, including the creation, storage, transfer and application of knowledge. For example, creating internal knowledge, acquiring

Y. Jia et al. (Eds.): *MDATA Cognitive Model: Theory and Applications*, LNCS 15470, pp. 24–58, 2025.
https://doi.org/10.1007/978-981-96-3528-3_2

external knowledge, storing knowledge in documents, updating knowledge, and sharing knowledge internally or externally [2].

Knowledge representation and knowledge management are interlinked and complementary. Through knowledge representation, knowledge in reality is represented in computable and storable figurative forms, so that knowledge management can organize, classify and store these figurative symbols or models to facilitate the subsequent use of knowledge. In addition, through the use of formal knowledge representations, knowledge in organizations becomes easier to understand and process, and allows for automated reasoning and analysis. Thus, knowledge representation provides an effective way of processing knowledge for knowledge management, enabling organizations to manage, utilize and share knowledge resources more effectively. For example, if a security centre monitors an attack event in the network, it needs to first transform this attack event into a form that can be recognized by a computer through a knowledge representation method, and then categorize the attack event through a knowledge management method and store it in the computer. When such an attack is encountered again, the previous attack can be queried and analyzed for an effective defense strategy.

1.2 Current Status of Research on Knowledge Representation Methods

Commonly used knowledge representation methods include predicate logic representation, generative rule representation, knowledge graph representation, deep learning representation, MDATA model representation, etc., and Fig. 1 shows the development history of these knowledge representation methods.

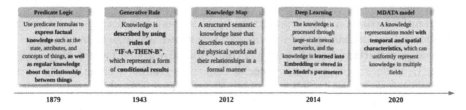

Fig. 1. Knowledge representation development history

1.2.1 Predicate Logic Representation Model

Predicate Logic Representation (PLR) is to use predicate logic formulas to represent factual knowledge such as the state, attributes and concepts of things, as well as regular knowledge of causal relations between things. Therefore, Predicate Logic Representation is a narrative knowledge representation method [3]. The general steps of representing knowledge with predicate logic mainly include: ① defining predicates, determining the exact meaning of each predicate and individual; ② assigning specific values to the variables in each predicate according to the things or concepts to be expressed; ③ according to the semantics of the knowledge to be expressed, using, for example, the words "and," "or". According to the semantics of the knowledge to be expressed, the predicates are connected by appropriate logical conjunctions such as "and", "or", "not", etc., so as to form a predicate formula.

For example, in the case of the OceanLotus attack, the behaviour of "sending a phishing email and releasing a remote Trojan connection backdoor" can be expressed using a predicate logic representation:

Connection (release remote Trojan, send phishing email, backdoor) ← Exploitation (send phishing email, vulnerability) ∧ Exploitation (release remote Trojan, vulnerability)

① Defining predicates:

Utilisation (A, C)

Utilisation (B, C)

Connections (A, B, D)

② Assign a value to the predicate formula variable as:

Exploitation (sending phishing emails, exploits)

Exploitation (release of remote Trojans, vulnerabilities)

Connections (releasing remote Trojans, sending phishing emails, backdoor programmes)

③ Connections are made through logical conjunctions:

Connections (releasing remote Trojans, sending phishing emails, backdoor programmes) ←

Exploitation (sending phishing emails, vulnerability) ∧ Exploitation (releasing remote Trojans, vulnerability)

Predicate Logic Representation has the following advantages:

① **Clear knowledge structure:** predicate logic representation provides a strict syntax and semantics, which can accurately describe various types of knowledge and relations;

② **Strong inference:** predicate logic representation supports complex logical operations and inference mechanisms, which can infer new knowledge from known facts;

③ **Good versatility:** logical inference, as a kind of formal reasoning method, has a strong generality, does not depend on any specific domain, and can describe the knowledge of different domains and disciplines, including mathematics, natural language, physics, biology, and so on.

Predicate logic representation in support of knowledge representation has the following shortcomings:

① **Complex knowledge representation process:** predicate logic representation of knowledge representation is usually more complex, requires the use of a large number of symbols and rules;

② **Weak knowledge representation ability:** predicate logic representation does not support uncertainty and fuzzy knowledge representation, and does not support spatio-temporal characteristics of the representation and relevance of the knowledge representation;

③ ③ **Poor computability:** the computational complexity of the predicate logic;

④ **Poor computability:** predicate logic representation has high computational complexity, low reasoning efficiency, and high computational cost for knowledge base querying and reasoning tasks containing large-scale knowledge.

1.2.2 Generative Rule Representation

Production Rule Representation (PRR) is a relatively simple way of representing knowledge by means of rules, usually using the "IF A-THEN B" statement, which represents a condition-result form [3]. Here, A describes the prerequisites of the rule and B describes the conclusion of the rule. Generative rule representations are mainly used to describe knowledge and state the control between various process knowledge, and the mechanisms of their interactions.

For example, in the OceanLotus attack, the behaviour of "the attacker first sends phishing emails and releases a remote Trojan connection backdoor, then the attacker launches a horizontal penetration attack on the intranet, and finally steals the data and sends it back" can be expressed by generative rule representation as follows:

① *IF* Successfully send phishing email *THEN* Release remote Trojan horse
② *IF* Successfully release the remote Trojan horse *THEN* connect to the backdoor programme
③ *IF* Successful connection to the backdoor programme *THEN* Intranet horizontal penetration attack
④ *IF* Infiltration attack completed *THEN* Stolen data returned

Generative Rule Representation has the following advantages:

① **Easy to be understood by human beings:** Generative Rule Representation can represent knowledge in natural language or near-natural language, which is simple, intuitive, easy to understand and write.
② **Bidirectional reasoning:** Generative Rule Representation can realize both forward and backward reasoning, which is suitable for solving different types of problems.

Generative rule representation has the following drawbacks in supporting knowledge representation:

① **Poor relevance of knowledge representation:** it cannot well represent complex structured knowledge, such as hierarchical, categorical and time-space relations.
② **Easy contradiction or redundancy between rules:** generative rule representation may lead to excessive number of rules, redundancy or contradiction, thus affecting its reasoning efficiency and correctness, relying on rule management techniques.

1.2.3 Knowledge Graph Representation

Predicate Logic Representation (PLR) is to use predicate logic formulas to represent factual knowledge such as the state, attributes and concepts of things, as well as regular knowledge of causal relations between things, therefore, Predicate Logic Representation is a narrative knowledge representation method [3]. The general steps of representing knowledge with predicate logic mainly include:

① Defining predicates, determining the exact meaning of each predicate and individual;
② Assigning specific values to the variables in each predicate according to the things or concepts to be expressed;
③ According to the semantics of the knowledge to be expressed, using, for example, the words "and", "or" According to the semantics of the knowledge to be expressed,

the predicates are connected by appropriate logical conjunctions such as "and", "or", "not", etc., so as to form a predicate formula.

For example, in the OceanLotus attack, "**a network system continued to receive phishing emails, the administrator of the web server opened the phishing emails, and the attacker exploited a Microsoft .NET Framework URL spoofing vulnerability (Vulnerability No. CVE-2011-3415) to redirect the administrator to a malicious URL for a phishing attack. The attacker exploited a malicious website Apache Web Server security vulnerability (vulnerability number CVE-2002-0840) to release a remote-control Trojan horse, which establishes a persistent connection with the attacker via a Trojan horse to the web server**". Using the knowledge graph ternary representation of this web attack event can be represented as:

<Vulnerability CVE-2002-0840, exists in, Web Server>
<Vulnerability CVE-2011-3415, exists in, Web Server>
<phishing file, exploit, vulnerability CVE-2011-3415>
<Remote Trojan, Exploit, Vulnerability CVE-2002-0840>
<backdoor programme, impact, web server>

① **Entity Extraction**, the following entities are extracted by named entity identification:

Vulnerability CVE-2002-0840
Vulnerability CVE-2011-3415
phishing document
remote Trojan horse (computing)
backdoor program
web server

② **Relation extraction**, the following relations are extracted from the corpus:

Vulnerability CVE-2002-0840 Entity Exists in Web Server Entity
Vulnerability CVE-2011-3415 Entity Exists in Web Server Entity
Phishing File Entity Exploit Vulnerability CVE-2011-3415 Entity
Remote Trojan Entity Exploit Vulnerability CVE-2002-0840 Entity
Backdoor Entities Affect Web Server Entities

③ **Constructing a ternary**, based on each relation

<Vulnerability CVE-2002-0840, exists in, Web Server>
<Vulnerability CVE2011-3415, exists in, Web Server>
<phishing file, exploit, vulnerability CVE2011-3415>
<Remote Trojan, Exploit, Vulnerability CVE2002-0840>
<backdoor programme, impact, web server>

In this way, using the knowledge graph representation, this knowledge can be represented as Fig. 2:

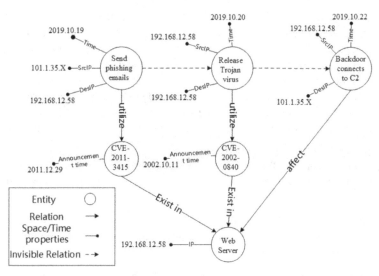

Fig. 2. Example of a Knowledge Graph

Knowledge graph representation has the following advantages:

① **Easy for humans to understand:** knowledge graph adopts a graph structure to represent the semantic relation between entities, which can accurately describe the information of entities, attributes, relations, etc.;

② **Strong knowledge scalability:** knowledge graph can be expanded and updated based on existing knowledge. When new knowledge needs to be added to the graph, it is only necessary to add a new node and the corresponding edge, without modifying the existing structure, thus ensuring the stability and scalability of the graph structure;

③ **Knowledge can be reasoned:** nodes and edges in the knowledge graph carry structural information, which can be used to improve the efficiency of knowledge utilisation by link prediction and other techniques node to node new relation knowledge.

Knowledge graph representation also suffers from the following shortcomings:

① **Poor spatio-temporal correlation:** the representation of knowledge graph for entities and relations is static, and cannot effectively describe the dynamic changes of entities and relations;

② **Poor computability:** when the data size of the knowledge graph and the complexity of the relations are increasing, the knowledge graph faces the challenges of high computational cost and poor real-time performance.

1.2.4 Deep Learning Representations

Deep learning representations usually refer to the processing and processing of knowledge by training models through large-scale neural networks, learning knowledge into vector representations or storing knowledge in the parameters of the model for knowledge management [5]. Common methods for learning knowledge into vector representations include Resnet, a deep convolutional neural network model that learns vector representations for image information, SIF, a natural language processing model that learns vector representations for sentences in text, and GCN, a graph convolutional neural network that learns representations for knowledge of graph structures.

The general steps of deep learning representation are: by using data samples to train the deep learning model, the knowledge is embedded in the parameters of the trained model, or transformed into vectors by the model. For example, for Knowledge Graph data, the general steps for learning knowledge vectors with deep representation are:

① **Text embedding:** transform words into vectors by word embedding;
② **Entity relation embedding:** fine-tune the vectors by neural network model;
③ **Non-linear mapping:** change the vector dimensions by fully connected neural network.

For example, the triad " Phishing File, Exploit, Vulnerability CVE2011-3415>" in the knowledge graph of the Hailian Flower Attack event is represented using deep learning representation, the process is:

① **Text embedding:** three-word vulnerabilities CVE2011-3415, exploits and phishing files in the corpus are textually embedded at the embedding layer to get preprocessed vectors.
② **Entity-relation embedding:** three vectors are fed into the neural network model to learn and get vectors with more features.
③ **Nonlinear mapping:** vector dimensions are processed through a fully connected layer to unify three vectors into the same dimension.

The process of the above deep learning representation is shown in Fig. 3:

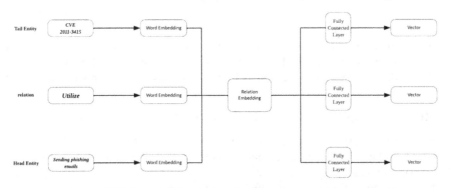

Fig. 3. Example of a deep learning representation

Deep learning representation has the following advantages:

① **Strong knowledge representation capability:** through the training of large-scale deep neural networks, more feature information of knowledge can be acquired.
② **Knowledge representation can be cross-modal:** deep learning representation can perform knowledge representation on different types of data such as image, text, and sound, thus supporting cross-modal knowledge representation and reasoning.

Deep learning representation also has the following shortcomings:

① **Poor knowledge interpretability:** the knowledge representation process of deep learning representation is black-box, which is difficult to explain and understand.

② **High knowledge representation learning cost:** deep learning representation requires a large amount of data and computational resources for training and optimisation, especially for large-scale knowledge representation tasks, which require the use of distributed computing and parallel processing;

③ **Poor correlative knowledge representation:** it can only deal with static knowledge, and it is difficult to represent knowledge with temporal and spatial information through a unified approach to knowledge representation.

1.3 Current Status of Research on Knowledge Management Methods

Knowledge base refers to a collection of knowledge consisting of concepts, facts and rules. Knowledge base management system refers to the computer software used to manage the knowledge base, which can achieve the functions of knowledge expression and storage, knowledge organization and updating, knowledge retrieval and reasoning. Most knowledge management methods are based on the knowledge base to build the corresponding knowledge management system, such as rule base, knowledge graph data management system, and model base management system. Figure 4 shows the relation between knowledge management methods and knowledge representation methods.

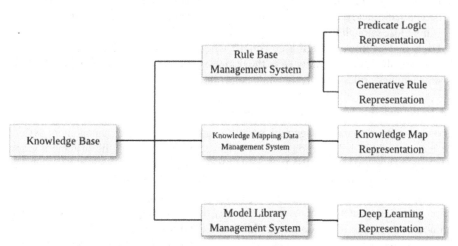

Fig. 4. Relation between Knowledge Management Methods and Knowledge Representation Methods

1.3.1 Rule Base Management System

A rule base management system [6] is a knowledge base management system for managing rules, consisting of a rule base and a management system kernel. A rule base is a collection of rules, which exists as a file system in the form of metadata encoding, or a database stored by a relational database. The management system kernel is a logical module for creating, editing and executing rules. Rule base management systems are commonly used to manage knowledge of predicate logic and generative rule representations. For example, Zeus [7], the rule management system of Meituan, is divided into an execution layer and a computation layer, where the execution layer obtains a collection of rules through specific business scenarios, and returns the results and corresponding decisions after the rules are executed. The computation layer performs the computation of rules during rule execution.

Advantages of the Rule Base Management System:

① **Functional modularity:** the management system kernel and the rules it executes are relatively independent. This means that the management system kernel can be used to handle problems in different industries without fundamental changes. At the same time, adding or modifying rules in the rule base will not affect the system kernel functionality;

② **Easy knowledge management:** As the system manages the rules it ensures easier updating of the rule base without the need for programmers to be involved, which reduces the cost of software operation and maintenance, and ensures that changes to the rules are based on the needs of the industry personnel.

Disadvantages of Rule Base Management System:

① **Difficult to use old knowledge effectively:** some knowledge of long time cycle can't be applied quickly, and the combination of offline rule base and real-time rule base is not close enough to realise the application of old knowledge.

② **High cost of knowledge management:** when the non-major business increases, a large number of rules unrelated to the business will be generated, and it is difficult to manage these rules effectively while controlling the cost.

1.3.2 Knowledge Graph Data Management System

Knowledge graph data management system is a knowledge base management system for managing knowledge graphs, which consists of an RDF tuple library and a graph data processing system [8]. The RDF tuple library stores information in the knowledge graph in the form of ternary groups, and the graph data processing system performs querying of the knowledge graph through the RDF graph query language. Knowledge graph data management systems are commonly used to manage knowledge represented in knowledge graphs. For example, WikiData [9], Wikipedia's massively linked knowledge graph knowledge base, stores massive amounts of information from Wikipedia, Freebase.Wikidata structures the data into a ternary format when storing it, and as of 2016, it already contains more than 24.7 million ternary groups, and at the same time, Wikidata supports editing of knowledge entries of these ternary groups, querying, and other operations.

Advantages of knowledge graph data management system:

① **Low cost of knowledge management:** support for large-scale knowledge graph distributed query, the existence of efficient distributed query processing algorithms, give full consideration to the storage and indexing structure, to reduce the knowledge graph query overhead;

② ② **Support for knowledge reasoning:** support for the ontology and knowledge reasoning, knowledge graph data and traditional relational data, one of the biggest differences is the representation of ontology and the intrinsic knowledge reasoning ability. Intrinsic knowledge reasoning capability. Knowledge graph data management system provides effective management of knowledge graph ontology and efficient reasoning function in the storage layer and query processing layer.

Disadvantages of Knowledge Graph Data Management System:

① **Difficulty in updating knowledge:** The real knowledge graph data will be constantly updated over time. The knowledge in the current knowledge graph data management system is read-only or one-way append, which makes it difficult to update and maintain large-scale knowledge graphs.

② **Difficulty of knowledge data integration:** it is difficult to meet the demand for data integration of multiple separately maintained knowledge graph knowledge bases or historical knowledge graph knowledge bases.

③ **Difficult to ensure knowledge consistency:** in the process of updating the knowledge graph, it is easy to introduce redundant knowledge entities and inconsistent relations between entities.

1.3.3 Model Library Management System

A model library management system is a software system that provides model storage, manipulation and retrieval [10]. It mainly consists of a model repository and a model library management system. The model repository stores a collection of associated models in a specific structure, while the model library management system handles model access and various management control software to achieve effective management of the model library. Model library management systems are commonly used to manage the knowledge of deep learning representations. For example, Alibaba's model library management system ModelScope [11], which enables machine learning model sharing, demo demonstrations, and access to datasets and data metrics. An interface and development environment are provided to upload and download relevant model files and obtain useful model and dataset metadata from ModelScope.

Advantages of the model library management system:

① **Easy knowledge storage:** models can be stored in the database, which simplifies both model retrieval and storage, and the combination of the model library and the database;

② **Good knowledge usability**: users do not need to know the information about the model itself, and can use the model conveniently through the interface provided by the system.

Disadvantages of the model library management system: since most of the models in the model library originate from the sharing of users, this leads to insufficient quality of the models and significant challenges in code consistency and reuse of model structures.

2 Requirements and Challenges of Knowledge Representation and Management

In the cybersecurity field, knowledge is a very important resource because it can improve cybersecurity and prevent cyberattacks. However, knowledge in the cybersecurity field is often characterised by its **giant scale**, **evolutionary nature** and **relevance**. Therefore, it is necessary to study and address the practical needs of knowledge representation and management in cyberspace security, and to analyze the challenges and difficulties faced by knowledge representation and management in the cybersecurity field.

2.1 The Need for Knowledge Representation and Management in the Cybersecurity Field

In order to make better use of cyberspace security knowledge and to support the detection and analysis of attack events in the cybersecurity field, there are several practical needs.

① The knowledge representation should be **human-understandable**. This means that a representation that can be expressed in natural language or other easily understandable forms is needed to describe the various concepts and entities in cyberssecurity field
② A **scalable** knowledge management approach to enable the management and organisation of large amounts of security-related knowledge, updated as security threats continue to evolve.
③ A **reasonably** embedded representation to enable the application of logical and other reasoning methods in the knowledge representation. This can help to better understand and analyze cyberspace security events and enable the rapid identification of potential security problems.
④ The knowledge representation should **support validated**, i.e., the results of reasoning should be able to be verified and interpreted. This ensures that analyzes and interpretations of cybersecurity incidents are accurate and reliable.
⑤ A knowledge representation method **that** supports **multi-dimensional semantics and temporal and spatial correlations**. A method is needed to describe the temporal and spatial relations between events and entities so that the temporal and spatial characteristics of cybersecurity events can be better understood. Thus, it reduces the false alarm rate of event research and judgement in the cybersecurity field, and relies on spatio-temporal correlation properties to support finding multi-step attacks.
⑥ Knowledge representations should be **computable**, not all knowledge representations are computable, computable knowledge representations are able to utilise computers and artificial intelligence techniques to process large amounts of security related knowledge and discover potential security threats.

2.2 Challenges and Difficulties in Knowledge Representation and Management in the Cybersecurity Field

According to these six characteristic demands faced by knowledge representation and management in the cybersecurity field, i.e., **human comprehensibility, reasonability, interpretability of reasoning results, knowledge extensibility, multi-dimensional**

semantics and spatio-temporal relevance, and computability. This section is divided into six subsections to discuss them in detail and to analyze the shortcomings of existing knowledge representation approaches (Sect. 1) in responding to these demands and the challenges of knowledge representation and management.

2.2.1 Human Comprehensibility

Human comprehensibility refers to the variety of knowledge, information and experience that humans can understand and grasp, which includes different expressions such as language, images and symbols. These representations should be easy to understand, express and use, and at the same time conform to human cognition and ways of thinking. However, different knowledge representations have different strengths and weaknesses in supporting human comprehensibility, for example:

- **Deep learning methods** have some more obvious limitations in terms of human comprehensibility. Firstly, the internal structure in deep learning models is often black-boxed, meaning that people cannot directly understand how the model makes decisions. Second, deep learning models usually require a large amount of data for training, which may come from different domains, languages or cultures, resulting in a lack of portability and generalisability of the model, as well as making it more difficult for people to understand and use the model. Finally, deep learning models tend to produce a large number of parameters and intermediate results, making them insufficiently interpretable and difficult to explain and understand intuitively.
- **Generative rule representations** are relatively better in terms of human comprehensibility because their rules are usually expressed in the form of natural language, which is easy for people to understand and use. However, generative rule representations also have some drawbacks, such as overlapping and conflicting rules, which can lead to ambiguity in people's understanding of the rules.
- **Knowledge graph** representations perform well in terms of human comprehensibility because they present knowledge in a graphical form that is easy for people to understand and use intuitively. Knowledge graphs can also be further improved in terms of their comprehensibility through semantic interpretation and visualisation tools.

In the cybersecurity field, knowledge representations face challenges in terms of human comprehensibility. This is because knowledge and experience in the cybersecurity field are usually abstract symbols and concepts that are difficult to be understood and used by non-specialists. Therefore, knowledge representation methods need to address the problem of how to transform abstract symbols and concepts into forms that are easy for people to understand and use. Forms such as natural language and graphical interfaces that are consistent with human cognition and ways of thinking should be adopted to present complex security knowledge and experience into forms that are easy to understand and use. This is of great significance for improving people's security awareness and capabilities and strengthening security protection in cyberspace.

2.2.2 Inferability of Knowledge

The reasonability of knowledge representation refers to the use of effective reasoning methods to process large-scale cybersecurity data and knowledge to extract useful information and knowledge from it. These reasoning methods can be machine learning techniques, logical reasoning, etc. Existing knowledge representation methods, although they can be applied to knowledge reasoning, still have some challenges and limitations. For example:

- Although **the predicate logic representation** is capable of symbolic logic reasoning, its reasoning process is more complex and computationally intensive, and therefore suffers from inefficiency when dealing with large-scale data.
- **Generative rule representations** have certain advantages in logical reasoning and can quickly perform matching and reasoning, but their expressive ability is relatively weak and difficult to represent complex relations and constraints.
- **Knowledge graph representation** can represent knowledge as a graphical structure of entities, attributes and relations, which can be applied to areas such as semantic reasoning and information extraction. However, the expressive and reasoning abilities of knowledge graphs still need to be further improved, such as how to deal with complex temporal and spatial relations.
- **Deep learning representations** can reason by learning patterns and laws in large-scale data, have good generalisation performance, and can handle large-scale and complex cybersecurity data and knowledge. However, deep learning methods have poor interpretability, making it difficult to clearly explain and understand their reasoning process and results.

Therefore, how to combine knowledge representation methods with reasoning methods requires research into new knowledge representation methods and reasoning methods to achieve the ability to process large-scale cybersecurity data and knowledge while maintaining reasonable linearity on such knowledge.

2.2.3 Interpretability of Reasoning Results

Interpretability of reasoning results refers to the ability to explain and illustrate the results of reasoning so that people can understand the process and results of reasoning, and verify and adjust them. In the cybersecurity field, the interpretability of reasoning results is particularly important because it concerns the accuracy and reliability of identifying and handling cyber threats and risks. **However, there are still some different defects and deficiencies in the interpretability of reasoning results in different knowledge representation methods, for example:**

- **Predicate logic representation, generative rule representation** and other knowledge representation methods often use mathematical formula-based calculation methods when reasoning, which can achieve efficient reasoning, but the reasoning results obtained by predicate logic representation and generative rule representation are often just simple "yes" or "no", without providing more details and explanations. "No", without providing more details and explanations.

- **Deep learning techniques** excel in handling large-scale data, but their internal reasoning process is black-box and cannot provide interpretable results. Logical reasoning has good interpretability, but when faced with complex knowledge and relations, its reasoning efficiency and accuracy are often insufficient to meet practical needs.

Therefore, knowledge representation methods need to be able to provide interpretable reasoning results while ensuring reasoning efficiency and accuracy. This is a challenge for knowledge representation. In order to address this challenge, knowledge representation methods that are more human-friendly and easy to understand and express, such as natural language-based representation methods, and some representation methods with visualisation capabilities, need to be adopted. At the same time, some techniques such as interpreters and validators are also needed to verify the correctness and reliability of the reasoning results.

2.2.4 Knowledge Scalability

Knowledge extensibility is critical in the cybersecurity field because knowledge and technologies in the cybersecurity field are constantly developing and evolving. As new attack methods and threats emerge over time, new knowledge and technologies need to be integrated into the existing knowledge base in a timely manner to better support new application scenarios and requirements. In addition, data and knowledge in the cybersecurity domain are usually dispersed across multiple sources and domains. Therefore, the extensibility of the knowledge representation also includes the ability to easily integrate knowledge from different sources and domains. This is important to enable more comprehensive and accurate security analyzes and decisions. However existing knowledge representation methods still have some limitations in terms of extensibility, for example:

- **Predicate logic and generative rule representations** are weak in terms of knowledge scalability. Predicate logic representations usually require manual design and definition of predicates, which becomes very difficult when facing new domains and applications. The rules of generative rule representations are usually designed for specific application scenarios or problems, so neither can be easily used in other domains or problems.
- **Knowledge graph representations** have a great advantage in terms of knowledge extensibility, allowing knowledge to be extracted from different sources and domains, and to organize and integrate this knowledge. In addition, knowledge graphs can be expanded and updated with new knowledge in an automated manner, thus keeping the knowledge base current and accurate. However, the disadvantages of knowledge graph representations are that they are time and resource intensive to build and maintain and require specialised domain knowledge.
- **Deep learning representations** are highly scalable and adaptable when dealing with large-scale data and knowledge, and can continuously improve their performance and performance through adaptive learning. However, deep learning representations are poorly interpretable and it is difficult to explain and account for their inference results, thus limiting their application in the cybersecurity field.

Therefore, in practical applications, it is necessary to choose the most suitable knowledge representation method according to specific problems and scenarios, and to make trade-offs and give and take between extensibility and interpretability. At the same time, new knowledge representation methods need to be explored and developed continuously to meet the ever-changing and developing needs in the cybersecurity field.

2.2.5 Multi-dimensional Semantics and Spatio-Temporal Relevance of Knowledge

In the cybersecurity field, the multi-dimensional correlation of data and knowledge is very strong, especially the multi-dimensional correlation of semantic and spatio-temporal information, as they can help to better understand and respond to cybersecurity threats. However, existing knowledge representations still have many challenges in supporting multi-dimensional correlations.

- Firstly, existing knowledge representation models are mostly used for the representation of static concepts, but lack the ability to model and express **dynamic spatio-temporal** concepts. For example, in the cyber security field, attack events usually have time-series characteristics, but existing knowledge representation methods do not represent these time-series characteristics well, which may lead to limitations in the understanding and response capabilities of cybersecurity threats.
- Secondly, cybersecurity data and knowledge themselves are highly complex and heterogeneous. These data and knowledge come from different data sources and knowledge domains with different data types and structures. For example, an attacker's behavioural pattern is usually influenced by multiple factors, including attack time, attack target, attack method, etc. These factors come from different data sources and knowledge domains, and need to be fused in order to get more accurate analysis results. Existing knowledge representation methods do not handle this complexity and heterogeneity well.
- In addition, the spatio-temporal characteristics of cybersecurity threats are usually closely related to geographical locations, such as the geographical locations of attack sources and attack targets. Existing knowledge representation methods do not represent this spatio-temporal characteristic correlation well, which may lead to certain uncertainties and errors in performing security analyzes and decision-making.

Therefore, how to take multi-dimensional correlation properties into account in knowledge representation and achieve the fusion of complex and heterogeneous data and knowledge is an important challenge in knowledge representation in the cybersecurity field.

2.2.6 Knowledge Computability

Data and knowledge in the cybersecurity field need to be computed and analyzed. Therefore, computable knowledge representations are needed to support these computations and analyzes. For example, representations such as logical expressions are used to support the computation and analysis of cybersecurity knowledge.

- **A logical expression** is a common method of representing computable knowledge. It can represent cybersecurity knowledge as a series of logical formulas so that computers can understand and process it. Logical expressions can represent features, rules, anomalies, etc. of cybersecurity threats and can be used for threat detection, threat intelligence analysis, security event response, etc.

- **Deep learning models** are also widely used in cybersecurity. Deep learning models can be used for threat detection, threat intelligence analysis, anomaly detection, and so on. For example, convolutional neural networks can be used to classify and identify network traffic, recurrent neural networks can be used to model and predict network behaviour, and deep trust networks can be used to detect and analyze malware.

Data in the cybersecurity field is usually very large and requires efficient data processing and computation. Therefore, efficient algorithms and computational methods are needed to process these data to ensure computational efficiency and accuracy. Meanwhile, data in the cybersecurity field usually have multiple types and formats, including structured data, semi-structured data and unstructured data. Therefore, computational methods and techniques suitable for different types of data are needed to effectively utilise these data. Table 1 demonstrates the knowledge representation methods and requirements against each other.

Table 1. Comparison of Knowledge Representation Methods and Requirements

	Human comprehensibility	Inferable	The results of the reasoning can be explained	Knowledge is scalable	Multi-dimensional association	Computable
Predicate Logic Representation	√	√		√		√
Generative Rule Representation	√	√	√			
Knowledge Graph	√	√	√	√		√
Deep Learning Knowledge Representation		√		√		√
MDATA Knowledge Representation	√	√	√	√	√	√

* Note: A √ indicates that the method has a strong characteristic; a blank indicates that the method does not have this characteristic, or that this characteristic is not prominent for the method.

3 Knowledge Representation and Management in MDATA

MDATA is a knowledge representation model that introduces temporal and spatial characteristics, which can effectively solve the problem of unified representation of multi-domain dynamic knowledge and associated fusion analysis. This section firstly introduces the definition and method of knowledge representation based on MDATA, then introduces MDATA's processing method of temporal and spatial information in data, and finally introduces MDATA's data indexing and storage compression management method.

3.1 MDATA Knowledge Representation

MDATA (Multi-dimensional Data Association and inTelligent Analysis) knowledge representation method describes cybersecurity event entities and inter-entity association relations through the quintuple <HEntity, Relation, TEntity, [Time 1, Time 2], [Space 1, Space 2]> to describe the cybersecurity event entities and the association relation between event entities, where HEntity denotes the head entity, TEntity denotes the tail entity, Relation denotes the relation between entities, Time denotes the temporal information, and Space denotes the spatial information.

MDATA knowledge representation can support unidirectional relation, bidirectional relation characteristics, in addition, there are temporal and spatial characteristics on the relation, so time and space information is added to each quintuple. By representing the temporal and spatial characteristics in this way, when the dynamic knowledge changes with the temporal and spatial characteristics, only the corresponding temporal and spatial characteristic values need to be modified without changing the information in the whole knowledge system, which can solve the problem of not being able to represent the dynamic knowledge in the traditional knowledge representation method.

For example, in the OceanLotus attack, "Beginning on 19 October 2019, a network system continued to receive phishing emails, which were opened by an administrator of a web server (IP 192.168.12.58), and the attacker exploited a Microsoft.NET Framework URL spoofing vulnerability (vulnerability number NET Framework URL spoofing vulnerability (vulnerability number CVE-2011-3415) to redirect the administrator to a malicious URL (IP 101.1.35.X) to carry out phishing attacks; on 20 October, the attacker used a malicious website Apache Web Server security vulnerability (vulnerability number CVE-2002-0840) to release a remote control Trojan horse and, on 22 October, through the Trojan horse on the web server to establish a persistent connection with the attacker (IP 101.1.35.X)". Expressed in MDATA multigroup representation as:

<Vulnerability   CVE2002-0840,   exists   on,   web   server,   [2002.10.11], [192.168.12.58]>

<Vulnerability   CVE2011-3415,   exists   in,   web   server,   [2011.12.29], [192.168.12.58]>

<phishing file, exploit, vulnerability CVE2011-3415, [2019.10.8, 2011.12.29], [101.1.35.X,192.168.12.58]>

<Remote Trojan, exploit, vulnerability CVE2002-0840, [2019.10.10, 2002.10.11], [101.1.35.X, 192.168.12.58]>

<backdoor   program,   impact,   web   server,   [2019.10.22], [101.1.35.X,192.168.12.58]>.

Where "[2002.10.11]", "[2011.12.29]", "[2019.10.8, 2011.12.29]", "[2019.10.10, 2002.10.11]", "[2019.10.11]" denote the temporal attributes of the knowledge, i.e., the time of generation of the attack program or vulnerability in the attack event, " [192.168.12.58]", "[101.1.35.X, 192.168.12.58]" denote the spatial attributes of the knowledge, i.e., the IP address of the source of the attack or the target of the attack in the attack event, and Fig. 5 illustrates the MDATA model legend representation:

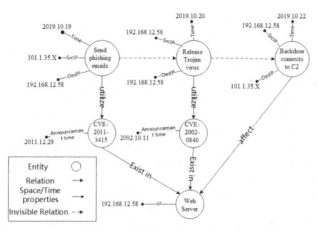

Fig. 5. MDATA model example

3.2 Joint Embedding Method for MDATA Models Based on Spatio-Temporal Information

In the previous section, MDATA knowledge in the form of a quintuple, i.e., <HEntity, Relation, TEntity, [Time], [Space]>, is defined. This MDATA knowledge representation can satisfy the dynamically interpretable and reasonable characteristics of cybersecurity knowledge, and has greater advantages and capabilities than traditional representations. However, in order to meet the demand of MDATA knowledge computable, the technical means of joint embedding of spatio-temporal information is introduced, which makes the static knowledge can be linked to spatio-temporal information for more accurate and efficient expression by embedding the spatio-temporal information of the knowledge in MDATA in the low-dimensional dense vector space at the same time, and then the MDATA knowledge can be fully utilized in a computational way. In this method, firstly, the entities and relations are encoded by the knowledge graph embedding model, and the temporal information [Time] and spatial information [Space] are encoded as feature vectors of fixed dimensions respectively. Then, this vector is added to the embedding vector of each entity and relation in the form of splicing information, which can better mine the potential semantic information in MDATA knowledge. The steps of the MDATA knowledge computation method based on joint embedding of spatio-temporal information are described in detail below:

Step 1: Extraction **of spatial and temporal information on entities and relations and their associations**

For example, if there exists a cybersecurity event under a certain moment t of a cybersecurity scenario, in which there is a TCP (Transmission Control Protocol) connection between the source IP address and the destination IP address associated with a certain specific attack, then the scenario can be extracted by matching the available knowledge base of cybersecurity knowledge and associate it with the corresponding spatio-temporal information, and define cybersecurity knowledge with an evolutionary type through the quintuple representation of MDATA, for example:

<attack, exploit, vulnerability, time, [src, dst]>

where t represents the point in time when the attack occurs, and src and dst represent the source and destination IP addresses associated with that cybersecurity evolution fact, respectively. This information helps to better understand the different spatio-temporal distributions caused by cyber attacks.

Step 2: **Encoding entity vectors and relation vectors**

Entity vectors and relation vectors can be obtained by knowledge graph embedding, specifically, a suitable knowledge graph embedding model needs to be selected, such as TransE [12], ConvE [13], RotatE [14] and so on. Then, all the knowledge graphs are converted into training data available to the embedding model, i.e., triples <HEntity, Relation, TEntity>, which can be viewed as labelled data samples, and thus input into the embedding model. During training, optimisation algorithms such as SGD are used to minimise these predefined loss functions of the embedding model. The embedding models need to be updated by continuously performing vector updates so that the embedding vectors of entities and relations can better represent the semantic associations between them. The final model learns to obtain the embedded representation vectors of entities and relations.

Step 3: **Encoding temporal and spatial information**

Spatio-temporal data contain rich temporal and spatial relations, such as association laws and topological structures. Therefore, many researchers have devoted themselves to exploring a method that can convert data into low-dimensional embedding vectors while preserving the spatial and temporal information of the data for model training and optimisation. The spatio-temporal feature embedding technique is a method based on vector space models, which is applied in the cybersecurity field to encode the temporal and spatial features in MDATA knowledge into low-dimensional vectors respectively. Specifically, the implementation steps of the technique are as follows:

① The data is processed, for example, by normalisation and standardisation, so as to unify the spatio-temporal data representing the knowledge associations.
② Features such as time series (e.g., time points) are extracted from spatio-temporal data, and the data at different time points are represented as a fixed-length vector by means of a time-varying mapping function, such as a cosine function or a periodic function such as a sine function.
③ Features such as spatial data (e.g., source and destination addresses) are extracted from the spatio-temporal data, and their structure is represented by the adjacency matrix, e.g., the adjacency matrix A can be used to represent the connectivity relation (association relation) between the IP address spaces, and then, the spatial features in the matrix are inputted into the graphical convolutional neural network structure, and the spatial embedding vectors of each IP address are finally obtained, where, the ith IP address in the The embedding vector in space can be calculated as follows:

Embedding$(i) = GCN(A, Y)$

Where GCN denotes graph convolution network and Y denotes feature vector in the adjacency matrix. The method performs a convolution operation on the adjacency matrix A and the individual feature vectors therein by means of a graph convolution network, which is continuously updated so as to obtain the spatial embedding vectors.

In spatio-temporal feature embedding, techniques such as cross-validation [15] and regularisation [16] are usually used to avoid overfitting and underfitting problems of the model and to finally obtain the embedded representation vectors of time series and spatial features.

Step 4: **Splicing feature vectors.**

After obtaining the encoded temporal and spatial feature vectors, these vectors are concatenated into entity and relation vectors to form new richer vector representations. For the convenience of description, assume that the entity embedding vector and the relation embedding vector are **e** and **r**, respectively, and the temporal and spatial embedding vectors are **a** and **b**, respectively, and the specific steps are as follows:

① The joint embedding vector of each entity can be represented as $\mathbf{e'} = [\mathbf{e}; \mathbf{a}; \mathbf{b}]$, where $[\mathbf{e}; \mathbf{a}; \mathbf{b}]$ represents the splice of three vectors.
② The joint embedding vector for each relation can be represented as $\mathbf{r'} = [\mathbf{r}; \mathbf{a}; \mathbf{b}]$, where $[\mathbf{r}; \mathbf{a}; \mathbf{b}]$ represents the splice of three vectors.

The final spatio-temporal joint embedding vectors that can be used for computation are shown in Fig. 6:

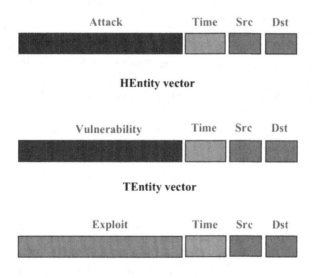

Fig. 6. Joint spatio-temporal embedding vector

Temporal and spatial information is critical to data analysis and mining efforts, e.g., in the cybersecurity field, an attacker usually launches an attack against an intended IP address at a specific time. By embedding temporal and spatial information into entities and relations, the entity and relation vectors can be made more specific and accurate, which is conducive to obtaining potential threat information through the computation of knowledge. In the following, the application process of the MDATA knowledge computation method based on the joint embedding of spatio-temporal information is still introduced by taking the Hailian Flower attack as an example. Firstly, the cybersecurity knowledge related to the attack is extracted, and by associating it with the spatio-temporal information corresponding to the occurrence of the attack, the following two MDATA knowledge are defined:

<Phishing email sent, exploit, CVE-2011-3415, 2019.10.19, [101.1.35.X, 192.168.12.58]>

<Release of remote control Trojan, exploit, CVE-2002-0840, 2019.10.20, [192.168.12.58, 192.168.12.58]>

In the above MDATA knowledge of the OceanLotus attack, there exist two kinds of attacks: sending email attack and releasing remote control Trojan, which have obvious sequential relation. A large number of ternary data (not limited to the OceanLotus attack, and as much as possible) are extracted from the cybersecurity knowledge base, and the classical TransE knowledge graph embedding model is selected for training (taking into account that the number of relations in the cybersecurity is much smaller than the number of entities, and the computational volume is large). After several rounds of iterative updating, the embedding vector of "sending phishing emails" is $(0.32, -0.68, 0.45, -0.11, -0.77, 0.96, -0.21, -0.87, 0.13, -0.55,...)$. The vector of "CVE-2011-3415" is $(0.02, -0.92, -0.09, 0.73, -0.53, 0.78, -0.42, -0.59, 0.39, 0.89, ...)$, the embedding vector of "Release Remote Control Trojan" is $(0.11, -0.82, 0.69, -0.27, -0.95, 0.78, -0.43, -0.7, 0.57, -0.49,...)$ The embedding vector of "CVE-2002-0840" is $(0.02, -0.77, -0.3, 0.73, -0.58, 0.84, -0.48, -0.33, 0.83, 0.55, ...)$. The "utilisation" of the The embedding vector for "utilisation" is $(0.88, -0.36, 0.63, -0.29, -0.98, 0.67, 0.24, -0.71, -0.46, 0.81, ...)$..

In the acquisition of temporal embedding vectors, the cosine function can be used to obtain time-varying features. Specifically, obtain a time series consisting of all time points in the OceanLotus attack scenario, divide it into n time points: $t_1, t_2 ..... t_n$, and map these time points into a fixed-length vector to represent the features of that time point, where the mapping function is shown below:

Embedding$(t_i) = \cos(2\pi t_i /T)$, $i \in [1, n]$

where T is the length of a time window, which is usually equal to half the length of the time series. This function maps each time point to a point in a two-dimensional plane and ensures that the distance between these points is fixed at adjacent time points.

In the acquisition of spatial embedding vectors, the IP address correlation graph in the scenario is constructed from data sources such as alarm logs or threat intelligence, so as to obtain the corresponding adjacency matrix, and the embedding vectors of all IP addresses are finally obtained by pooling layer aggregation after using GCN network modelling, and the spatial embedding vectors of the corresponding IP addresses are finally obtained by looking up the corresponding spatial embedding vectors through the IPs to obtain the embedding vectors of "101.1.35. X" is $(-0.36, 0.58, -0.14, 0.89, -0.47, 0.23, -0.99, 0.12, -0.68, 0.56,...)$. And the embedding vector for "192.168.12.58" is $(-0.34, 0.98, -0.29, 0.76, -0.57, 0.43, -0.18, 0.61, -0.72, 0.35 ...)$..

Information of potential value in the cybersecurity field can be obtained through the interactive calculation of eigenvalues between vectors. For example, whether the relation is the same or not and whether there is any correlation between IP addresses in the cybersecurity facts. Specifically, in the case of Hai Lianhua attack described above, the "exploit" relation not only exists in two MDATA knowledge, but also consists of the embedding vectors of the "exploit" relation itself, the time embedding vector, the embedding vector of the source address and the embedding vector of the destination address, which can be stitched together. It can extract the feature vectors of the two cybersecurity knowledge about the "use" relation itself, and by subtracting the modulus, if we get a value with zero modulus, then we can judge that the same relation exists in the two cybersecurity knowledge. In the determination of IP address relation, we can extract the spatial feature vectors of the same dimension in the joint embedding vectors of the two relations, and calculate the cosine similarity between them [17] to judge the relation, and the specific calculation method is as follows:

$$\text{cosine}(\mathbf{m}, \mathbf{n}) = \text{dot}(\mathbf{m}, \mathbf{n}) / (\text{norm}(\mathbf{m}) * \text{norm}(\mathbf{n}))$$

where $\mathbf{m}$ and $\mathbf{n}$ are source-address embedding vectors of the same dimension or destination-address embedding vectors of the same dimension, respectively, $\text{dot}(\mathbf{m}, \mathbf{n})$ is the dot product of vectors $\mathbf{m}$ and $\mathbf{n}$, and $\text{norm}(\mathbf{m})$ and $\text{norm}(\mathbf{n})$ denote the L_2 norms of vectors $\mathbf{m}$ and $\mathbf{n}$, respectively.

In addition, IP address correlation and analysis can be achieved by extracting features in the same dimension of the joint embedding vectors of entities. For example, in the knowledge of the "Release Remote Trojan Horse" attack described in the Hailian attack, the embedding vectors of the attack in the low-dimensional space consist of the embedding vector of the entity, the time embedding vector, the source address embedding vector, and the destination address embedding vector. The embedding vector of the attack in the low-dimensional space consists of the embedding vector of the entity, the time embedding vector, the source address embedding vector, and the destination address embedding vector. It helps security analysts to achieve the tracking and determination of security time in cyberspace.

The above introduces the computational model of MDATA knowledge from the perspective of knowledge embedding in MDATA, and focuses on the practicality in cybersecurity in conjunction with the case study due to the highly evolutionary nature of knowledge in the cybersecurity domain. The analysis shows that the spatio-temporal joint embedding method based on the MDATA model not only makes the description of entities and relations in vector space more accurate, but also supports higher-level knowledge reasoning **and inference**, which helps cybersecurity experts better understand the nature and mechanism of cyber-attacks, and discover potential attack threats. At the same time, the method is also **interpretable** with inference results, which can present the inference results to the user in an interpretable way so that the user can understand the principles and logic behind the inference results. In addition, the knowledge embedding method based on the MDATA model has high knowledge **scalability**, which allows new knowledge to be easily added to the model, thus continuously improving the accuracy and performance of the system. Meanwhile, the **multi-dimensional semantics and spatio-temporal correlation** also enable the model to better handle complex cybersecurity problems, including the temporal and spatial characteristics of attacks. Finally, the method is also highly **computable**, allowing knowledge embedding and reasoning processes to be implemented through computer programmes, leading to efficient and accurate cybersecurity analysis and prediction.

In summary, the knowledge embedding method based on MDATA model has a wide range of practicality and application value in the cybersecurity field, which can help us to better understand and deal with cybersecurity problems, and improve the level and capability of cybersecurity.

3.3   MDATA Model Characterisation

The MDATA model addresses six characteristic needs faced by knowledge representation and management in cybersecurity, each of which is detailed below:

① **Human Comprehensibility:** The comprehensibility of the MDATA model is reflected in the way of knowledge representation.MDATA adopts a graph structure for knowledge representation, which can clearly show the entities in the knowledge, the relation between the entities, and the spatial and temporal information of the events. Compared with traditional relational databases, MDATA is able to display knowledge more intuitively in the form of graph structure that is easier for people to understand. In addition, MDATA supports visual presentation, making it easier for people to navigate and understand the relations between knowledge. For some complex knowledge domains, MDATA's comprehensibility advantage is especially obvious.

② **Knowledge Reasonability:** The reasonability of MDATA model stems from the relation mining technology it adopts.MDATA uses the semantic features of relations to mine and analyze entities and inter-entity relations in knowledge to improve the reasoning ability and value of the knowledge.MDATA also supports a variety of inference algorithms, such as rule-based reasoning, logic-based reasoning, and statistical-based reasoning.

③ **Interpretability of Reasoning Results:** the interpretability of the reasoning results of MDATA model is reflected in the quintuple representation. The MDATA quintuple contains information such as entity, relation, time, space, etc., which can be represented by the graph structure. In addition, MDATA also supports visual interpretation, presenting the results of knowledge reasoning in a visual way, making it easier for people to understand and accept the reasoning results.

④ **Knowledge Scalability:** the scalability of MDATA model is reflected in its multi-level graph structure.MDATA adopts a multi-level graph structure for knowledge representation, which associates and fuses the knowledge of different domains and dimensions on the main graph, thus solving the problem of the difficulty of unified representation of multi-domain knowledge, and improving the quality and credibility of data.

⑤ **Multi-dimensional Semantics of Knowledge Representation Associated with Spatio-temporal Characteristics:** MDATA introduces spatio-temporal characteristics into knowledge representation, adding spatio-temporal characteristics to relations and attributes in knowledge, so as to be able to express dynamic knowledge more accurately. For example, for a certain event, it is possible to know not only what it is and which entities it is related to, but also the time and place of its occurrence, as well as other related events before and after the occurrence of the event. This representation of spatio-temporal characteristics facilitates a more comprehensive understanding and analysis of knowledge, especially when dealing with knowledge related to time and space.

⑥ **Knowledge Computability:** The MDATA model can be combined with knowledge representation learning methods, thus significantly improving the computational efficiency of knowledge. Traditional knowledge representation learning methods, such as graph-based representation learning and word embedding, usually require complex computations on large-scale knowledge bases, such as graph matching, graph inference, and embedding similarity computation. These computations are of high complexity and require large computational resources and time, limiting their application on large-scale knowledge bases. In contrast, the MDATA model combines knowledge representation and computation by introducing spatio-temporal properties and the structure of multilevel graphs, which achieves efficient computation of knowledge. For example, in the MDATA model, by embedding knowledge as vectors with spatio-temporal characteristics, efficient relational reasoning and attribute computation can be carried out through the operations between the vectors. In addition, the MDATA model can further improve the computational efficiency by dispersing the processing and querying tasks of large-scale knowledge bases to multiple computational nodes through distributed computation.The efficient computational capability of the MDATA model makes it feasible to be applied on large-scale knowledge bases, and also provides strong support for real-time reasoning and application scenarios for knowledge representation and reasoning. This computability of knowledge representation makes the MDATA model have great potential in practical applications, especially in handling large-scale knowledge and complex reasoning tasks, where it shows superior performance.

However, the MDATA model still faces some technical challenges. For knowledge graphs that deal with a large number of entities and complex relations, the computational complexity of the MDATA model is still high and requires more efficient algorithms and hardware support. Despite the advantages of MDATA model in improving computational efficiency, the computational complexity is still a challenge for huge knowledge graphs containing a large number of entities and complex relations. In practical applications, such as social networks, medical knowledge bases, and financial domains, knowledge graphs may contain millions or even tens of millions of entities and complex relation networks, and for the MDATA model, dealing with such large-scale graphs may require long computation time and a large amount of computational resources. To address this challenge, future research can make further improvements in the algorithms and hardware support of MDATA models. For example, optimisation methods based on techniques such as graph neural networks, distributed computing, and approximate computing can be explored to improve the computational efficiency of the MDATA model in processing large-scale knowledge graphs. In addition, the use of high-performance computing hardware such as GPUs and TPUs can also be used to accelerate the computational process of the MDATA model and improve its ability to process large-scale knowledge graphs.

In conclusion, MDATA model has the advantages of human comprehensibility, knowledge reasonability, interpretability of reasoning results, knowledge extensibility, spatio-temporal characteristic correlation, and computability of knowledge representation, which can be adapted to the needs of knowledge modelling in different domains and at different levels. However, when dealing with large-scale complex relational data, the computational efficiency still needs to be improved.

3.4 MDATA Knowledge Management

In MDATA knowledge management, knowledge is classified and managed by indexing key data information in the knowledge to support rapid retrieval, analysis and exploitation of security knowledge. Since knowledge in MDATA can be represented as a quintuple: <head entity, relation, tail entity, time, space>, an index is built for a cybersecurity event knowledge based on its time, space, spatio-temporal information, semantics and relation.

The time and spatial information in the quintuple record two entries each. For an attack event, the entries for the spatial information are the source and destination IP addresses of the attack, and the temporal information is the time of the attack, while for a vulnerability exploit, the entries for the temporal information are the time of creation of the vulnerability and the time of the attack exploiting the vulnerability, and the spatial information is the IP address of the asset.

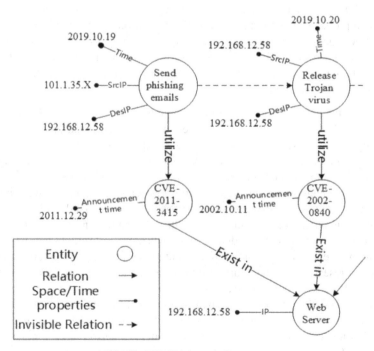

Fig. 7. MDATA knowledge map.

The MDATA Asset Vulnerability Attack Diagram shown in Fig. 7 below contains four sets of MDATA knowledge, namely, <Send Phishing Email, Exploit, CVE-2011-3415, (2019.10.19, 2011.12.29), (101.1.35.X, 192.168.12.58)>, <CVE -2011-3415, presence, web server, (2011.12.29, -nan), (192.168.12.58, -nan)>, <Release Remote Control Trojan, exploit, CVE-2002-0840, (2019.10.20, 2002.10.11), (192.168.12.58 (192.168.12.58)>, <CVE-2002-0840, presence, web server, (2002.10.11, -nan) >, and are referred to as the first through fourth quintets in that order. The following section describes the indexing structure of MDATA from three perspectives: temporal, spatial, and spatio-temporal, using the four quintuples of this Fig. as examples.

3.4.1 MDATA Model Index Construction Method Based on Temporal Characteristics

MDATA time information entries, only one of which needs to be indexed. In the case of an attack event that exploits a vulnerability, the time of the attack event is indexed, and in the case of an event in which a vulnerability exists, the time of the publication of the vulnerability is indexed. At the same time, MDATA-based time information entries can help us better understand the **temporal sequence and time characteristics** of cyber-security events, as well as support higher-level time-related **knowledge reasoning and inference**. By building an index of temporal information, we can retrieve and query time-related knowledge and information more quickly, improving the efficiency and accuracy of data processing. For example, in the event of an attack that exploits a vulnerability, we can build an index of the occurrence time of the attack event, so that we can more accurately analyze and predict the trend and evolution pattern of the attack event. In the case of vulnerabilities, we can index the publication time of the vulnerability, so that we can better track and monitor the evolution of the vulnerability, and take timely measures to prevent and deal with it.

In addition, the MDATA-based temporal information entries also have high **knowledge scalability and multi-dimensional semantics, which allow** new time-related knowledge to be easily added to the model, thus continuously improving the accuracy and performance of the system. At the same time, the temporal correlation also enables the model to better deal with complex cybersecurity issues, including the temporal sequence of attacks.

Finally, the method is also highly **computable**, allowing for the indexing and querying of temporal information through computer programmes, leading to efficient and accurate cyber security analysis and prediction. This computability is important because cyber attacks are increasing in number and complexity and must be addressed with the power of computers.

B+ Tree Index [18]: B+ Tree is a multiplexed balanced query tree optimised for disk storage, the index structure has the following features: ① The non-leaf nodes (index nodes) hold the keyword data of the index, such as time information, and the leaf nodes hold pointers to the complete data. ② The leaf nodes have pointers to the next leaf node, forming an incrementally sorted single linked table to facilitate range queries. (iii) The keyword data in each index node is in sequential order. ④ The right pointer of an index node points to an index node point that is greater than or equal to its keyword, and the left

50 Y. Jia et al.

pointer points to an index node with a smaller keyword than. ⑤ The maximum number
of keywords per node is m, and there are at most m + 1 pointers (in the example, m =
2).

The B+ tree construction process for MDATA knowledge is shown in Fig. 8. ① First,
a B+ tree is created with a root node containing two data in sequential order. (ii) The
first quintuple is merged with the original root node, and the root node splits due to the
time of the first quintuple being ordered second among the three data, the first quintuple
rises to be the root node and points to the two child nodes. (iii) The second quintet has
a smaller time than the root node and is therefore inserted into the left child node of the
root node. (iv) The third quintuple, again after comparison with the root node, is inserted
into the right child node of the root node, which splits, and the third quintuple rises to
the root node. ⑤ The fourth quintuple enters as it is smaller than the smallest keyword
of the root node and hence is inserted into the leftmost node of the root node and causes
the leftmost child node of the root node to split and the fourth quintuple rises up to the
root node causing the root node to split further to produce two intermediate nodes.

The B+ tree index lookup process of MDATA is shown in Fig. 8, e.g., to find the
fourth quintuple <CVE-2002-0840, Existing, Web Server, (2002.10.11, -nan)>, first
compare the time of the vulnerability's release, 2002.10.11, with the time of the root
node, 2019.10.19, and the result is less than. So turn to look up the left child of the root
node and compare it with the time 2002.10.11 of that node, the result is equal. So turn
to look up the right child node of that node and find the pointer corresponding to the
complete data in that leaf node and you can read the corresponding knowledge based on
the pointer.

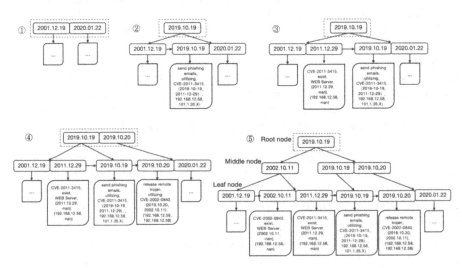

Fig. 8. Schematic diagram of B+ tree indexing

3.4.2 Spatial Characteristics Based Index Construction Method for MDATA Models

As an example of a cybersecurity incident, in Fig. 7, the source IP address 101.35.X sent a phishing email to the destination address 192.168.58 on the day of 2019.10.19. The IP address needs to be searched for the source IP address that initiated the attack, and it can be analyzed whether the address also initiated an attack on other assets of the system, and it can also be searched for the destination IP address that was attacked to find other vulnerabilities in that address. Using the **knowledge extensibility** of the MDATA model, new event information and knowledge can be continuously added to the model index for better discovery of new threats and attacks. At the same time, using the **multi-dimensional semantics and spatial correlation** of the MDATA model, attack behaviours with spatial characteristics can be more accurately described and analyzed, helping to improve the detection and prevention capabilities of cybersecurity.

Prefix Tree Indexing [19]**: a prefix** tree is a data structure that stores strings to form prefix matching paths. Each node in the tree represents a common prefix and forms a prefix with its ancestor nodes, and the strings represented by the node's descendant nodes all have an identical string prefix. Using the prefix tree index can quickly locate the data corresponding to the IP address of the spatial information.

As shown in Fig. 9, a prefix tree is formed by the spatial information in MDATA knowledge. When searching for the source IP address "101.1.35.1" data of the attack, you can locate the third child node of the root node by the IP prefix "101.1.35", and then locate the first child node of that node by the remaining string "1" to the first child node of that node. By placing the same prefix string in one node, the retrieval time can be reduced.

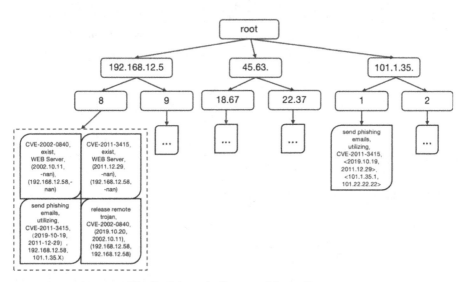

Fig. 9. Schematic diagram of the prefix tree

3.4.3 MDATA Model Indexing Method Based on Spatio-Temporal Properties

In addition to indexing time and space separately, **spatio-temporal data** can also be indexed at the same time, such as the need to query a certain point in time, a certain IP suffered by the attack data, you need to establish an index on the spatio-temporal data in order to quickly find. In this way, the spatio-temporal **correlation and computability** of the MDATA model can be used to quickly find the attack data that meets the requirements. At the same time, due to the **interpretability of the reasoning** results of the MDATA model, the retrieval results can be presented intuitively through visualisation, which is convenient for users to understand and reason. The following describes the spatio-temporal data index building method based on MDATA:

Z3 Index [20] : encodes two-dimensional spatial and temporal points into one-dimensional space, which speeds up spatio-temporal range queries for point objects. Z3 indexes can be created for objects with spatial and temporal attributes. Geospatial is the IP address boundaries (0.0.0.0, 255.255.255.255). Time starts at 1970-01-01 00:00:00 (computational epoch time) and is sliced by a fixed time period, each of which has a defined boundary. The time period can be set to day, week, month, year. a time period is denoted by T, with T.s denoting the start of the period and T.e denoting the end of the period. In a time period, the Z3 index first separates T from the middle (T.m) and encodes 0 if the time point is less than T.m, otherwise encodes 1. It then divides the IP boundaries according to the same dichotomous rule. Thus, the Z3 index can be used with two-bit encoding (time before and IP after) to represent the region where the spatio-temporal point is located.

As shown in Fig. 10, if you look for the space-time point p (t:10, IP: 192.168.12.58), it is in the "01" region (t:0, IP:1) at the first level r = 1, and is in the "11" sub-region of the "01" region at the second level r = 3, and finally in the "10" region of the "0111" region at the maximum level r = 3. Subregion "11" in the second layer, and finally in the "10" region of the "0111" region at the maximum layer r = 3. Finally, p is denoted by "011110".

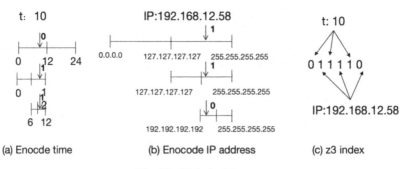

(a) Enocde time   (b) Enocode IP address   (c) z3 index

Fig. 10. Z3 Index Diagram

3.5 Index Compression

When the amount of data in KM continues to grow, the amount of data in the indexes also expands. Such as in the Mysql database performance optimisation is used, the first several layers of the B+ tree nodes into memory, so that when reading data can ensure that part of the IO is carried out in memory, do not have to access the disk each time to improve performance. When the amount of data in the index is further inflated and reaches a point where the memory can not be placed, the performance of data retrieval is bound to be affected. Thus the benefits of compressed indexing include saving disk space, increasing the utilisation of caching techniques, speeding up the transfer of data from disk to memory and loading more indexed data in the content. In data index compression, the key-value types of the index are usually differentiated, using different compression methods. For example, numeric types can be compressed using into byte encoding, string types can be compressed using string compression algorithms based on public prefixes, or general compression algorithms can be used. This method can provide great help in the **expandability and computability** of knowledge management, at the same time, in order to ensure **the reasonability and the interpretability of the reasoning results**, it is necessary to compress the indexed data while retaining the key data features and structural information to facilitate the reasoning and interpretation of the results.

3.5.1 Huffman Coding

Statistical character frequency compression algorithm, the most commonly used is **Huffman coding** [21]. This coding method is a coding method proposed by Huffman in 1952, which is a generalised entropy coding algorithm for lossless data compression, and is usually used to compress character data with a relatively high repetition rate. The principle is based on the probability of occurrence of characters to construct for each character prefix unique code word with the shortest average length. That is, characters with high frequency of occurrence are represented by shorter codes, while characters with low frequency of occurrence are represented by longer codes. Compression algorithms based on statistical character frequency are usually suitable for scenarios where the frequency of occurrence of characters is not uniform, and if certain characters occur more frequently, they can be encoded using shorter code words. As shown in Fig. 11 when indexing spatial information for compression, the frequency of occurrence of characters in an IP address can be counted and encoded. The encoding process is to determine a unique prefix code through the traversal process from the root node to the leaf nodes, and the characters that appear more frequently are encoded using a shorter prefix code.

Huffman coding is performed for the IP addresses (192.168.12.58, 101.1.35.1) in Fig. 7. As shown in Fig. 11, a total of nine different characters appear in the two IP addresses, and their frequency of occurrence is given in the coding table, so the corresponding Huffman tree can be constructed from this frequency table.

Huffman's tree building process is shown in Fig. 12, firstly, the character frequencies counted in the frequency table in Fig. 11 are extracted as a frequency pool, and each time, the two smallest weight values from the frequency pool are selected as child nodes, and their weights are added to generate a parent node until all the values in the frequency pool are used up. The specific process is as follows: ① In Fig. 11(a), the two smallest

① Input spatial information :
101.1.35.1
192.168.12.58

② Count character frequency :

character	frequency
'1'	7
'.'	6
'2'	2
'5'	2
'8'	2
'0'	1
'3'	1
'6'	1
'9'	1

Fig. 11. Statistical character frequency compression algorithm

weight values 1 and 1 are selected to generate a parent node with weight value 2, and a new weight value 2 will be added to the frequency pool, ② In Fig. 11(b), the two smallest weight values 1 and 1 are selected to generate a parent node with weight value 2, and a new weight value 2 will be added to the frequency pool, ③ In Fig. 11(c), the two smallest weight values 2, 1 are selected to generate a new parent node, and the new parent node will be added to the frequency pool, and the new parent node will be added to the frequency pool. Minimum weights 2, 2, to generate a parent node with weight value 4, and will add a new weight value 2 in the frequency pool. The rest of the process is similar and will not be repeated, and repeat the operation until all the weights in the frequency pool have been used up.

As shown in Fig. 12(h), the minimum prefix encoding of each character in a Huffman tree can be obtained by starting from the root node of the Huffman tree and recording the weight values of the edges passed along the way until its corresponding leaf node, e.g., the weight of the character '1' is 7, and the encoding is the two edges passed from the root node to its corresponding leaf node The corresponding encoded value is '01'. Taking the ip value 101.1.35.1 as an example, after Huffman coding in the coding table of Fig. 12(h), its coded value is "01 1100 01 10 01 10 1101 0010 10 01", as shown in the coding table of Fig. 12(h). It can be calculated that a total of ($7 \times 2 + 6 \times 2 + 2 \times 3 + 2 \times 4 \times 3 + 1 \times 4 \times 4 = 72$) bits are needed for encoding after Huffman encoding. The original IP address has 9 different characters, so it originally required 4 bits per character for preservation.$2^4 > 9$, while the original two IP addresses have a total of 23 characters, so a total of 92 bits are required for preservation. From this calculation, Huffman coding can compress the index data of spatial information. The query process after index compression is as follows, the data to be queried can be encoded with Huffman coding first, and then queried with the encoded values, and the query process is as described in the prefix tree indexing in Sect. 3.3.2.

3.5.2 Public Prefix Based String Compression Algorithm

The public prefix based string compression algorithm [22] is to save the IP address in the MDATA spatial index with a string, for the index compression of string type. The public prefix compression algorithm is used, the compression process is shown in

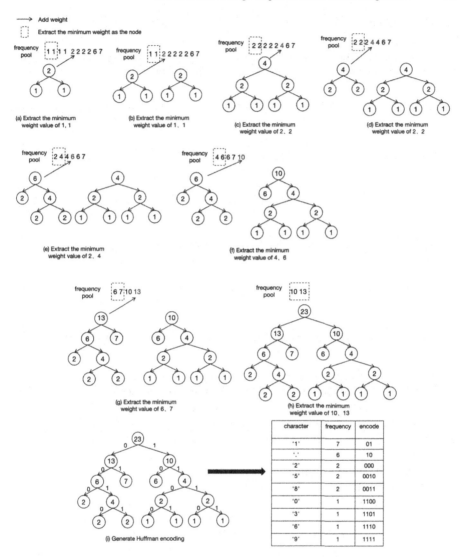

Fig. 12. Schematic diagram of Huffman coding

Fig. 13, all the key value strings in accordance with the character order of the sorting arrangement on the numerical axis, the numerical axis is divided into intervals, each interval of the string has a longest public prefix, the longest public prefix is assigned a coded value. As in the Fig., the public prefix "198.168.12" is assigned a coded value of "0110" for compression (the coding method can be referred to Hu-Tucker coding [23]), and then the public prefix strings are replaced interval by interval. The public prefix string is then encoded by substituting the public prefix string interval by interval. The public prefix encoding and its corresponding encoding value constitute a dictionary, in the index query process, the first query data in the dictionary is converted to the corresponding encoding value, and then use the encoding value in the index structure for the query, the search process as shown in Sect. 3.3.2. The public prefix-based string compression algorithm is applicable in the index compression of spatially typed data because IP addresses of a subnet, usually enjoy repeated public prefixes.

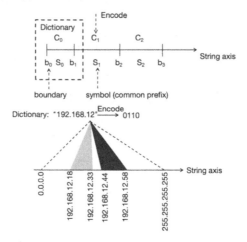

Fig. 13. String compression algorithm based on public prefixes

In addition to the methods introduced above, there are also BWT [24] (Burrows-Wheeler Transform) algorithm through BWT transform can gather the duplicate characters in the index together, and then encode the duplicate characters with the swimmer to simplify the index and improve the compression effect, and FSE [25] (Finite State Entropy) encoding and other methods to compress the index to reduce the storage space of the index.

The above introduces the management method of MDATA model from the perspectives of MDATA's knowledge representation, construction of spatio-temporal indexes, and index compression. In addition to the above aspects, it is worthwhile to pay attention to the fact that when the amount of MDATA data continues to grow, in order to meet the requirements of higher availability, security, fault tolerance and capacity of the system, it is necessary to carry out a distributed design of the entire knowledge management system to improve the system's expansion performance. For example, multi-copy backup improves the fault tolerance and crash recovery capability of the system, distributed consensus algorithm using master-slave replication improves the single-point fault tolerance of the system, and data slicing method is used to route the data to different clusters in order to improve the data processing performance of individual clusters.

4 Summary

This chapter mainly analyzes the needs and challenges faced by knowledge representation and management in the cybersecurity field. Considering human comprehensibility, reasonability, interpretability of reasoning results, knowledge scalability, multi-dimensional semantics with spatio-temporal correlation and computability, we propose a quintuple knowledge representation method based on the multi-dimensional correlation cognitive MDATA model, and combine it with the spatio-temporal data characteristics to design and implement a knowledge management method to support spatio-temporal and spatial efficient querying. Specifically, our approach abstracts cybersecurity event knowledge into quintuples, i.e., head entity, tail entity, relation, time and space, which is easy for human to understand and reason, and can support knowledge extension. Meanwhile, we also designed a joint embedding method of spatio-temporal information supporting the MDATA quintet and an indexing method of spatio-temporal properties, which enable us to quickly query security event knowledge with spatio-temporal relevance. Through these methods, we can achieve accurate real-time research and judgement of cybersecurity event knowledge, as well as the effective use of knowledge, which provides theoretical and technical guarantee for the prevention and response of cybersecurity events.

References

1. Bench-Capon, T.J.M.: Knowledge Representation: An Approach to Artificial Intelligence. Elsevier, Amsterdam (2014)
2. Alavi, M., Leidner, D.E.: Knowledge management and knowledge management systems: Conceptual foundations and research issues. MIS Q. 107–136 (2001)
3. Nian, Z.G., Liang, S., Ma, F.L., et al.: Research and application of knowledge representation. Comput. Appl. Res. **187**(05), 234–236+286 (2007)
4. Chaudhri, V., Baru, C., Chittar, N., et al.: Knowledge graphs: introduction, history and perspectives. AI Mag. **43**(1), 17–29 (2022)
5. LeCun, Y., Bengio, Y., Hinton, G.: Deep learning. Nature **521**(7553), 436–444 (2015)
6. Guo, J.J., Liu, Y., Zhang, X., et al.: Implementation and application of rule base management system. China Digit. Med. **12**(05), 59–61+52 (2017)
7. https://tech.meituan.com/2020/05/14/meituan-security-zeus.html
8. Liu, B., Wang, X., Liu, P., et al.: KGDB: a knowledge graph database management system with unified model and language. J. Softw. **32**(03), 781–804 (2021). https://doi.org/10.13328/j.cnki.jos.006181
9. https://www.wikidata.org/wiki/Wikidata:Main_Page
10. Dolk, D.R., Konsynski, B.R.: Knowledge representation for model management systems. IEEE Trans. Softw. Eng. (6): 619–628 (1984)
11. https://www.modelscope.cn/home
12. Bordes, A., Usunier, N., Garcia-Duran, A., Weston, J., Yakhnenko, O.: Translating embeddings for modelling multi-relational data. In: Advances in Neural Information Processing Systems, vol. 26 (2013)
13. Dettmers, T., Minervini, P., Stenetorp, P., Riedel, S.: Convolutional 2D knowledge graph embeddings. In: Proceedings of the AAAI Conference on Artificial Intelligence, vol. 32, no. 1 (2018)
14. Sun, Z., Deng, Z.H., Nie, J.Y., et al.: RotatE: knowledge graph embedding by relational rotation in complex space. arXiv preprint arXiv:1902.10197 (2019)
15. Efron, B., Gong, G.: A leisurely look at the bootstrap, the jackknife, and cross-validation. Am. Stat. **37**(1), 36–48 (1983)
16. Evgeniou, T., Pontil, M., Poggio, T.: Regularization networks and support vector machines. Adv. Comput. Math. **13**, 1–50 (2000)

17. Rahutomo, F., Kitasuka, T., Aritsugi, M.: Semantic cosine similarity. In: The 7th International Student Conference on Advanced Science and Technology ICAST, vol. 4, no. 1, p. 1 (2012)
18. Shi, E., Gu, D.Q., Feng, D., et al.: Research and optimisation of B+ tree indexing mechanism. Comput. Appl. Res. **34**(6), 1766–1769 (2017)
19. Leis, V., Kemper, A., Neumann, T.: The adaptive radix tree: ARTful indexing for main-memory databases. In: 2013 IEEE 29th International Conference on Data Engineering (ICDE), pp. 38–49. IEEE (2013)
20. Li, R., He, H., Wang, R., et al.: JUST: JD urban spatio-temporal data engine. In: 2020 IEEE 36th International Conference on Data Engineering (ICDE), pp. 1558–1569. IEEE (2020)
21. Moffat, A.: Huffman coding. ACM Comput. Surv. (CSUR) **52**(4), 1–35 (2019)
22. Zhang, H., Liu, X., Andersen, D.G., et al.: Order-preserving key compression for in-memory search trees. In: Proceedings of the 2020 ACM SIGMOD International Conference on Management of Data, pp. 1601–1615 (2020)
23. Hu, T.C., Tucker, A.C.: Optimal computer search trees and variable-length alphabetical codes. SIAM J. Appl. Math. **21**(4), 514–532 (1971)
24. Manzini, G.: An analysis of the burrows wheeler transform. J. ACM (JACM) **48**(3), 407–430 (2001)
25. Moffat, A., Petri, M.: ANS-based index compression. In: Proceedings of the 2017 ACM on Conference on Information and Knowledge Management, pp. 677–686 (2017)

MDATA Knowledge Acquisition

Yan Jia[(✉)] and Aiping Li

National University of Defense Technology, Changsha 410073, China
jiayanjy@vip.sina.com, liaiping@nudt.edu.cn

Knowledge acquisition is one of the three parts of MDATA model. Knowledge acquisition mainly studies the process of human acquiring knowledge. It covers the steps of human cognition and processing information, and includes knowledge extraction and knowledge deduction. Knowledge extraction mainly studies the process of extracting entities, relationships and spatio-temporal attributes from big data in cyberspace. Knowledge deduction mainly studies the process of deducing new knowledge from known knowledge, which involves the complement of missing knowledge and the inference method of unknown knowledge in MDATA knowledge base.

Firstly, in Sect. 1, the concepts of knowledge acquisition and traditional knowledge extraction and inference methods are introduced. In Sect. 2, starting from the requirements of knowledge acquisition, such as interpretability and verifiability, the challenges of traditional knowledge extraction and inference are expounded. Section 3 introduces the automatic extraction methods for MDATA models, including entity and relationship extraction and spatio-temporal attribute extraction. Section 4 introduces the inference methods for MDATA models, including the inference methods for relationships between unknown entities and temporal relationships between events. Finally, Sect. 5 summarizes this chapter.

1 Research on Knowledge Acquisition

1.1 Basic Concepts of Knowledge Acquisition

Knowledge Acquisition (KA) is a process that aims to study how to obtain the knowledge needed for solving problems from various sources and convert it to computers. By studying human knowledge acquisition behavior, we can better understand human cognition and processing steps of information, as shown in Fig. 1. Knowledge acquisition is a process from data to information, and then to knowledge processing, in which data is the original material, information is the logical data after processing, knowledge is to refine the association between information to complete the current task, and wisdom is concerned about the future with the ability to predict.

Y. Jia et al. (Eds.): *MDATA Cognitive Model: Theory and Applications*, LNCS 15470, pp. 59–85, 2025.
https://doi.org/10.1007/978-981-96-3528-3_3

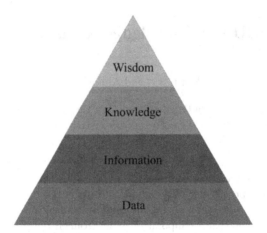

Fig. 1. Schematic diagram of DIKW framework.

For example, in the traditional knowledge acquisition method, for the corpus "on March 6, 2022, an attacker carried out a code execution attack to download a malicious payload by using the remote code execution vulnerability (CVE-2017-0199) existing in Microsoft Office 2010 version." If the knowledge representation chosen by the user is a triplet of knowledge graph, the triplet of knowledge graph "<code execution attack, exploitation, remote code execution vulnerability>, <remote code execution vulnerability, exists in, Microsoft Office 2010>" can be extracted.

MDATA Knowledge Acquisition is the process of studying how to extract knowledge with huge scale, evolution and correlation from big data in cyberspace, which is in line with the knowledge representation of MDATA model. There are two kinds of MDATA knowledge acquisition methods, one is extraction method, and the other is deduction method, corresponding to induction operator and deduction operator respectively.

Induction Operator is the operator composition of extracting knowledge based on big data in cyberspace, which includes entity extraction, relationship extraction and spatio-temporal attribute extraction operators. Among them, entity extraction identifies and extracts named entities such as attacks, vulnerabilities and assets. Relation extraction is responsible for the association between entities. Attribute extraction is responsible for extracting the spatio-temporal information of entities and relations, to complete the knowledge extraction function of MDATA. The **Deduction Operator** is based on the known cyberspace security knowledge to the unknown knowledge, including the deduction method of the entity, knowledge, and spatio-temporal attributes oriented to the cyberspace security relationship, to complete the MDATA knowledge deduction function.

For example, for the corpus "On October 20, 2019, an attacker used a malicious Apache Web Server security vulnerability (vulnerability number CVE-2002–0840) to release a remote-control Trojan, and established a persistent connection with the attacker through the Trojan program to the web server (IP 201.11.145.X) on October 22." If the knowledge representation chosen by the user is the MDATA knowledge model, such as the MDATA knowledge representation method in Sect. 3.1, the five-tuple of MDATA knowledge can be extracted "<attacker, exploit, Apache Web Server security vulnerability, 2019.10.20>, <attacker, establish persistent link, web server, 2019.10.22, 201.11.145.X>" etc.

In the above knowledge acquisition example, the new MDATA five-tuple knowledge of "<web Server, existence, Apache Web Server security vulnerability, 2019.10.22, 201.11.145.X>" can be deduced by using the knowledge of two MDATA five-tuples.

In the following, the existing methods of knowledge extraction and knowledge deduction are introduced.

1.2 Existing Knowledge Extraction Methods

The earliest knowledge extraction methods are manual methods, that is, knowledge acquisition methods based on manual communication between knowledge engineers. However, these methods rely on many manual processing of knowledge, and cannot realize large-scale and automatic knowledge extraction. With the development of deep learning technology, the use of deep learning related technologies for knowledge extraction has made significant progress, and the degree of automation and accuracy have been greatly improved. Knowledge extraction based on deep learning is mainly divided into named entity recognition, relation extraction and entity linking. This section introduces the related work of these technologies.

1.2.1 Named Entity Recognition Technology

Entities are the most basic elements of knowledge graph. Named Entity Recognition (NER) technology extracts meaningful entities and their categories from text, which mainly includes names of people, places, and organizations. Named entity recognition (NER) technology using deep learning model mainly uses two main types of technologies for entity recognition. The first is label classification, and the other is to use span to enumerate all words that may be entities in a sentence [1, 2]. Nowadays, there are also many industrial tools that can be directly used, such as StanfordCoreNLP, NLTK, etc.

Neural network-based named entity recognition methods first extract the content of the text into a vector form, and then use neural networks to learn and optimize these vectors. During the learning process, the neural network will automatically capture the context information and learn the semantic representation of the entity. Each token in the extracted text is passed through the neural network corresponding to a score function, and its output is the score of the entity position, which is used to evaluate which entity the token belongs to. Finally, the extracted entities are obtained according to the division of tokens and entities.

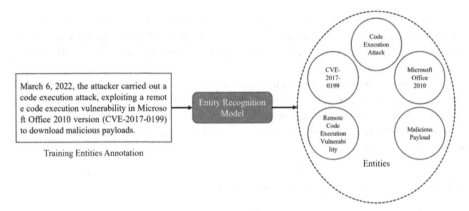

Fig. 2. An illustration of named entity recognition.

The corpus "On March 6, 2022, an attacker performed a code execution attack to download a malicious payload using a remote code execution vulnerability (CVE-2017-0199) in Microsoft Office 2010." As an example, the overall extraction process is shown in Fig. 2. It can be divided into tokens in word units, which are input into the neural network to obtain a low-dimensional vector representation. The output label of "remote" is the beginning of the entity, "code execution" is the middle of the entity, and "vulnerability" is the end of the entity, that is, the extracted entity is "remote code execution vulnerability". The specific process is as follows:

Step 1: Annotate the entities in the training text. For example, the first character of "code execution attack" is labeled as the beginning of the entity B-TECH, TECH denotes the entity type;

Step 2: Divide the extracted sentence into character tokens. For example, the text of "code execution attack" is divided into tokens and its corresponding position representation and input into the encoder;

Step 3: Map the input text into a low-dimensional vector representation using a pre-trained language model. For example, the text in the example goes through the second step to obtain a low-dimensional vector representation through a multi-layer encoder;

Step 4: Use a linear classifier to perform multi-label classification on the low-dimensional representation vector, score the low-dimensional vector corresponding to each token through the linear classifier, and divide the sentence into entities according to the highest score.

According to the above steps, the word "code" in "code execution attack" corresponds to the label B-TECH, indicating that "code" is the beginning of the entity "code execution attack" with type "TECH". While "O" means that the corresponding character is not an entity. The classifier is used to determine the entity boundary, and the highest B-TECH score is obtained for "code", the highest I-TECH score is obtained for "code execution attack", which represents the middle part of the entity, and the highest E-TECH score is obtained for "attack", which represents the end of the entity. Therefore, the entity "code execution attack" can be extracted.

The main advantages of the proposed method include: ① **Automaticity:** it can automatically learn and discover patterns and rules in the data, without manually designing features or rules; ② **High accuracy:** when dealing with a large amount of data, it can automatically capture the patterns and rules in the data, thereby improving the accuracy of the model. The disadvantages are: ① **High training data requirement:** high data demand and a large amount of data are required for training, especially for entity extraction of cybersecurity knowledge graph, a lot of manual labeling of cyberspace security entities is required.

1.2.2 Relation Extraction Technology

Relation extraction technology is to automatically extract the semantic relationship between every two entities in the text of a given named entity, and the goal is to obtain the r in the entity-relation triple (h, r, t). Relation extraction is a key step in the construction of knowledge graph, and provides important support for the application of knowledge graph. Relation extraction techniques can be divided into two categories according to whether a relation type is given or not. Limited relation extraction techniques know the set of all relations and transform relation extraction into a classification problem. The relation category of open relation extraction is not predefined, and the system automatically finds and extracts the relation type from the text.

Generally, unsupervised clustering methods are used to conduct research [3]. Limited by the difficulty of regularizing the clustering results themselves and the low recall rate of low-frequency instances, the extraction effect is generally poor, and it is difficult to directly use it to construct knowledge graphs. At present, relation extraction methods based on supervised methods are the most widely and fully studied. Taking reference [4] as an example, it is one of the first works to use deep neural networks for relation extraction. This method introduces a position vector to determine the position of the entity corresponding to the relation to be extracted. Then, the corresponding entity representation and position vector of the relation to be extracted are input into the neural network. Finally, the output of the neural network is a score function, which is used to indicate the existence of a certain relationship between two entities.

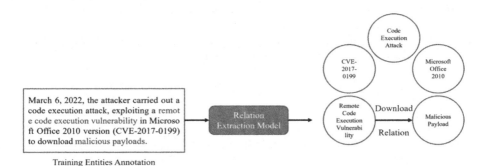

Fig. 3. An illustration of relation extraction.

Take the corpus "On March 6, 2022, an attacker carried out a code execution attack to download a malicious payload using the remote code execution vulnerability (CVE-2017-0199) in Microsoft Office 2010 version" as an example. As shown in Fig. 3, to extract the relationship between "remote code execution vulnerability" and "malicious payload", the relationship extraction process with supervised training is as follows:

Step 1: Annotate the corpus between entities "code execution attack" and "remote code execution vulnerability" as describing the relationship "using";
Step 2: Input the head entity, tail entity and labeled relationship description into the encoder to obtain a low-dimensional vector representation.
Step 3: The low-dimensional vectors are pooled and input to the classifier for scoring, and the highest score is output as the final relation.

For example, for the above entity and corpus description, the score of the relationship "using" is higher than that of other relations, so the relationship between entities is "using".

The advantages of using deep learning algorithms for relation extraction are as follows: ① **Automaticity:** to automatically learn and discover patterns and rules in data, manual feature engineering is not needed; ② **High accuracy:** the accuracy of relation extraction based on deep learning training is generally high. Disadvantages: ① **Label dependency:** This supervised learning-based relation extraction relies on many labeled corpuses.

1.2.3　Entity Linking Technology

Entity linking is a technology that maps a mention to the corresponding entity on the knowledge graph, and removes the ambiguity and ambiguity of the mention. Entity linking technology generally includes two parts: candidate entity generation and candidate entity ranking (entity disambiguation). Related work mainly focuses on the entity disambiguation part.

Take reference [5] as an example, this work is the earliest work that proposes to use deep neural networks for entity linking. The first step of entity linking is to use named entity recognition technology to identify entities in the text. The second step is to expand the query and display the synonyms of the entity. The third step generates candidate entities, and finds all relevant entities in the knowledge base according to the results of the second step expansion query. Finally, this work uses CNN to perform feature comparison and select the most similar entities as linked entities.

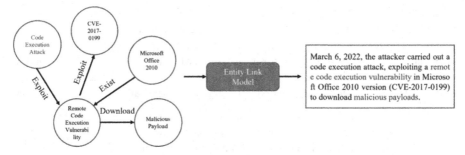

Fig. 4. An illustration of entity linking.

Taking the corpus "on March 6, 2022, an attacker carried out a code execution attack to download a malicious payload by using the remote code execution vulnerability (CVE-2017-0199) existing in Microsoft Office 2010 version" as an example, the overall entity linking process is shown in Fig. 4. Assuming that there is a constructed cyberspace security knowledge graph, linking the "code execution attack" in the graph with the corresponding entity in this text can be performed as follows:

Step 1: Use named entity recognition technology to extract the cyberspace security entities in this text;
Step 2: Then, the synonyms of "code execution attack" are added to the candidate set.
Step 3: Finally, the entities in the knowledge graph are compared with the entities in the candidate set, that is, the entities in the knowledge graph are corresponding to the entity "code execution attack" in the text. The entity with the highest feature similarity is the corresponding entity.

The advantages of using deep learning for entity linking are: ① **High accuracy:** compared with the traditional machine learning method, there is no manual feature engineering and high accuracy; The disadvantages are: ① **label dependency:** it is a problem of insufficient labeled data; ② **Insufficient transferability:** the entity linking task only has relatively high quality labeled data in a very limited number of domains, so how to make full use of the labeled data or even do not need the labeled data to complete the entity linking is an important challenge.

1.3 Existing Methods for Knowledge Inference

At present, many researches focus on knowledge deduction, and a series of knowledge deduction methods have been formed in practice. In this book, they are mainly summarized as logic-based methods, production rule-based methods, deep learning-based methods, and knowledge graph-based methods.

1.3.1 Methods Based on Predicate Logic

Logic-based deduction refers to the direct use of first-order predicate logic, description logic and other methods to represent and deduce rules formulated by experts, and such methods have the characteristics of high accuracy and strong interpretability [6].

According to the different representation of rules, logic-based inference methods can be divided into first-order predicate logic-based inference and description logic-based inference. The former uses first-order predicate logic to represent rules predefined by experts and then deduces them in propositional units, while the latter achieves knowledge deduction by determining whether a description satisfies logical consistency.

The general steps of knowledge deduction based on predicate logic are as follows:

Step 1: Determine the premise and conclusion: First determine the premise and conclusion that need to be inferred, usually expressed in symbols;

Step 2: Convert to standard form: Convert the premise and conclusion to the standard form of predicate logic respectively, that is, use all quantifiers, predicates and variables, and arrange them in a specific order;

Step 3: Apply the logic rules: Use the logic rules to derive the relationship between the premise and the conclusion. These rules include deduction, induction, and resolution, among others;

Step 4: Perform deduction: Use known facts and assumptions to deduce the relationship between the premise and the conclusion, looking for evidence that makes the conclusion true;

Step 5: Test the results: Test the conclusions obtained to ensure their correctness and validity.

Suppose we have mastered a predicate logic $P1 \wedge P2 \rightarrow P3$, such as P1 = (OceanLotus, utilization, CVE-2011-3415, 2019.10.19, 192.168.12.58), P2 = (CVE-2011-3415, existence, web server, 2011.12.29, 192.168.12.58), P3 = (OceanLotus, control, web server, 2019.10.19, 192.168.12.58), then in this case we can deduce new knowledge P3 based on the logic we already have.

Its advantages mainly include: ① **High reliability:** logic-based knowledge deduction can express knowledge in formal language, through logical rules and knowledge representation, deduction, and draw new knowledge conclusions. These conclusions have high accuracy and reliability, which can help people better understand the knowledge and the field; ② **Strong interpretability:** logic-based knowledge deduction has good interpretability, which can clearly show the deduction process and results. This is very important for decision makers and professionals, which can help them understand the process and results of the deduction.

However, it also has the following drawbacks: ① **Low efficiency:** logic-based knowledge deduction requires complex logical calculation and deduction, which requires a lot of computing resources and time, and has low processing efficiency; ② **Narrow scope of application:** logic-based knowledge deduction is mainly suitable for formal knowledge and domain, and the deduction effect is not good for informal knowledge and domain; ③ **The difficulty of knowledge representation:** logic-based knowledge deduction needs to express knowledge in logical language, which requires professional knowledge and skills. For non-professionals, knowledge representation is difficult.

1.3.2 The Method Based on Production Rule Deduction

A production rule is an "IF THEN" statement in the following form: "IF A THEN B". Where "IF" denotes the precondition and "THEN" denotes the conclusion [7]. In the knowledge deduction based on production rules, the system will deduce new knowledge by matching the preconditions of the rules according to the existing knowledge base and rule base, to complete the deduction process.

The general steps of the knowledge inference process based on production rules include:

1. Determine the goal of inference: define the conclusion to be deduced;
2. Define the knowledge representation form: represent the knowledge of the problem domain as a set of production rules, each of which includes preconditions and conclusions, such as: "if the preconditions, then the conclusion";
3. Build the rule base: compose the rule base of the production rules and store them in the computer;
4. Determine the known conditions: input the known conditions of the problem domain into the computer;
5. Match rules and perform derivation: select production rules from the rule base that match the known conditions, execute the derivation process, and draw new conclusions;

Add the new conclusion to the known condition, and repeat step 5 until the target conclusion is deduced or the new rule can no longer be applied.

During inference, the inference engine selects a rule from the rule base and tries to match its preconditions to facts in the knowledge base. If the match is successful, the rule can be applied and new facts can be obtained from the conclusion of the rule. These new facts can in turn be added to the knowledge base to continue the inference process.

When the preconditions are met, the conclusion can be reached by applying the production rule. For example, "IF (OceanLotus, utilize, CVE-2011-3415, 2019.10.19, 192.168.12.58) AND (CVE-2011-3415, exist, web server, 2011.12.29, 192.168.12.58), THEN (OceanLotus, Control, web Server, 2019.10.19, 192.168.12.58) ". If we know cyberspace security incident (OceanLotus, exploitation, CVE-2011-3415, 2019.10.19, 192.168.12.58) and cyberspace security incident (CVE-2011-3415, exists in, web server, 2011.12.29, 192.168.12.58), then this deduction mechanism can be used to deduce the possible cyberspace security events based on the knowledge already mastered (OceanLotus, Control, web server, 2019.10.19, 192.168.12.58).

The advantages of this mechanism include: ① **High flexibility:** the form of production rules is very flexible, and it is easy to add, delete or modify rules, so that the system is more suitable for different tasks and environments; ② **Strong interpretability:** because the production rules are in a form that can be understood by people, the deduction system based on production rules is usually easier to explain and debug.

However, it has the following drawbacks: ① **Difficulty in contradiction detection:** since the number of production rules is large, there may be contradictions between different rules, which will lead to wrong conclusions in the system; ② **The completeness is difficult to ensure:** the deduction system based on production rules usually needs a large number of rules to cover all cases, but even if there are many rules, it is difficult to completely cover all cases, which will lead to incomplete conclusions in the system; ③ **Low efficiency of inference:** Due to the large number of production rules, the process of matching rules needs a lot of computing resources, which will lead to low efficiency of inference.

1.3.3   Deep Learning Based Methods

The main idea of deep learning-based knowledge inference is to use the distributed representation and deep architecture of deep learning to model the fact triples of knowledge graph [8]. Its goal is to enable computers to infer new facts from known facts just like humans do. The main idea is to input a large amount of structured and unstructured data into the deep learning model, and infer new knowledge by learning and discovering patterns and rules in it.

Neural network-based inference methods first represent the fact tuples in the knowledge graph in the form of vectors, and then use neural networks to learn and optimize these vectors. During the learning process, the neural network will automatically learn the semantic relationships and connections between entities and relations, so as to obtain more accurate vector representations. The whole neural network is constructed into a score function, and its output is the score of the fact tuple, which is used to evaluate the credibility and relevance of the tuple. Finally, the inference results are obtained by sorting and filtering according to the scores.

Security events <code execution attack, using, ?, [2021.2.1, 2021.3.1], {45.63.114.152, 91.229.77.192}> for example, the general steps of knowledge inference based on deep learning are as follows:

1. Data preparation: collect and process the data involved in inference, such as the collection of cyberspace security events and related attributes, text collections, etc.
2. Knowledge representation: transform data into embedded vector form that neural network can process. In this example, entities "code execution attack" and relations "using" are represented by vectors.
3. Model selection and training: select the appropriate deep learning model according to the type of question and the characteristics of the data, and train it with the training data, so that it can deduce the question and output the correct answer;
4. Inference process: Use the trained model to infer new inputs to (code execution attack, using, ?, [2021.2.1, 2021.3.1], {45.63.114.152, 91.229.77.192}) in the known entities, relations, temporal and spatial attributes as input data, which are imported into the network through the vector of input data. According to the existing knowledge and training data, the system will use the neural network to calculate and analyze to draw a specific conclusion or produce a prediction/answer.
5. Output results: according to the existing information, deduce the corresponding calculation or prediction, and output the results. In some scenarios, it is necessary to manually verify whether the answer is correct. The whole process requires continuous iteration, optimization, and update to improve its efficiency and accuracy.

Its advantages include: ① **Support for automatic learning:** the knowledge inference model based on deep learning can automatically learn and discover patterns and rules in data without manually designing features or rules; ② **Wide range of adaptation:** the knowledge deduction model based on deep learning can deal with various types of data, including text, image, video and audio, and has strong adaptability. ③ **High accuracy:** When dealing with a large amount of data, the knowledge deduction model based on deep learning can automatically capture the patterns and rules in the data, thereby improving the accuracy of the model.

It also has the following shortcomings: ① **High data demand:** deep learning models require a large amount of data to train, otherwise the model is prone to overfitting and other problems; ② **Poor interpretability:** deep learning models are usually black box models, which are difficult to explain the decision-making process and results of the model. ③ **Limited inference ability:** the inference ability is usually based on existing knowledge and patterns, which is difficult to deal with new problems and unknown situations, and the inference ability is limited.

1.3.4 Knowledge Graph Based Methods

Knowledge deduction based on knowledge graph refers to the process of discovering new knowledge and relationships through deduction and logical inference using the information such as entities, attributes, relationships and rules in the knowledge graph, aiming at deducing new facts or identifying incorrect knowledge based on the existing knowledge graph facts [9]. Entities, attributes, and relationships are represented as graph structures in knowledge graphs, where entities and attributes are usually represented as nodes, and relationships are usually represented as edges. Based on the knowledge graph, the unknown nodes (entities) and edges (relationships) can be inferred according to the known nodes and edges in the graph.

The general steps of knowledge inference based on knowledge graph are as follows:

1. Construct a knowledge graph: construct a knowledge graph with related entities and relationships in the domain to be inferred;
2. Problem representation: the problem to be solved is expressed in natural language or other forms, and it is transformed into a machine-understandable form;
3. Problem matching: matching the problem with entities and relations in the knowledge graph to find potentially related entities and relations;
4. Finding paths: Finding paths connecting questions and answers. For knowledge graph-based inference, paths are usually represented by relationships between entities. Algorithms can be used to find the shortest or most likely paths;
5. Follow the path: After finding the path, move gradually according to the relationships along the path and follow the corresponding restrictions, such as entity type, relationship type, etc.
6. Deduction: When the required entity of the problem is reached, a conclusion is drawn based on the various available evidence.

The cyberspace security knowledge graph can be constructed based on the security events that have been mastered, and the unknown security events can be further inferred. For example, <remote code execution vulnerability, exists in, ?, [2021.1.1, 2021.3.1], 192.168.10.1>, which means we want to extrapolate between "[January 1, 2021, March 1, 2021]", which occurs at "IP: 192.168.10.1 "remote code execution vulnerability" is "present" in some software, code, or platform.

Its advantages include: ① **High efficiency:** the relationships between entities, relationships and attributes in the knowledge graph have been established, which can be directly inferred, avoiding a lot of calculation and search, thus improving the efficiency and accuracy of inference; ② **Good interpretability:** the structure and relationship of the knowledge graph can be intuitively explained and understood, which can help people better understand the results of the deduction. The interpretability of the path-based method is stronger, while the interpretability of the embedding and deep learning based method is slightly weaker. ③ **Better scalability:** the knowledge graph is extensible, and new entities, attributes and relationships can be continuously added to improve the coverage of the knowledge base and the accuracy of the deduction.

At the same time, it also has the following drawbacks: ① **High construction cost:** the construction of knowledge graph requires a lot of human and material resources, and requires a lot of data cleaning and processing; ② **The completeness is difficult to guarantee:** the knowledge graph may be incomplete, that is, the knowledge base does not contain all the entities, attributes and relationships, which may lead to the inaccuracy of the inference results. ③ **The complexity of processing unstructured data:** knowledge graph can only deal with structured data. For unstructured data (such as natural language text), additional processing and transformation are needed, which will increase the complexity of inference. ④ **Need further verification and evaluation:** In the construction process of knowledge graph, there may be incomplete, erroneous, inaccurate data sources and other problems. To ensure the accuracy and reliability of the inference results, further verification and evaluation are needed, including manual verification, experimental verification, comparative verification and other methods, to improve the credibility and reliability of the inference results.

2   The Requirements and Challenges

From the perspectives of how to extract and summarize knowledge from huge and complex cyberspace big data and apparent events, how to deduce new cyberspace security event knowledge based on partial cyberspace security event knowledge, and how to ensure the spatio-temporal characteristics of cyberspace security event knowledge, knowledge extraction and deduction face a series of difficulties and challenges. Therefore, it is necessary to study and solve the actual needs of knowledge extraction and deduction in cyberspace security, and analyze the challenges and difficulties faced by knowledge acquisition technology in the field of cybersecurity.

2.1   Requirements for Knowledge Acquisition Technologies

With the expansion and complexity of the scale and structure of cyberspace, cybersecurity knowledge is becoming more hidden and complex. Cyberspace security knowledge acquisition and deduction have their own unique practical requirements, which are elaborated as follows.

① Cybersecurity knowledge should be **accessible**. The premise and foundation of the knowledge in the field of cybersecurity are based on cyberspace big data and performance events, and cyberspace big data must be obtainable to provide the premise and foundation for the acquisition of cybersecurity knowledge.
② The knowledge fully acquired by the network should be **interpretable**. The discovery and early warning of cyberspace security events need to give users interpretable results. Although the pure deep learning-based method has great improvement in automatic acquisition and accuracy, it has shortcomings in interpretability.

③ The knowledge fully acquired by the network should be **correct**. Cyberspace security event analysis and early warning is different from the general knowledge in traditional fields. The correctness needs to be verifiable, that is, in the same application scenario, users can reproduce and verify the correctness of the acquired cyberspace security knowledge.

④ Cyberspace security knowledge sources should **support multi-modal data fusion**. The data in cyberspace contains both structural and unstructured information such as Common Vulnerabilities and Exposures (Cves), as well as attack information exploited in blogs and papers. Therefore, users need to support multimodal data fusion for information extraction.

⑤ The knowledge acquired by cyberspace security should **support semantic multi-dimensional spatio-temporal correlation**. Unlike traditional knowledge in other fields, knowledge in the field of cyberspace security should support the semantic features of multidimensional space and time correlation, that is only at a certain time and certain semantic limit of the space, to obtain the support of the related knowledge of cyberspace security has practical application value.

2.2   The Challenges of Knowledge Acquisition and Inference

According to the five requirements of knowledge acquisition and inference in the field of cyberspace security, which are **acquisition, interpretability**, **correctness, multi-modal data fusion**, and **supporting semantic multi-dimensional spatio-temporal association, ** the difficulties and challenges of existing knowledge acquisition and inference methods are analyzed.

2.2.1   Knowledge Accessibility

Knowledge accessibility refers to all kinds of data, information and knowledge that human beings can grasp, including different ways of expression such as language, images and symbols. In order to extract knowledge, the data must be accessible to human beings, and can also meet the computational complexity of human processing knowledge.

However, different knowledge acquisition and inference methods have different advantages and disadvantages in terms of data availability, such as:

- **Predicate logic and production rules based knowledge acquisition methods** have high requirements in terms of human accessibility, because whether propositional logic or rules, they also need to manually understand cyberspace security corpus, extract propositional logic or production rules in a manual way, and remove the overlapping and conflict problems of rules, which leads to low efficiency of proposition and rule acquisition.
- The **deep learning based method** has been significantly improved in the acquisition and deduction of knowledge. However, deep learning models usually require a large amount of data for training, which may come from different fields, languages or cultures, resulting in the lack of portability and universality of the model, and increasing the difficulty for people to understand and use the model.
- The **knowledge graph method** also has a high degree of automation in terms of knowledge accessibility, because it presents knowledge in a graphical form, which is

easy for people to intuitively understand and use. However, there is the possibility of redundant and false knowledge. However, due to the particularity of the cyberspace security field, its correctness needs to be confirmed manually, which will affect the efficiency of knowledge acquisition.

In the field of cyberspace security, the accessibility of knowledge acquisition is facing challenges, and it is also an important bottleneck that limits the field of cybersecurity artificial intelligence. With the rise of deep learning and knowledge graph methods, the automaticity of knowledge acquisition has been greatly improved. However, due to the particularity of knowledge in the field of cyberspace security, manual verification is still needed, which limits the efficiency of knowledge acquisition.

2.2.2 Interpretability

The interpretability of knowledge acquisition refers to the ability to explain and explain the extracted and inferred knowledge, so that people can understand the acquired knowledge, verify and adjust it. In the field of cyberspace security, the interpretability of knowledge is particularly important because it relates to the accuracy and reliability of the knowledge about cyber threats and risks. However, the existing methods still have some different defects and deficiencies in the interpretability of knowledge, such as:

- **Predicate logic and production rules based knowledge acquisition methods** need to be acquired manually in terms of extraction, and are generally interpretable by preproducing explanatory texts for propositions and rules. However, in the aspect of deduction, the method based on mathematical formula or rule matching reasoning is often used. Generally, the explanation of knowledge deduction can be realized by backtracking the reasoning chain and predicting the reasoning text, so as to have a certain interpretability.
- **Deep learning based methods** perform well in dealing with large-scale data. However, when training large-scale data, their internal learning process and inference process are black box, which cannot provide interpretable results. Therefore, although deep learning technology has the characteristics of high automation and good accuracy in knowledge acquisition, its lack of interpretability also limits its application.
- **Knowledge graph based method** performs well in the understandability of the acquired knowledge, because it presents the knowledge in a graphical form, which is easy for people to intuitively understand and use. Knowledge graphs can also be further improved by semantic interpretation and visualization tools.

Therefore, knowledge acquisition methods need to be able to provide interpretability for acquired knowledge while ensuring automatic acquisition and accuracy. This is also a challenge for knowledge acquisition. In order to solve this challenge, it is necessary to adopt knowledge acquisition methods that are easier for human to understand and express, such as natural language-based representation methods and some representation methods with visual functions.

2.2.3 Correctness

The correctness of knowledge acquisition refers to the need to ensure that the acquired knowledge is correct, and the support is verified and adjustable according to the characteristics of the cyberspace security field. In the field of cyberspace security, the correctness of knowledge is particularly important, because it is related to whether the knowledge of cyber attack and defense is accurate and reliable. However, there are still some different defects and deficiencies in the correctness of knowledge in the existing methods, such as:

- **Predicate logic and production rules based knowledge acquisition methods**, the correctness of propositional logic requires technologies such as interpreters and verifiers to verify the correctness and reliability of the reasoning results. The correctness and completeness of the manually sorted propositional logic are verified by a complete set of logical deduction methods. As the production rules are also manually arranged, a set of grammar checking and knowledge refinement tools are also needed to detect the contradictions, redundancy, omission and other errors between the production rules.
- The correctness verification of the knowledge acquired by the **deep learning based methods**, because of its internal black box, in terms of verification, the current method leaves a part of the training data as validation data to verify the correctness of the acquired knowledge, but due to its lack of interpretation, people have the problem of lack of confidence in the use of the knowledge acquired by deep learning. But due to its lack of interpretation, people have insufficient confidence in using the knowledge acquired by deep learning.
- In the aspect of the correctness verification of knowledge acquisition, the **knowledge graph-based method** is somewhat like the correctness and completeness of production rules. Before the newly extracted and deduced knowledge is put into the cyberspace security knowledge base, in addition to verifying its own correctness, it also needs to detect and verify the contradictions and redundancy of the existing knowledge in the knowledge base to ensure the correctness of the cyberspace security knowledge base.

Therefore, different knowledge acquisition methods have certain means to verify the correctness of knowledge at present, but there are also problems of insufficient automation and low efficiency, which is also a challenge for knowledge acquisition. To solve this challenge, it is necessary to adopt more automatic and intelligent verification methods for the correctness and completeness of knowledge, and provide more efficient verification methods for the correctness of knowledge.

2.2.4 Multi-modal Data Fusion

The sources of cyberspace security knowledge acquisition need to support multi-modal data sources, support structured, semi-structured and unstructured data, and support multimedia pictures, audio and video data, etc. In the field of cyberspace security, the diversity of knowledge sources is an important factor to be considered. However, the existing knowledge acquisition methods still have some different defects and deficiencies in supporting multimodal data fusion, such as:

- The **predicate logic and production rules-based knowledge acquisition methods,** because the method based on predicate logic and production rules is mainly dependent on artificial methods, therefore, the two methods are dependent on experts and knowledge engineers for the artificial understanding of multimodal data, through the expert understanding of cyberspace security field knowledge, propositional logic and production rules are obtained and fused. Is to support multiple modal data fusion, but has the problem of inefficient.
- **Deep learning-based methods** have strong expansibility and adaptability in extracting and deducing knowledge from large-scale data, and their performance and performance can be continuously improved by means of adaptive learning. Therefore, deep learning-based methods can support multi-modal data fusion if the multi-modal data are labeled. However, due to deep learning knowledge interpretability is poorer, it is difficult to explain the result and explanation, which limits its application in the field of security in cyberspace.
- **Knowledge graph-based method,** can support to get the data source of multimodal fusion, support from different sources and modal data acquisition of knowledge, and knowledge integration and organization. In addition, the knowledge graph can also expand and update new knowledge in an automated way, to maintain the timeliness and accuracy of the knowledge base. However, the disadvantages of knowledge graph representations are that their construction and maintenance require a lot of time and resources, and they require professional domain knowledge to be manually verified.

Therefore, different knowledge acquisition methods are currently supported in terms of multimodal knowledge fusion, but there are also problems of insufficient automation and low efficiency, which is also a challenge for knowledge acquisition. To solve this challenge, it is necessary to adopt more automated and intelligent methods to support the acquisition and fusion of multimodal cyberspace security knowledge.

2.2.5 Support Semantic Multi-dimensional Spatio-Temporal Associations

In the field of cyberspace security, the extraction of multi-dimensional associations with inferred data and knowledge, especially with spatio-temporal information characteristics, because they can help to better understand and respond to cyberspace security threats. However, existing knowledge acquisition methods still have many challenges in supporting semantic multidimensional spatio-temporal associations, such as:

- **Predicate logic and production rules-based knowledge acquisition methods,** the acquired knowledge representation models are mostly used to represent static concepts, but lack the ability to model and express dynamic spatio-temporal concepts. For example, in the field of cyberspace security, attack events usually have the characteristics of time series, but the existing knowledge representation methods cannot represent these time series characteristics well, which may lead to limitations in the understanding and response ability of cyberspace security threats.
- **Deep learning-based methods,** cyberspace security big data and knowledge themselves are highly complex and heterogeneous. For example, the attacker's behavior pattern is usually affected by multiple factors, including attack time, attack target, attack method, etc. These factors come from different data sources and knowledge

fields, and need to be fused to obtain more accurate analysis results. The existing deep learning-based methods have certain temporal and spatial embedding representation methods, but they cannot handle the complexity and heterogeneity of semantic multi-dimensional spatio-temporal correlation well.

- **Knowledge graph-based methods,** the spatio-temporal characteristics of cyberspace security threats are usually closely related to geographical locations, such as the geographical locations of attack sources and attack targets. The existing methods of obtaining knowledge graph triples cannot represent this spatio-temporal correlation well, which may lead to certain uncertainties and errors in security analysis and decision-making.

Therefore, how to support semantic multi-dimensional spatio-temporal associations into knowledge extraction and inference, and realize the fusion of complex and heterogeneous data and knowledge, is an important challenge faced by knowledge representation in the field of cyberspace security. A MDATA knowledge acquisition method that supports spatio-temporal attributes and semantic associations is needed to construct a MDATA cybersecurity knowledge base that supports certain inferences and can require manual verification to provide knowledge support for the analysis of cyberspace security events.

3 Automatic Knowledge Extraction Method

Compared with traditional knowledge extraction, MDATA-oriented automatic knowledge extraction method also considers the spatio-temporal information characteristics of knowledge to adapt to the characteristics of cyberspace security. MDATA-based knowledge extraction mainly uses induction operators to extract knowledge from massive data in cyberspace security, including entity extraction, relationship extraction, and spatio-temporal attribute extraction. The inductive operator knowledge acquisition method is a kind of explicit knowledge extraction method, which includes structural/semi-structural data extraction, natural language data extraction and spatio-temporal attribute extraction. The induction operator of MDATA specifically proposes the cyberspace security ontology model based on the characteristics of cyberspace security entities to extract entities and relations from structured/semi-structured data. The distant supervision relation extraction of natural language data such as cyberspace security threat intelligence is used to supplement the missing knowledge in structured/semi-structured data. Finally, a spatio-temporal extraction strategy for cyberspace security entities is used to supplement the spatio-temporal attributes. In this section, the algorithm of MDATA induction operator for knowledge acquisition is introduced in detail. The general framework is shown in Fig. 5.

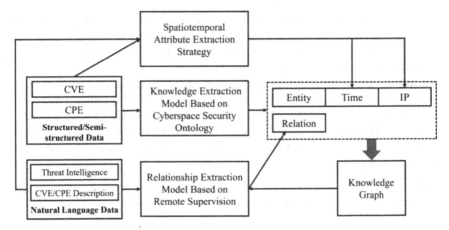

Fig. 5. The framework of automatic knowledge extraction for MDATA model.

3.1 MDATA Knowledge Extraction Method Based on Cyberspace Security Ontology Model

This section primarily elucidates the process of knowledge extraction from databases of vulnerabilities and Trojans, utilizing the MDATA cognitive model grounded in the cyberspace security ontology. It aims to acquire pertinent details concerning the entities of cyberspace security, including their attributes and values, as well as the interconnections that define their relationships.

The knowledge extraction of cyberspace security knowledge base includes extracting the relationship between entities from its unstructured data and extracting entities and entity attribute values from its structured data. For example, the unstructured description of "vulnerability CVE-2021-36744" in the knowledge base CVE reads: "TrendMicroSecurity (Consumer) 2021 and 2020 are vulnerable to a directory connection vulnerability that may allow an attacker to exploit the system to escalate privileges and create denial of service.", from which the relationship between the vulnerability and privilege escalation attacks and the relationship between the vulnerability and denial of service attacks can be obtained. The structured description of "vulnerability CVE-2021-36744" is: "CVSS value: 4.6; Vulnerability type: Denial Of Service; Corresponding CWE ID: 59; Access complexity: Low". This is shown in Fig. 6. Among them, CVSS value, vulnerability type, corresponding CWE ID and access complexity are common attribute names, and entities and their attribute values can be directly extracted according to their attribute names.

Vulnerability Details : CVE-2021-36744

Trend Micro Security (Consumer) 2021 and 2020 are vulnerable to a directory junction vulnerability which could allow an attacker to exploit the system to escalate privileges and create a denial of service.

Publish Date: 2021-09-06 Last Update Date: 2022-07-12

Collapse All Expand All Select Select&Copy   Scroll To Comments External Links
Search Twitter Search YouTube Search Google

- CVss Scores & Vulnerability Types

CVSS Score	6.5
Confidentiality Impact	Partial (There is considerable informational disclosure.)
Integrity Impact	Partial (Modification of some system files or information is possible, but the attacker does not have control over what can be modified, or the scope of what the attacker can affect is limited.)
Availability Impact	Partial (There is reduced performance or interruptions in resource availability.)
Access Complexity	Low (Specialized access conditions or extenuating circumstances do not exist. Very little knowledge or skill is required to exploit.)
Authentication	Not required (Authentication is not required to exploit the vulnerability.)
Gained Access	None
Vulnerability Type(s)	Denial Of Service
CWE ID	59

Fig. 6. Information of vulnerability CVE-2021-36744.

Since the relationship between cyberspace security entities is relatively simple, such as "vulnerability will lead to attack", and there is no explicit expression of the relationship in the description, the relationship between vulnerability and attack is clarified by constructing an ontology model, and entities are extracted based on the ontology model, and then the relationship between entities is obtained. And because the correspondence between entities is uncertain, such as "vulnerability CVE 2019-14847: a defect is found in samba 4.0.0 before samba 4.9.15 and Samba 4.10.10 before samba4.10.x. An attacker can crash an ADDCLDAP server through directory synchronization, resulting in a denial of service. Permissions cannot be elevated for this issue." Both vulnerabilities are "denial of service", but the former is also described as "permissions elevated". The ontology classification is dynamically optimized to ensure that the correct relationship between entities is extracted.

In this section, with the help of ontology modeling [10] and entity recognition model [11], a cyberspace security knowledge extraction method based on ontology model is proposed. The extraction process is shown in Fig. 7. Firstly, at the concept level, the cyberspace security ontology-instance model is constructed and classified. Secondly, in the data layer, the ontology features were combined with the named entity recognition model to identify entities, and the ontology-instance model was optimized by the categories of identified entities. Finally, the relationships between entities are obtained based on the relationships in the ontology-instance model.

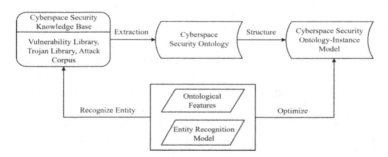

Fig. 7. MDATA knowledge extraction based on cyberspace security ontology model.

Combined with the previous example, the extraction process of the relationship between "vulnerability CVE-2021-36744" and "denial of service attack" is as follows:

Step 1: Construct a coarse-grained cyberspace security ontology model at the conceptual level, and specify the relationship between "vulnerability" and "attack" as "cause" in the model;

Step 2: In the instance layer, the named entity recognition model is used to identify the vulnerability name "CVE-2021-36744" and the combination of attack names "denial of service" and "lifting all limits", and the combination of attack names is optimized to "denial of service" according to the position of negative words.

Step 3: The "vulnerability" in the ontology model is further refined into "denial of service vulnerability", and the "attack" is further refined into "denial of service attack". The relationship of "cause" is inherited between the instance of the denial-of-service vulnerability and the denial-of-service attack.

According to the above algorithm, "CVE-2021-36744" as an instance of denial of service vulnerability inherits the relationship between "denial of service vulnerability" and "denial of service attack", and then extracts a new knowledge <CVE-2021-36744, causes, DOS attack>.

The MDATA knowledge extraction based on the cyberspace security ontology model introduced in this subsection can identify the entities and relationships in the cyberspace security ontology through the named entity recognition of the structured/semi-structured corpus, and construct the progressive cyberspace security MDATA knowledge base.

3.2 MDATA Relation Extraction Algorithm Based on Remote Supervision

Through the previous section, the CVE vulnerability information and CPE asset information can be extracted through the MDATA-based induction operator, such as "CVE-2011-3415", "web server" and other entities. This vulnerability information can be associated and matched through the relationships and patterns defined in the cyberspace security ontology, forming cyberspace security knowledge.

It is impossible to construct complete MDATA cyberspace security knowledge and restore security events only through semi-structured/structured extraction of asset information and vulnerability information. There are other relationships between entities in the corpus that need to be extracted, such as <"send phishing email", "exploit", "CVE-2011-3415">, etc. These relationships exist in unstructured corpus such as threat intelligence and CVE vulnerability description. To capture the relationships between entities to construct a complete security event, it is necessary to extract such relationships.

For the relation extraction in MDATA cyberspace security knowledge base, labeling the relation data requires more effort, and the annotator needs to have certain cyberspace security knowledge to distinguish the annotation relationship between two cyberspace security entities. To solve the above problems, this book proposes a distant supervision relation extraction model, which can use the constructed cyberspace security knowledge graph to automatically label the relationship. The process of relation extraction is shown in Fig. 8.

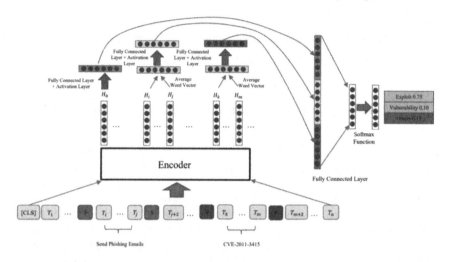

Fig. 8. MDATA relation extraction with remote supervision.

For the corpus to be extracted, such as "Since October 19, 2019, a network system has been receiving phishing emails. The administrator of the web server (IP 192.168.12.58) opened the phishing email. The attacker used Microsoft.NET Framework URL spoofing vulnerability (vulnerability number CVE-2011-3415) to direct the administrator to a malicious URL (IP 101.1.35.X) for phishing." Distant supervision relation extraction of unstructured corpus information can be carried out through the following algorithm steps.

Step 1: The entity in the knowledge graph is matched with the text to be extracted through the entity linking technology, and the textual description of the two entities in the text is corresponding to the relationship. For example, "send phishing email" and "CVE-2011-3415" in the MDATA cyberspace security library can be aligned with the corresponding entities in the text.

Step 2: annotate the text containing the entity by the aligned entity. The relationship between the constructed MDATA cyberspace security library entity "send phishing email" and "CVE-2011-3415" is "exploit", so the text description in the middle of the aligned entity in the text is labeled as the description of the relationship "exploit".

Step 3: Input the sentence containing the head and tail entities into the low-dimensional vector representation of the sentence obtained in the encoder. The sentence obtained in step 2 is input into the encoder, and the low-dimensional representation vector of the sentence is obtained by the encoder.

Step 4: Finally, the relation represented by the sentence is scored through the fully connected layer. The score for "exploit" is 0.75, the score for "vulnerability" is 0.10, and the score for remaining relationship is 0.15. Therefore, the relationship between "send phishing" and "CVE-2011-3415" is "exploit."

Through this method, the entity relationship in the unstructured text information of threat intelligence describing security events is extracted, to supplement the MDATA cyberspace security knowledge extracted in Sect. 3.1. At the same time, the MDATA cyberspace security library that has been constructed and verified manually is used to solve the problem of less text annotation of cyberspace security data by means of distant supervision. However, this method still has the problem of large noise of labeled data, and the extracted knowledge needs to be further verified.

3.3 Spatio-Temporal Attribute Extraction Method of MDATA Based on Entity Link

Compared with the general knowledge graph, the knowledge representation of MDATA model adds the description of spatio-temporal information. In addition to extracting entities and relations, MDATA recursive operators also need to extract spatio-temporal attributes of entities and relations. Although previous works on named entity recognition and open-source tools can accurately identify time and IP address [2], for MDATA-based knowledge representation, the extraction of temporal and spatial (IP address) attributes needs to be aligned with the corresponding entities and relations. For example, the OceanLotus attack describes "From October 19, 2019, a network system continues to receive phishing emails. The administrator of the web server (IP = 192.168.12.58) opened the phishing email. The attacker used Microsoft.NET Framework URL spoofing vulnerability (vulnerability number: CVE-2011-3415) to redirect the administrator to a malicious URL (IP: 101.1.35.X) for phishing attacks".

The existing entity extraction methods can extract the time attribute of "October 19, 2019", but the extraction cannot determine which entity relation pair this time attribute belongs to. Based on the analysis and summary, it is found that most of the temporal attributes and spatial attributes of entities and relationships in threat intelligence texts and analysis reports are near the entities. For example, "IP is 192.168.12.58" in the description is the spatial attribute of the nearby entity "web server". Therefore, for the automatic extraction of temporal attributes in the cyberspace security knowledge graph, a simple and effective strategy based on entity link temporal and spatial attribute extraction method is used, and the extraction process is shown in Fig. 9.

Step 1: The entities "spear attack" and "malicious attachment" to be extracted for temporal attribute are matched in the text to determine the corresponding positions through entity linking technology.

Step 2: Set the window length t, and set the t text sentences before and after the entity as the extraction object of the time attribute. If the extracted text is set to 1, the next sentence containing the time attribute "2019" will be listed as the extraction range of the corresponding time attribute of <harpoonattack, exploitation, malicious attachment>.

Step 3: The extraction range is determined, and the entity extraction method is used to extract the time attribute and IP attribute. The extracted time attribute corresponds to the link attribute, <harpoon attack, exploitation, malicious attachment, [2019]>. For the same security event may be described in different reports, multiple time attributes can be used for calibration.

Step 4: Repeat steps 1–3 to align and extract spatial attributes IP using entity links.

Through the spatio-temporal extraction strategy, the time attribute and IP attribute in the secure time described by unstructured text are corresponding to the corresponding entities. At present, it is a challenge to accurately align entities and spatio-temporal

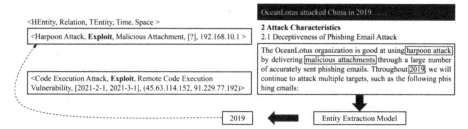

Fig. 9. Spatio-temporal attribute extraction of MDATA based on entity linking.

attributes in MDATA cyberspace security knowledge extraction, and there is no special model that can accurately correspond this relationship. Through the spatio-temporal attributes and entities corresponding to this strategy, the time of manual extraction is reduced and the efficiency is improved. At the same time, there is a certain noise that needs further research.

4   Knowledge Deduction Method in MDATA Model

The traditional knowledge deduction methods for MDATA are no longer applicable because they consider the spatio-temporal information characteristics of knowledge to adapt to the characteristics of cyberspace security. MDATA-oriented knowledge deduction methods need to use the abundant information from the known cyberspace security events to infer the unknown events according to the regular characteristics between cyberspace security events. At present, only the unknown knowledge missing in the cyberspace security knowledge base is completed to make the knowledge base more complete. However, the inference of unknown attacks still needs more in-depth research. According to the specific task of inference, it can be further divided into MDATA knowledge inference oriented to cyberspace security relationship, MDATA knowledge inference oriented to cyberspace security event sequence, and so on. The general framework diagram is shown in Fig. 10.

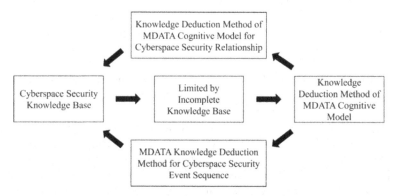

Fig. 10. Knowledge deduction framework in MDATA model.

4.1 MDATA Knowledge Deduction Method for Cyberspace Security Relations

MDATA knowledge inference for cyberspace security relationship is based on MDATA model to infer the relationship in unknown security events that may occur, such as the security event <release remote Trojan,?, CVE-2002–0840, 2019.10.20, 192.168.12.58>.

Although traditional knowledge deduction methods have certain interpretability, they cannot effectively deal with the rich spatio-temporal information in MDATA model, and cannot form an understandable deduction chain for MDATA model. Therefore, based on the TLogic model [12], this section introduces a knowledge deduction method of MDATA for cyberspace security relations based on time series random walk.

The main process of inference is as follows:

Step 1: Firstly, the temporal random walk should be extracted from the MDATA spatio-temporal knowledge base. For the rules of length, the walks of length $l+1$ should be sampled.

Step 2: Extract temporal logic rules. Define temporal logic rules as first-order Horn clauses, and a cyclic temporal logic rule of length L is defined as: $(e_1, r_h, e_{l+1}, t_{l+1}, s_{l+1}) \leftarrow \wedge_{i=1}^{l}(e_i, r_i, e_{i+1}, t_i, s_i)$, where the temporal constraint of is $t_1 \leq t_2 \leq \cdots t_l < t_{l+1}$, the left part of $\leftarrow$ is the head of the rule, and the right part is the body of the rule;

Step 3: Define a confidence function for rule learning, and solve the confidence conf(r) for all rules with length and rule head as relation r;

Step 4: For each security event query $q = (e_s, ?, e_o, t_q, s_q)$, to be inferred, select a convex combination of the confidence and time difference $t_q - t_1$ of the rule $f(r) = a \cdot conf(r) + (1 - a) \cdot exp(-\lambda(t_q - t_1))$ as the score function, where $\lambda > 0$ and $a \in [0, 1]$;

Step 5: Select the rule with the highest score, corresponding to the generated candidate entity, as the result of deduction.

This inference method does not need to rely on neural network for training, and has strong interpretability. In step 4, the convex combination of confidence and time difference $t_q - t_1$ of rules is chosen because the score function should be designed so that the candidate entities generated by the rules with high confidence have high scores, and the rules used should be as close to the time of the query to be inferred as possible to ensure that the rules that are valid in recent time are used in the inference.

In this example, when the security event <Intranet lateral penetration, ?, CVE-2018-16509, 2020.11.1, (192.168.12.58, 192.168.12.143)> the relations, in turn, after more than five steps in learning and using rules, final selection with high confidence and close time and effective rules, The candidate relationship (in this case, entity "use") corresponding to this rule is taken as the result of deduction.

Obtains the full push performance of security incidents <Intranet horizontal permeability, the use of CVE-2018-16509, 2020.11.1, (192.168.12.58, 192.168.12.143)>.

The MDATA knowledge inference method for cyberspace security relationship introduced in this section can deduce some unknown relationships in cyberspace security events through the effective use of known cyberspace security event information, and further complete and enrich our MDATA spatio-temporal knowledge base.

4.2 MDATA Knowledge Deduction Method for Cyberspace Security Event Sequence

The inference of cyberspace security event sequence mainly focuses on the sequence of multiple event entities in the cyberspace security event. For example, in the example below, the sequence of two event entities "send phishing email" and "release remote Trojan horse" is important information in the analysis of cyberspace security events, which has more important deduction value.

The traditional knowledge inference model cannot effectively deal with the rich spatio-temporal information in the MDATA model, so it cannot deduce the sequence of pairs of event entities in cyberspace security events. To address this, we introduce a binary classification-based MDATA knowledge deduction method for cyberspace security event sequences, as shown in Fig. 11.

The main steps of inference are as follows:

Step 1: Collect, sort and clean data, extract data from the mastered spatio-temporal knowledge base of MDATA model, and extract pairs of event entities, such as <head, tail>, and their order as a label (1 or 0);

Step 2: Using the knowledge representation based on deep learning, the embedding vectors of head and tail are obtained, denoted as **h** and **t**, respectively. The embedding vectors of each pair of head and tail are differentiated in turn, namely **h-t**, which is used as the input data for training.

Step 3: The inference of cyberspace security event sequence is regarded as a binary classification task, and the appropriate model is selected, such as logistic regression, support vector machine, decision tree, random forest, neural network and other models. The training data is used to train the model, and the parameters are adjusted and optimized to improve the accuracy and robustness of the model, and a trained binary classifier is obtained.

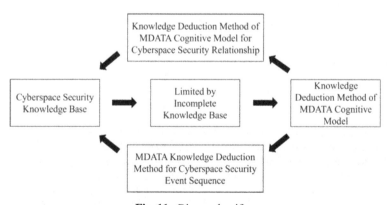

Fig. 11. Binary classifier.

Step 4: Extrapolate using the trained binary classifier. Whenever the order of two event entities (such as <head, tail>) needs to be determined, the embedding vectors of the two entities (obtained by deep learning-based knowledge representation) are extracted and subtracted as the input data of the classifier, and the output of the classifier is used as the inference result. The output is 1, which means "head before tail". If the output is 0, then "tail before head".

The MDATA knowledge inference method for cyberspace security event sequence introduced in this section is based on the knowledge representation based on deep learning, and the sequence of two different cyberspace security event entities is simplified into a binary classification task, which is easy to operate and execute. Because this method is model-independent, in the actual inference, the classification model can be selected according to the actual needs of logistic regression, support vector machine, decision tree, random forest, neural network and other classification models.

The inference of cyberspace security event sequence introduced in this subsection is mainly for the order of the multiple event entities in the cyberspace security event. Further exploring the sequence law of cyberspace security events is conducive to mining more unknown information in the analysis of cyberspace security events.

5 Summary

This chapter introduces the concept of knowledge acquisition, and introduces the existing methods of knowledge extraction and knowledge inference from traditional manual methods to deep learning based methods. In the face of the characteristics of cyberspace security, the requirements and challenges of knowledge extraction and knowledge deduction are summarized. In this chapter, we propose a knowledge extraction method and a knowledge inference method based on MDATA model. We comprehensively introduce the entity extraction method, relation extraction method and knowledge extraction method based on spatio-temporal attributes of MDATA model, and the knowledge inference method based on MDATA for cyberspace security relationship and event entity temporal relation. This paper provides theoretical and technical support for knowledge acquisition, accurate and real-time analysis of cyber security events, and knowledge utilization.

References

1. Lample, G., Ballesteros, M., Subramanian, S., et al.: Neural architectures for named entity recognition (2016)
2. Baevski, A., Edunov, S., Liu, Y., et al.: Cloze-driven pretraining of self-attention networks. In: Proceedings of the 2019 Conference on Empirical Methods in Natural Language Processing and the 9th International Joint Conference on Natural Language Processing, EMNLP-IJCNLP 2019, Hong Kong, China, 3–7 November 2019, pp. 5359–5368 (2019)
3. Hasegawa, T., Sekine, S., Grishman, R.: Discovering relations among named entities from large corpora. In: Proceedings of the 42nd Annual Meeting of the Association for Computational Linguistics, Barcelona, Spain, 21–26 July 2004, pp. 415–422 (2004)
4. Zeng, D., Liu, K., Lai, S., et al.: Relation classification via convolutional deep neural network. In: COLING 2014, 25th International Conference on Computational Linguistics, Proceedings of the Conference: Technical Papers, Dublin, Ireland, 23–29 August 2014, pp. 2335–2344 (2014)

5. Francis-Landau, M., Durrett, G., Klein, D.: Capturing semantic similarity for entity linking with convolutional neural networks (2016)
6. Tian, L., Zhang, J., Zhang, J., et al.: Knowledge graph: representation, construction, reasoning and knowledge hypergraph theory. J. Comput. Appl. **41**(8), 26 (2021)
7. Fan, Y., Chen, C., Bo, J.: Structured representation and management of production decision rules. Microcomput. Inf. (31), 3 (2009)
8. Zhang, Y., Guo, W., Lin, S., et al.: A survey on the combination of deep learning and knowledge reasoning. Comput. Eng. Appl. **58**(01), 56–69 (2012)
9. Guan, S., Jin, X., Jia, Y., et al.: Knowledge map-oriented knowledge reasoning research progress. J. Softw. **29**(10), 2966–2994 (2018). https://doi.org/10.13328/j.carolcarrollnkijos.005551
10. Syed, Z., Padia, A., Finin, T., et al.: UCO: a unified cybersecurity ontology. In: Proceedings of the AAAI Workshop on Artificial Intelligence for Cyber Security, pp. 1–8. AAAI Press, Palo Alto (2016)
11. Qin, Y., Shen, G.W., Zhao, W.B., et al.: A network security entity recognition method based on feature template and CNN-BiLSTM-CRF. Front. Inf. Technol. Electron. Eng. **20**(6), 872–884 (2019)
12. Liu, Y., Ma, Y., Hildebrandt, M., et al.: TLogic: temporal logical rules for explainable link forecasting on temporal knowledge graphs (2021)

Knowledge Utilization of MDATA Cognitive Model

Yan Jia[1]([✉]) and Jianye Yang[2]

[1] National University of Defense Technology, Changsha 410073, China
jiayanjy@vip.sina.com
[2] Guangzhou Univeristy, Guangzhou 510006, China
jyyang@gzhu.edu.cn

Knowledge utilization is a component of the MDATA cognitive model. In the field of cybersecurity, we can leverage the knowledge stored in the MDATA cognitive model knowledge base to achieve comprehensive, accurate, and real-time analysis of cybersecurity incidents. This involves graph computation methods such as subgraph matching, reachable path query, and label-based subgraph queries.

The rest of this chapter is organized as follows. Section 1 introduces the basic concepts of knowledge utilization and discusses how to map the knowledge utilization of the MDATA cognitive model to graph computing techniques. Section 2 discusses the difficulties and challenges brought by the data characteristics in the field of cybersecurity to knowledge utilization. Section 3 provides a detailed description of the knowledge utilization methods of the MDATA cognitive model. Section 4 concludes the chapter.

1 Basic Concepts and Related Techniques of Knowledge Utilization

1.1 Basic Concepts of Knowledge Utilization

Knowledge utilization refers to the process of using proper algorithms for mining and analyzing the knowledge in a knowledge base to accomplish user-specified tasks or functions across different application scenarios. Cybersecurity events exhibit characteristics such as large scale, highly dynamic, and interrelated. A critical task of knowledge utilization of MDATA cognitive model is to conduct comprehensive, accurate, and real-time assessments to the cybersecurity events using the knowledge in MDATA knowledge base. Three important assessment methods are categorized as below.

Category 1: Detection of Known Multi-Step Attacks. When attackers execute multi-step attacks, they need to finish several fixed single-step attacks. For example, in the OceanLotus attack, attackers first send phishing scams and release remote control trojans to connect to backdoor programs, then conduct lateral penetration attacks within the intranet, and finally steal and exfiltrate data. Therefore, we can establish relationships between attack events through spatial and temporal constraints to form an attack pattern which contains multiple security event entities. The pattern for the OceanLotus attack is shown in Fig. 1. In real application scenarios, the cybersecurity events are generated in a rapid manner, which form a large graph where vertices represent entities and edges represent relationships between entities. Figure 2 shows a part of the MDATA cognitive

Y. Jia et al. (Eds.): *MDATA Cognitive Model: Theory and Applications*, LNCS 15470, pp. 86–112, 2025.
https://doi.org/10.1007/978-981-96-3528-3_4

model knowledge base. This graph is formed by correlating real-time detected cyberattack behaviors. Multi-step attack event detection can be accomplished using subgraph matching, which finds the isomorphic subgraphs of the OceanLotus attack pattern within the cybersecurity event graph. An isomorphic subgraph is a subgraph where there exists an injective mapping from its vertices to the vertices in the pattern.

Category 2: Reachability Querying between Events. When assessing a multi-step attack event, it is often necessary to frequently check whether two single-step events are related or reachable. For example, in the OceanLotus attack, a security analyst needs to check in real-time whether a specific "phishing email" security event is related or reachable to a specific "data exfiltration" security event in the MDATA cognitive model knowledge base. This can be done using reachability query technology in graph computing, which utilizes a two-hop index structure to achieve constant-time reachability queries.

Third Category: Analysis of Unknown Multi-Step Attacks. When analyzing unknown multi-step attack events, suspicious labels can be used to perform correlation analysis of cybersecurity incidents and present subgraph structures in the MDATA cognitive model knowledge base. After analysis and processing by security analysts, unknown multi-step attack events and their templates can be uncovered. This task can be achieved by label-based subgraph query in graph computing.

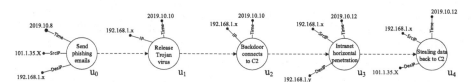

Fig. 1. OceanLotus Attack Template

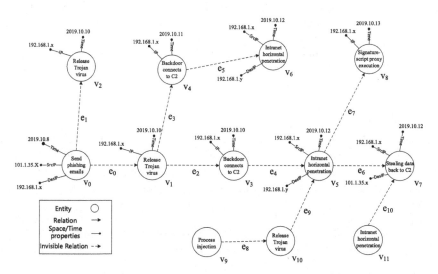

Fig. 2. Example of Security Event Graph

1.2 Subgraph Matching

Subgraph Matching is a prominent research topic in the field of graph data management and analysis. Its primary objective is to identify all subgraphs in a given data graph that are isomorphic to a query graph. Subgraph Matching has a wide range of applications. For instance, in the field of cybersecurity, by constructing a provenance graph model from computer system kernel logs, subgraph matching algorithms can be used to detect complex attack behaviors [1]. The following sections will first present relevant concepts and definitions, and then introduce mainstream subgraph matching algorithms.

1.2.1 Concepts and Definitions of Subgraph Matching

A graph $G = (V, E, L_V, L_E)$ consists of a set of vertices V and a set of edges E representing the relationships between them. The vertices and edges have labels, forming the label sets L_V and L_E for vertices and edges, respectively.

Definition 4.1 (Isomorphic Subgraph). Given a query graph Q and a subgraph g of a data graph G, if all vertices and edges in Q can be found in g with a one-to-one mapping, and the labels of the mapped vertices and edges are also identical, then g is called an isomorphic subgraph of Q.

Definition 4.2 (Subgraph Matching). Given a query graph Q and a data graph G, the goal of the subgraph matching problem is to extract all subgraphs in G that are isomorphic to Q.

Example 4.1: Consider the example of the graph the OceanLotus attack template (i.e., the query graph) and the network attack event graph as shown in Fig. 1 and Fig. 2, respectively. For simplicity, we only consider vertex labels here. Since the vertex labels in the query graph u_0, u_1, u_2, u_3, u_4 are "sending phishing emails," "releasing remote Trojan," "backdoor program connecting to C2," "lateral movement within the intranet," and "stealing data back to C2," respectively, there is one isomorphic subgraph in the data graph that satisfies the vertex labels and edge structure relationships of the query graph, which is $\{v_0, v_1, v_3, v_5, v_7\}$.

1.2.2 Subgraph Matching Methods

Subgraph matching is an NP-complete problem [2], and achieving efficient subgraph matching on large-scale graph data is a highly challenging task. Existing subgraph matching algorithms can be broadly divided into join-based and exploration-based methods [3]. Since the former is inefficient when dealing with large-scale sparse graphs, most algorithms adopt exploration-based strategies. Many of the current exploration-based algorithms have been developed from the widely used subgraph matching algorithm VF2 [4]. The following sections will first introduce the VF2 algorithm and then discuss the mainstream optimization methods.

(1) The VF2 Algorithm

VF2 employs a recursive approach to match vertices in the query graph sequentially. During the matching process, intermediate results are stored in a vertex pair matching structure. Initially, this vertex matching structure is empty. Then, a vertex is selected from the query graph, and its candidate matching vertices in the data graph are calculated. Next, each vertex in this candidate matching set is considered in turn, forming a matching vertex pair with the query graph vertex and adding it to the vertex pair matching structure. This creates a new matching branch and extends the matching result. As the recursion progresses, when the size of the vertex pair matching structure equals the size of the query graph, a complete matching result is formed, and that matching branch terminates. Overall, the entire search space forms a recursive search tree, where an internal node represents an intermediate matching result, and a leaf node, with a depth equal to the number of vertices in the query graph, represents a complete matching result.

(2) Steps of the VF2 Algorithm

To better introduce the specific process of the algorithm, we first introduce some basic concepts.

$l(u)$: Label of vertex u;

$d(u)$: Degree of vertex u, i.e., the number of neighbors of u;

$C(u)$: Candidate matching vertices of vertex u in the data graph;

M: Intermediate matching result, i.e., pairs of matching vertices between the query graph and the data graph;

$p(u, v)$: A pair of matching vertices.

The specific steps of the algorithm are as follows:

Step 1: Initialize the intermediate matching result M as empty.

Step 2: First, we select a vertex u from the neighbors of the matched vertices in the query graph as the next matching vertex. A common selection rule is to choose the vertex with the least frequent label in the data graph. Then, calculate the candidate matching vertex set $C(u)$ in the data graph, where $C(u)$ includes neighbors of already matched vertices in the data graph under the current matching branch, which have the same label as u.

Step 3: Then, for each vertex $v \in C(u)$, we create a matching vertex pair $p(u, v)$ with vertex u, and add it to the intermediate matching result M. Thus, a new matching branch is formed.

Step 4: Last, we recursively execute the new matching branch. If the size of M is the same as the size of the query graph Q, output a matching result. Otherwise, repeat Step 2.

To help readers better understand the VF2 algorithm, we next use the running example shown in Fig. 1 and Fig. 2 to illustrate the main idea. Recall that, Fig. 1 depicts a OceanLotus attack template, which includes five single-step attack events, namely sending phishing emails, releasing remote Trojans, backdoor programs connecting to C2, lateral movement within the internal network, and extracting data to send back to C2. Through spatiotemporal constraints, the attack event relationships shown in Fig. 1 are established, forming a query graph Q with five vertices. Figure 2 is a part of an MDATA knowledge base, which includes multiple event entities. Through spatiotemporal constraint relationships, a data graph G is formed. For the convenience of algorithm description, unique identifiers are attached to event entities in the query graph and the data graph, namely $u_0, u_1, ..., u_4$ and $v_0, v_1, ..., v_{11}$, respectively. Next, we use VF2 to search for subgraph matches of the query graph Q over the data graph G. According to the specific steps of the algorithm, the detailed description of this example algorithm is as follows.

Step 1: Initially, set the intermediate matching result M to be empty;

Step 2: Since all vertices in the query graph are unmatched at the beginning, it is only necessary to select the vertex with the lowest label frequency in the data graph. The entity event "stealing data to send back to C2" (i.e., u_4) appears only once in the data graph, so u_4 is chosen first. Then, calculate the candidate matching vertex set $C(u_4)$ in the data graph G, which is $\{v_7\}$;

Step 3: Consider each vertex in $C(u_4)$ in turn, i.e., v_7, form a matching vertex pair $p(u_4, v_7)$, and add $p(u_4, v_7)$ to M. Thus, a new matching branch is generated;

Step 4: Since the matching result M contains only one vertex pair, the algorithm continues;

Step 5: Select a vertex from the neighbors of u_4, which has only one neighbor u_3, an entity event of lateral movement within the internal network. Calculate the matching vertex set $C(u_3)$ in the data graph. Because v_7 is an already matched vertex in this branch, its unused neighbor vertices are v_5 and v_{11}. Among them, only v_5 has the same label as u_3. Therefore, $C(u_3) = \{v_5\}$;

Step 6: Consider each vertex in $C(u_3)$ in turn, i.e., v_5, form a matching vertex pair $p(u_3, v_5)$, and add $p(u_3, v_5)$ to M, entering a new matching branch;

Step 7: BY repeating the above steps, we shall obtain a complete matching subgraph $\{v_0, v_1, v_3, v_5, v_7\}$.

(3) Optimized Algorithms

To improve computation efficiency, many algorithms are proposed to optimize the matching order and refine the candidate vertex sets. Below, we briefly introduce the mainstream optimization techniques.

1) Matching Order Techniques.

A reasonable matching order can terminate the invalid search branches in an early stage. The main idea is to prioritize the query vertices with fewer candidate vertices and iteratively match the remaining query vertices by expanding the neighborhood, thereby narrowing the search space early and improving matching efficiency. As mentioned above, VF2 [4] uses a simple and effective matching order where the vertex labels are matched in ascending order of their frequency in the data graph, meaning that query vertices with less frequent labels in the data graph are matched first. On this basis, vertices with the highest degree can be prioritized for matching because a vertex with a high degree has relatively fewer candidate vertices. For large query graphs, Bi et al. [5] decompose the query graph into a dense core structure and peripheral vertices, and then match the core structure first and the remaining vertices later. Han et al. [6] use a dynamic matching order, where the matching order of vertices is dynamically adjusted during the enumeration process. These matching orders have their pros and cons, and exhibit different performance regarding different data distribution.

2) Candidate set filtering techniques.

The widely used candidate filtering techniques are vertex label and vertex degree, which require that, for a query vertex u, its candidate vertex v in the data graph must satisfy the conditions $l(v) = l(u)$ and $d(v) \geq d(u)$.

Neighbor label frequency rate filter [5, 7] states that for a query vertex u, its candidate vertex v in the data graph must meet the neighbor label frequency rate condition [5, 7], meaning that for any label type among u's neighbors, the number of neighbors of that label type must be fewer than the number of neighbors of the same label type for v.

Neighborhood matching filter [8] illustrates that for a query vertex u and data vertex v, if all neighbors of u can find corresponding matching vertices among the neighbors of v, then v is a candidate vertex for u; otherwise, it is not.

Substructure-based filters [5, 7] generate candidate vertex sets through the intersection of multiple neighbors and construct a tree index structure to further refine the candidate vertex set.

The above candidate set filtering methods can be used in combination, and the computational overhead of the filtering methods themselves must be comprehensively considered.

1.3 Reachable Path Computation

Reachable path computation has been a hot research topic in the field of graph analysis. Its objective is to determine whether there exists a directed path in a given graph that allows vertex u to reach vertex v Reachable path computation typically includes two aspects: reachability queries and shortest reachability path queries. The former only needs to determine if the vertices are reac-hable, while the latter requires returning the shortest reachable path.

1.3.1 Concepts of Reachability Query

In a directed graph $G(V, E)$, vertices are connected by directed edges. A reachable path refers to a sequence that starts from vertex u(the starting point), passes through any number of vertices on G (excluding the two vertices u and v), and reaches vertex v (the endpoint). For any two adjacent vertices i and j in the vertex sequence, there always exists a directed edge G in $e \in$ E such that $e = (i, j)$.

Definition 4.3 (Reachability Query). Given a directed graph $G(V, E)$ and two query vertices u and v, a reachability query aims to determine whether there exists a reachable path from in G.

Definition 4.4 (Shortest Reachable Path Query). Given a directed graph $G(V, E)$ and two query vertices u and v, the objective of a shortest reachable path query is to return the shortest reachable path from u to v in G.

Considering the knowledge graph in Fig. 2, vertices v_0 and v_7 are reachable, while v_2 and v_7 are not reachable because there is no directed path from v_2 to v_7.

1.3.2 Reachability Query Algorithms

A straightforward approach to compute reachable paths is to directly apply methods such as depth-first search, breadth-first search, or shortest path algorithms. However, such methods often have high time complexity. For instance, the time complexity of Dijkstra's algorithm is $O(n^2)$, where n is the number of vertices in the graph. Obviously, this direct calculation approach is not suitable for application scenarios with large-scale graph data and frequent queries.

To improve query efficiency, index-based methods have been proposed. The aim of these methods is to design an index to store information about whether vertices in the graph are reachable. This allows transforming the reachability path computation problem into a problem of using indexes to solve reachable path queries, thus significantly reducing query time. Next, we will introduce one algorithm based on two-hop indexes, namely the Cohen algorithm [9], followed by discussions on optimization algorithms.

1. Main Idea of Cohen Algorithm

For a vertex v in the graph, a two-hop index will record two pieces of information: one is the set of vertices that can reach v, and the other is the set of vertices that v can reach. To determine if the query vertex u is reachable from v, it is sufficient to check if one of the following three conditions holds:

1) v is in the set of vertices reachable from u.
2) u is in the set of vertices that can reach v.
3) The intersection of the set of vertices reachable from u and the set of vertices that can reach v is not empty.

When any of these three conditions is met, we consider u is reachable to v. Obviously, query efficiency is linearly related to the lengths of these two sets in the index. Therefore, a good two-hop index should minimize the average length of these two sets while ensuring query correctness. Cohen et al. [9] prove that it is NP-hard to obtain the minimum two-hop index and propose a greedy algorithm based on transitive closure. The core idea of this algorithm is to select vertices with higher degrees as central nodes for the two-hop index, aiming to minimize the index size while maintaining query correctness as much as possible.

2. Computation Steps of Cohen Algorithm

To better describe the algorithm steps, we first introduce some basic concepts.

$L_{in}(v)$: Set of vertices in the directed graph that can reach vertex v.

$L_{out}(v)$: Set of vertices in the directed graph that vertex v can reach.

T: Transitive closure of the graph, where $T_{i,j} = 0$ indicates i is not reachable from j, and $T_{i,j} = 1$ indicates i is reachable from j.

The transitive closure of the graph is an $n \times n$ matrix T with elements 0 or 1, recording the reachability of vertices in the graph. The algorithm first performs matrix multiplication on the adjacency matrix of the graph with itself for n times to obtain the transitive closure of the graph. Then, it maintains a max-heap, where each element is of the form (v_i, d_i), where v_i represents the value of the element, and d_i represents the sum of all elements in the i-th row and i-th column of the transitive closure, i.e., $d_i =$

$\sum_{j=1}^{n} \left(T_{i,j} + T_{j,i}\right)$. The algorithm extracts the top element (v_i, d_i) from the max-heap and performs the following steps:

Step 1: If $T_{i,j} = 1$, add vertex v_j to $L_{out}(i)$. Similarly, if $T_{k,i} = 1$, add vertex v_k to $L_{in}(i)$ of v_i.

Step 2: Set all elements in the i-th row and i-th column of the transitive closure matrix T to 0 and update the max-heap.

Step 3: Repeat steps 1 and 2 until the construction of the two-hop index is completed, i.e., the max-heap is empty.

We use Fig. 2 as an example to illustrate how to construct the two-hop index.

First, the transitive closure of the graph is constructed based on the adjacency matrix of Fig. 2, as shown in Table 1.

Table 1. Construction of the Transitive Closure of the Graph

	v_0	v_1	v_2	v_3	v_4	v_5	v_6	v_7	v_8	v_9	v_{10}	v_{11}
v_0	1	1	1	1	1	1	1	1	1	0	0	0
v_1	0	1	0	1	1	1	1	1	1	0	0	0
v_2	0	0	1	0	0	0	0	0	0	0	0	0
v_3	0	0	0	1	0	1	0	1	1	0	0	0
v_4	0	0	0	0	1	0	1	0	0	0	0	0
v_5	0	0	0	0	0	1	0	1	1	0	0	0
v_6	0	0	0	0	0	0	1	0	0	0	0	0
v_7	0	0	0	0	0	0	0	1	0	0	0	0
v_8	0	0	0	0	0	0	0	0	1	0	0	0
v_9	0	0	0	0	0	1	0	1	1	1	1	0
v_{10}	0	0	0	0	0	1	0	1	1	0	1	0
v_{11}	0	0	0	0	0	0	0	1	0	0	0	1

Next, we initialize the max-heap based on the sum of all elements in each row and column where each vertex resides. Table 2 shows the initial values of each vertex and the sum of elements in their corresponding rows and columns. At this point, the top element of the heap is $(v_0, 9)$.

Then, extract the top element from the max-heap and perform the following operations.

Table 2. Initial Max-Heap Structure

vertex	v_0	v_1	v_2	v_3	v_4	v_5	v_6	v_7	v_8	v_9	v_{10}	v_{11}
value	9	8	2	6	4	8	4	8	7	5	5	2

① Extract (v_0, 9) from the max-heap and update $L_{out}(v_0)$ and $L_{in}(v_0)$, while the rest of the indices remain empty. The two-hop index structure at this point is shown in Table 3.

Table 3. Two-Hop Index Structure after Extracting Heap Top (v0, 9)

Vertex ID	L_{in}	L_{out}
v_0	ϕ	$v_1 v_2 v_3 v_4 v_5 v_6 v_7 v_8$
v_1	ϕ	$v_3 v_4 v_6$
v_2	ϕ	ϕ
v_3	ϕ	ϕ
v_4	ϕ	ϕ
v_5	ϕ	ϕ
v_6	ϕ	ϕ
v_7	ϕ	ϕ
v_8	ϕ	ϕ
v_9	ϕ	ϕ
v_{10}	ϕ	ϕ
v_{11}	ϕ	ϕ

① Set all elements in the 1st row and 1st column of the transitive closure matrix to 0 and update the max-heap. Table 4 shows the vertices in the max-heap and their corresponding values at this point, where the top element of the heap is (v_5, 7).

Table 4. Max-Heap Structure after Extracting Heap Top (v0, 9)

vertex	v_1	v_2	v_3	v_4	v_5	v_6	v_7	v_8	v_9	v_{10}	v_{11}
value	7	1	5	3	7	3	7	6	5	5	2

Next, repeat the above operation. First, extract (v_5, 7) from the max-heap, update $L_{out}(v_5)$ and $L_{in}(v_5)$, while the rest of the indices remain unchanged, then update the max-heap. The two-hop index structure at this point is shown in Table 5.

Table 5. Two-Hop Index Structure after Extracting Heap Top (v5, 7)

Vertex ID	L_{in}	L_{out}
v_0	ϕ	$v_1v_2v_3v_4v_5v_6v_7v_8$
v_1	ϕ	$v_3v_4v_6$
v_2	ϕ	ϕ
v_3	ϕ	ϕ
v_4	ϕ	ϕ
v_5	$v_1v_3v_9v_{10}$	v_7v_8
v_6	ϕ	ϕ
v_7	ϕ	ϕ
v_8	ϕ	ϕ
v_9	ϕ	ϕ
v_{10}	ϕ	ϕ
v_{11}	ϕ	ϕ

Finally, repeat the above process until the max-heap is empty. At this point, the construction of the two-hop index structure is completed, as shown in Table 6.

Next, we can utilize the constructed index to perform reachability queries. Based on the conditions for determining the reachability between two vertices, we find that vertex v_9 is reachable from v_8 because $v_9 \in L_{in}(v_8)$. However, v0 is not reachable from v_{11} because $L_{in}(v_{11}) = \emptyset$, $v_{11} \notin L_{out}(v_0)$, and $L_{out}(v_0) \cap L_{in}(v_{11}) = \emptyset$. That is none of the three conditions is satisfied.

Table 6. Final Two-Hop Index Structure

Vertex ID	L_{in}	L_{out}
v_0	ϕ	$v_1v_2v_3v_4v_5v_6v_7v_8$
v_1	ϕ	$v_3v_4v_6$
v_2	ϕ	ϕ
v_3	ϕ	ϕ
v_4	ϕ	ϕ
v_5	$v_1v_3v_9v_{10}$	v_7v_8
v_6	ϕ	ϕ
v_7	$v_1v_3v_9v_{10}v_{11}$	ϕ
v_8	$v_1v_3v_9v_{10}$	ϕ
v_9	ϕ	ϕ
v_{10}	ϕ	ϕ
v_{11}	ϕ	ϕ

2 Optimization Algorithm

The Cohen algorithm requires computing the transitive closure, temporarily storing it in memory, and maintaining a max-heap. This not only has high time complexity but also requires a significant amount of storage space during index construction. Here, we introduce an optimization algorithm called TF-Label [10], which does not require computing the transitive closure and has higher efficiency in the index construction phase. The TF-Label algorithm decomposes the directed graph into a series of strongly connected components (SCCs), where vertices within an SCC are mutually reachable. Therefore, the reachability problem between vertices is transformed into a reach-ability problem between SCCs. Each SCC is treated as a new vertex, transforming the directed graph into a directed acyclic graph (DAG).

The TF-Label algorithm constructs the index on the DAG using topological sorting, with the following steps:

Step 1: Obtain the topological sorting of the DAG. In the topological sorting, any ancestor vertex of a vertex will precede it, and any descendant vertex will follow it.

Step 2: According to the topological sorting, add the incoming neighbors set $N_{in}(v)$ of vertex v to $L_{in}(v)$, and add the outgoing neighbors set $N_{out}(v)$ to $L_{out}(v)$.

Step 3: According to the reverse topological sorting, for each vertex w in $L_{out}(v)$, calculate the union of $L_{out}(w)$ and $L_{out}(v)$, i.e., $L_{out}(v) = L_{out}(w) \cup L_{out}(v)$. Similarly, for each vertex w in $L_{in}(v)$, calculate the union of $L_{in}(w)$ and $L_{in}(v)$, i.e., $L_{in}(v) = L_{in}(w) \cup L_{in}(v)$. The algorithm completes.

2.1 Label-Based Subgraph Query

When performing association analysis on vertices in graph data, queries based on vertex or edge labels and constraints to refine the associated subgraph are referred to as label-based subgraph queries. Given a set of event labels, this method can uncover the dependencies between specific events within the knowledge base, aiding users in obtaining complex attack templates.

2.1.1 Concepts and Definitions of Label-Based Subgraph Queries

A labeled graph $G = (V, E, L_V, L_E)$ consists of a vertex set V and an edge set E representing the relationships between them. Both vertices and edges have labels, forming vertex label set L_V and edge label set L_E. Additionally, edges can have weight, which is defined ad-hoc to the specific application context. For example, in a road network, weight might represent the travel time or distance. Given a path p in the graph. Its length is the sum of the edge weights along the path, denoted as $len(p)$. Given two vertices $u, v \in V$, the distance $dist(u, v)$ between two vertices is the length of the shortest path connecting them. In an unweighted graph with security events, the distance between two vertices is defined as the path with the fewest hops.

Definition 4.5 (Label-Based Subgraph Query). Given a graph $G = (V, E, L_V, L_E)$, a query label set $Q = \{l_1, \ldots, l_k\}$ and an optimization function ϕ, the goal of the label-based subgraph query problem is to return a subgraph g of G that satisfies the following conditions:

1) The labels of vertices in g cover the query label set Q.
2) Among all subgraphs satisfying condition 1, g optimizes the function ϕ.

The optimization function ϕ can have different definitions. The widely applied is the Steiner Tree structure [15], where g is a Steiner tree, and the sum of distances from all leaf nodes to the root node is minimized.

For example, considering the security event graph shown in Fig. 2, if the query label set $Q = \{$Phishing Email, Data Exfiltration$\}$, the subgraph g returned would be $\{v_0, v_1, v_3, v_5, v_7\}$, This subgraph is essentially a Steiner tree with v_0 as the root node.

2.1.2 Label-Based Subgraph Query Methods

When the Steiner Tree is the optimization function, the label-based subgraph query is an NP-complete problem [2]. Therefore, many algorithms adopt heuristic strategies to obtain approximate solutions. A classic method is the backward search algorithm proposed by Bhalotia et al. [11], known as BANKS-I. Below, we first introduce the BANKS-I algorithm and then present the optimization algorithms.

(1) Main Idea of BANKS-I
  The algorithm uses a traversal approach to obtain a tree structure that includes the query labels. First, it builds a traverse iterator for each vertex containing the query labels, then performs backward traversal from these iterators, and finally, when all traversal iterator containing the query labels converge at a common vertex, a query result is obtained.
(2) Computation Steps of BANKS-I
  To better introduce the specific steps of the algorithm, we first introduce some basic variables.
    $l(v)$: The label of vertex v, also referred to as the labeled vertex.
    $hit(l)$: The set of vertices with label l, also known as the candidate vertex set for label l.
    $C(l)$: The set of reachable vertices for label l, that is, the vertices in $C(l)$ can reach any vertex with label l through a path.

The specific steps of the algorithm are as follows.
  Step 1: Identify the candidate vertex set of all labels in the query label set $Q = \{l_1, \ldots, l_k\}$, as $H = hit(l_1) \cup \cdots \cup hit(l_k)$;
  Step 2: The algorithm constructs $|H|$ traversal iterators and performs a single-source shortest path query, using each vertex in H as the source. During the algorithm's execution, it maintains k clusters $C(l_1), \ldots, C(l_k)$, recording the reachable vertices for each query label.
  Step 3: In each expansion iteration, the algorithm first selects a vertex v from the already visited vertices. Then, among all incoming neighbors of v, selects a vertex u and adds it into all clusters that containing v. Thus, the algorithm completes a backward expansion. Meanwhile, the incoming edges of u that have not been visited are marked visible for further expansion.
  Step 4: If a newly expanded vertex u becomes a common vertex for k clusters, i.e., u can reach all k query label vertices, the tree with u being the root is considered as the query result. The algorithm stops; otherwise, it repeats step 3.

To help readers better understand the algorithm, we illustrate it using Fig. 2. Suppose the query label set $Q = \{$Phishing Email, Data Exfiltration$\}$. The detailed steps of the BANKS-I are as follows:

Step 1: Initially, the candidate vertex sets for all labels are hit(Phishing Email) $= \{v_0\}$ and hit(Data Exfiltration) $= \{v_7\}$. Therefore, $H = \{v_0, v_7\}$.

Step 2: We construct two traversal iterators to execute two single-source shortest path algorithms with v_0 and v_7 as the sources, respectively. At the same time, we maintain two clusters C(Phishing Emai) $= \{v_0\}$ and C(Data Exfiltration) $= \{v_7\}$.

Step 3: Since v_0 and v_7 have no common edges but have incoming edges, i.e., $v_5 \rightarrow v_7$ and $v_{11} \rightarrow v_7$, both v_5 and v_{11} are added to the clusters that v_7 belongs to. Thus, C(Data Exfiltration) $= \{v_5, v_7, v_{11}\}$.

Step 4: The algorithm repeats step 3, and adds $v_3, v_{10}, v_1, v_9, v_0$ to the cluster C(Data Exfiltration) sequentially. At this point, v_0 is the common vertex of the clusters C(Phishing Email) and C(Data Exfiltration). Therefore, the query result is the tree containing vertices $\{v_0, v_1, v_3, v_5, v_7\}$ with root node v_0 and leaf node with v_7.

(3) Optimization Algorithm

To improve computational efficiency, the BANKS-I algorithm introduces a heuristic search strategy during expansion. This strategy prioritizes the unvisited nodes that are closest to the leaf nodes (i.e., the label nodes) during the expansion process. This approach can lead a more balanced resulting tree.

3   Requirements and Challenges of Knowledge Utilization

Because the MDATA cognitive model knowledge base is in essence a large graph, knowledge utilization in such large graphs involves many graph computation operations, which presents great difficulties and challenges, as manifested in the following aspects.

First, due to large scale data and high computation complexity of the problem itself, how to achieve real-time computation is challenging. According to the "2020 China Internet Network Security Report" released by the National Computer Network Emergency Response Technical Coordination Center, there are over a hundred million types of attacks, a hundred thousand types of vulnerabilities, and nine hundred thousand resources with their complex combinations in cyberspace. It is evident that the scale of the knowledge graph is massive. On the one hand, the computational complexity of the problem itself is high. For example, subgraph matching is a typical NP-hard problem, which implies that the computational complexity is exponential to the size of the knowledge graph. While reachability query is not NP-hard, it is also polynomial to the graph size. The label-based subgraph query is also NP-hard. On the other hand, in real-world applications, it is usually required to handle the queries in real-time. Therefore, how to achieve real-time computation is a challenging task in knowledge utilization.

Second, because knowledge evolves constantly, how to support dynamic updates of knowledge is essential. To efficiently utilize the knowledge in a knowledge base, the graph computation algorithms often employ proper data structures to store intermediate results (referred to as intermediate result storage structures) to trade off the storage space and computation time. However, frequent knowledge update is a critical feature of cybersecurity data. To ensure the correctness of computational results, it is necessary to maintain the intermediate result storage structures, which inevitably bring computational overhead. Therefore, for frequent update cybersecurity data, designing and utilizing proper intermediate result storage structures poses another challenge in knowledge utilization.

Third, because knowledge exhibits semantic, temporal, and spatial correlations, integrating semantic and spatiotemporal information is crucial. In the field of cybersecurity, knowledge often involves strong spatiotemporal relationships. Taking the OceanLotus attack for example, the entire attack process typically includes steps such as phishing email delivery, releasing remote control Trojan, connecting backdoor programs, lateral movement within the network, and data exfiltration. These steps usually have spatial correlations; for instance, the destination IP address of the phishing email is the same as the source IP address of the released remote control Trojan. Moreover, these steps have a sequential order. When utilizing knowledge, integrating such spatiotemporal information into computation models to enable comprehensive and accurate analysis of these cybersecurity events is a challenging task.

4 Methods of Knowledge Utilization of MDATA

4.1 Subgraph Matching Method of MDATA

In practical application systems, network security data is often presented in the form of attack event streams, requiring highly real-time analysis. To achieve this goal, the MDATA model employs subgraph matching methods on streaming graphs.

4.1.1 Concepts of Subgraph Matching Over Streaming Graphs

An attack event stream $\langle a_1, a_2, ..., a_i \rangle$ consists of a series of attack events, where a_i represents the i-th attack event, corresponding to an event entity in the MDATA knowledge base. Before performing streaming graph matching, MDATA converts the event stream into a streaming graph to identify the implicit relationships between attack event entities. As shown in Fig. 2, a streaming graph is formed by the attack event stream consisting of sending phishing emails, releasing remote trojans, backdoor program connections, lateral movement within the intranet, and data exfiltration. Generally, a streaming graph is composed of a series of edges. For instance, the streaming graph of the OceanLotus attack shown in Fig. 2 is represented as $\langle v_0 \rightarrow v_1, v_1 \rightarrow v_3, v_3 \rightarrow v_5, v_5 \rightarrow v_7 \rangle$.

Definition 4.6 (Continuous Subgraph Matching). Given a query graph Q and a data streaming graph $G = \langle e_0, e_1, ..., e_i \rangle$, where $e_i = (v, v')$ denotes the insertion of an edge(v, v'), the aim of continuous subgraph matching is to compute in real-time the newly generated matching subgraphs of the query graph Q in the current data graph as each edge e_i arrives.

Example 4.4: Given the OceanLotus attack query graph Q and the data streaming graph as shown in Fig. 1 and Fig. 2, respectively, assuming the order of edges is $\langle e_0, e_1, ..., e_8 \rangle$, a complete OceanLotus attack event emerges when e_6 arrives, which is a subgraph induced by vertex set $\{v_0, v_1, v_3, v_5, v_7\}$.

4.1.2 Continuous Subgraph Matching Algorithms

In recent years, a string of research efforts have been devoted to the subgraph matching problem over streaming graphs [12–14]. The general computation framework is as follows. First, a data structure is constructed to store intermediate matching results; then, for each newly inserted edge, this intermediate storage structure is updated, and new matching results are computed based on this structure accordingly. This framework for subgraph matching on streaming graphs does not need to invoke the subgraph matching algorithm to recompute matching results every time the graph is updated, thereby significantly enhancing the matching efficiency. Based on this computational framework, this section proposes a streaming graph subgraph matching algorithm with temporal constraints, called TC-Match. This algorithm addresses the challenges and difficulties discussed in Sect. 2, namely achieving real-time computation of knowledge utilization, supporting dynamic updates of knowledge, and considering temporal constraints in the query graph during the matching process. The main ideas of the algorithm will be introduced first, followed by a detailed description of the algorithm's steps.

(1) Main Idea of TC-Match

TC-Match employs a pruning strategy to reduce the search space. When a new edge arrives, the algorithm creates an entity for this edge and stores it in the intermediate storage structure. It also maintains a boolean state information for this entity. During subsequent matching searches, the entity is considered as a starting point for subgraph search only if its state information is set to 1, following a specific search order. If the edges in the query graph involve temporal constraints (one edge appearing before/after another edge), and the incoming edge does not satisfy these temporal constraints, the algorithm will discard the incoming edge.

(2) Computation Steps of TC-Match

To ease the illustration of TC-Match, we first introduce some variables.

$l(u)$, $l(v)$: Labels of vertex u or v;

$e(u, u')$, $e(v, v')$: Labels on the edges of the query graph or the data graph;

$C(u, u')$: Candidate matching edges in the data graph for the edge (u, u') in the query graph;

$C(u)$: Candidate matching vertices in the data graph for the vertex u in the query graph;

$\phi(u, u')$: Search order starting from the edge (u, u');

$\varphi(u)$: Pruning order starting from the vertex u;

$\phi(u)$: Search order starting from the vertex u;

$\prec$: Temporal constraints on the edges in the query graph;

M: Intermediate matching results, i.e., the search space for subgraph matching;

$E(v, v', s)$: Transform the edge (v, v') into an entity in the intermediate results M, with the entity state recorded as s;

$E(v, s)$: Transform the vertex v into an entity in the intermediate results M, with the state recorded as s;

R: Output results, i.e., the pairs of matching vertices and edges between the query graph and the data graph.

The specific algorithm steps are as follows:

Step 1: Initialize the intermediate matching results M as empty;

Step 2: Generate the search order ϕ starting from the last temporal edge in the query graph, ultimately traversing all edges in the query graph;

Step 3: For an incoming update edge (v, v', e) with source vertex v, target vertex v', and edge label e, if the update edge $(l(v), l(v'), e)$ does not match any $(l(u), l(u'), e)$ in the query graph, discard the update edge; otherwise, create an entity $E(v, v', s)$ for the update edge (v, v', e);

Step 4: Check the temporal constraints $\prec$ of the entity $E(v, v', s)$. If the preceding temporal entity of $E(v, v', s)$ does not exist, discard the update edge; otherwise, store $E(v, v', s)$ in the corresponding $C(u, u')$ in the intermediate results M;

Step 5: Create bidirectional links for all neighboring entities of $E(v, v', s)$;

Step 6: Check if the neighborhood of the entity $E(v, s)$ is complete. If it is not complete, set the status information s of the entity $E(v, s)$ to 0; otherwise, set it to 1;

Step 7: If the status information s of the entity $E(v, v', s)$ is 1, perform subgraph search in the intermediate results M according to the search order $\phi(u, u')$ starting from (v, v'), and save the search results in the output results R;

Step 8: If the size of R matches the query graph, output the matching results in R; otherwise, repeat steps 4 to 6.

To help readers better understand this algorithm, we consider the running examples in graphs shown in Fig. 1 and Fig. 2. TC-Match computes the matching subgraphs of the query graph Q over the data graph G, with the temporal constraint $\{(u_0, u_1) \prec (u_1, u_2) \prec (u_2, u_3) \prec (u_3, u_4)\}$. The detailed steps are as follows.

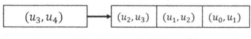

Fig. 3. Search Order

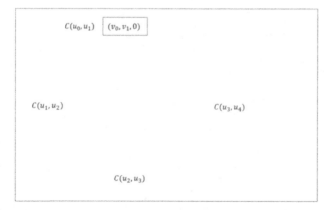

Fig. 4. Intermediate Results After Inserting Update Edge (v_0, v_1, e_0)

Step 1: Initially, set the intermediate matching result M to empty;

Step 2: Generate a search order starting from the last temporal edge in the query graph and eventually traversing all edges in the query graph. Since (u_3, u_4) is the only last temporal edge, the search order is shown in Fig. 3;

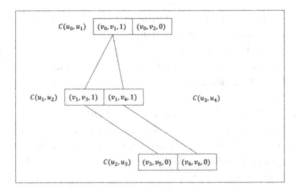

Fig. 5. Intermediate Results Before the Arrival of Update Edge (v_5, v_7, e_6)

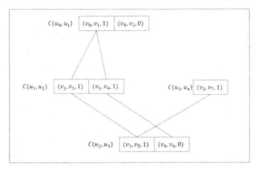

Fig. 6. Intermediate Results After Inserting Update Edge (v_5, v_7, e_6)

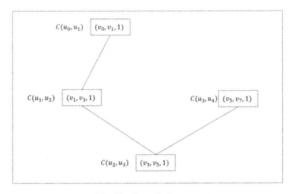

Fig. 7. Search Results

Step 3: When edge (v_0, v_1, e_0) arrives, it is found that the labels $(l(v_0), l(v_1))$ of this update edge are the same as those in the query graph $(l(u_0, u_1))$. Therefore, this update edge is converted into entity $E(v_0, v_1, 0)$;

Step 4: Entity $E(v_0, v_1, 0)$ has a mapping relationship with (u_0, u_1), and (u_0, u_1) is the first temporal edge in the temporal constraint, thus satisfying the temporal constraint. Therefore, entity $E(v_0, v_1, 0)$ is saved into $C(u_0, u_1)$ in the intermediate result M;

Step 5: Since entity $E(v_0, v_1, 0)$ currently has no neighbors, no bidirectional links are created, as shown in Fig. 4;

Step 6: When edge (v_0, v_2, e_1) arrives, it is found that the labels $(l(v_0), l(v_2))$ of this update edge are the same as those in the query graph $(l(u_0, u_1))$. Therefore, this update edge is converted into entity $E(v_0, v_2, 0)$ and saved into $C(u_0, u_1)$ in the intermediate result M;

Step 7: When edge (v_1, v_3, e_2) appears, it is found that the labels $(l(v_1), l(v_3))$ of this update edge are the same as those in the query graph $(l(u_1, u_2))$. Therefore, this update edge is converted into entity $E(v_1, v_3, 0)$ and saved into $C(u_1, u_2)$ in the intermediate result M;

Step 8: Since the preceding temporal edge of (u_1, u_2) is (u_0, u_1), and $C(u_0, u_1)$ contains entities $E(v_0, v_1, 0)$ and $E(v_0, v_2, 0)$, entity $E(v_1, v_3, 0)$ satisfies the temporal requirement. Therefore, entity $E(v_1, v_3, 0)$ is saved into $C(u_1, u_2)$ in the intermediate result M;

Step 9: Since entity $E(v_0, v_1, 0)$ is a neighbor of $E(v_1, v_3, 0)$, a bidirectional link is created between $E(v_1, v_3, 0)$ and $E(v_0, v_1, 0)$;

Step 10: Since the neighborhood of entity $E(v_0, v_1, 0)$ is satisfied, the state information of this entity is set to 1, i.e., $E(v_0, v_1, 1)$. However, since the state information of the update edge entity $E(v_1, v_3, 0)$ is not 1, the search step is skipped.

When other edges in Fig. 2 are inserted after (v_1, v_3, e_2), the intermediate results are updated accordingly. However, there is no complete matching result generated until the insertion of (v_5, v_7, e_6). In the following, we use this update edge as an example to elaborate the matching step.

Step 1: The intermediate result before the update of (v_5, v_7, e_6) is as shown in Fig. 5;

Step 2: When (v_5, v_7, e_6) arrives, it is found that the labels $(l(v_5), l(v_7))$ of this edge are the same as those in the query graph $(l(u_3), l(u_4))$. Therefore, this update edge is converted into entity $E(v_5, v_7, 0)$;

Step 3: After temporal judgment and bidirectional link operations, since the neighborhood of entity $E(v_5, v_7, 0)$ is complete, the state information of this entity is set to 1, i.e., entity $E(v_5, v_7, 1)$, as shown in Fig. 6;

Step 4: Since entity $E(v_5, v_7, 1)$ is both an update edge entity and its state information is 1, subgraph search is performed according to the search order $\{(u_3, u_4), (u_2, u_3), (u_1, u_2), (u_0, u_1)\}$ starting from (u_3, u_4). The matching result is finally stored in R, i.e., $\{(v_5, v_7), (v_3, v_5), (v_1, v_3), (v_0, v_1)\}$, as shown in Fig. 7.

4.2 Reachability Path Calculation Method of MDATA

In many real-world applications, edges in the graph often have specific labels to represent the types of relationships between vertices. The meanings of these labels are determined by the specific application scenarios. For example, in the field of cybersecurity, edge labels represent operation types of events (such as phishing email delivery, lateral movement within the network, etc.). The reachability path calculation on such graphs is referred to as label-constrained reachability query. In other words, given query vertices u and v, and a label set L, the label-constrained reachability query asks whether there exists a reachable path from u to v in G, and the labels on the path is a subset of L. This approach confines the labels on the path within a certain range, enabling more precise reachability queries. Thus, the challenge brought by the semantic and spatiotemporal correlations of knowledge in knowledge utilization is addressed. Below, we use an example to illustrate the two-hop index based method P2H [15].

Consider the network security event graph shown in Fig. 2. Given the path label set Σ = {phishing email, remote control Trojan, backdoor program, internal penetration}, it can be observed that vertex v_0 is reachable to v_7, vertex v_0 is also reachable to v_6, but v_9 is not reachable to v_7.

1. Main Idea of P2H

To better describe the algorithm concept, let's introduce some basic variables:

$L_{in}(v)$: The set of vertices in the directed graph that can reach vertex v.

$L_{out}(v)$: The set of vertices in the directed graph that vertex v can reach.

$(u, \mathcal{L}_u)$: An entry in $L_{in}(v)$ or $L_{out}(v)$, denoting that u is reachable to or from v under the constraint of the label set $\mathcal{L}_u$.

Query $(u, v, \mathcal{L}_{uv})$: A label-constrained reachability query, where the three parameters are the source vertex u, the destination vertex v, and the label constraint set $\mathcal{L}_{uv}$.

Λ: The set consisting of existing labels in the knowledge graph.

A: Edge label indicating the source event as "phishing email delivery".

B: Edge label indicating the source event as "release of remote control Trojan".

C: Edge label indicating the source event as "backdoor program connection".

D: Edge label indicating the source event as "internal network lateral movement".

E: Edge label indicating the source event as "proxy execution of signed script".

F: Edge label indicating the source event as "process injection".

P2H constructs an index based on a two-hop index. For each vertex, P2H maintains two entry sets $L_{in}(v)$ and $L_{out}(v)$. An entry $(u, \mathcal{L}_u)$ in $L_{in}(v)$ and $L_{out}(v)$ denotes that u is reachable to or from v under the constraint of the label set $\mathcal{L}_u$. The algorithm's idea is to use a greedy strategy to iteratively visit all vertices in descending order of vertex degree. In an iteration when u is visited, a forward breadth-first search and a backward breadth-first search are performed. The path label set $\mathcal{L}_u$ from vertex u to vertex v is added to $L_{in}(v)$ and $L_{out}(v)$ of vertex v. However, if at this point, it can be determined using the already obtained partial two-hop index that u is reachable to v under the constraint of $\mathcal{L}_u$, then the recording $(u, \mathcal{L}_u)$ can be skipped. By using this pruning technique, the P2H index structure can be constructed as small as possible.

2. Computation Steps of P2H

The P2H algorithm optimizes the construction strategy of the index by applying three pruning rules during index construction. Its characteristic is to improve the efficiency of label-constrained reachability queries by constructing a special two-hop index. When the forward breadth-first search from vertex u expands to vertex v, the following three pruning rules are applied:

Pruning Rule 1: If vertex v has been traversed before, there is no need to add $(u, \mathcal{L}_u)$ to $L_{in}(v)$, because if vertex u is reachable to v under the label constraint $\mathcal{L}_u$, then $(v, \mathcal{L}_u)$ has already been added to $L_{out}(u)$.

Pruning Rule 2: If the current query Query $(u, v, \mathcal{L}_{uv})$ can answer correctly based on the already constructed index, then it is safe to skip recording $(u, \mathcal{L}_u)$.

Pruning Rule 3: If there exists an element $(u, \mathcal{L}'_u)$ in $L_{in}(v)$, satisfying $\mathcal{L}'_u \subseteq \mathcal{L}_u$, then there is no need to record $(u, \mathcal{L}_u)$.

Similar pruning techniques are applied during the backward breadth-first search.

We illustrate how to construct the P2H index using Fig. 2 as an example. The specific steps are as follows:

Step 1: Sort the vertices of the graph in descending order of degree. The result is shown in Table 7.

Table 7. Degree Distribution of Vertices in Fig. 2

vertex	v_5	v_1	v_0	v_3	v_4	v_7	v_{10}	v_2	v_6	v_8	v_9	v_{11}
degree	4	3	2	2	2	2	2	1	1	1	2	1

Step 2: Following the order in Table 7, we first perform forward breadth-first search and backward breadth-first search starting from vertex v_5. Then, we add the index entries consisting of v_5 and its path labels to the two-hop index of the remaining vertices. The resulting two-hop index structure is shown in Table 8.

Table 8. Two-Hop Index after Adding v5 to the Remaining Vertices

Vertex ID	L_{in}	L_{out}
v_0	ϕ	(v_5, ABC)
v_1	ϕ	(v_5, BC)
v_2	ϕ	ϕ
v_3	ϕ	(v_5, C)
v_4	ϕ	ϕ
v_5	ϕ	ϕ
v_6	ϕ	ϕ
v_7	(v_5, D)	ϕ
v_8	(v_5, D)	ϕ
v_9	ϕ	(v_5, BF)
v_{10}	ϕ	(v_5, B)
v_{11}	ϕ	ϕ

Step 3: Perform a second traversal, starting from v_1, conducting both forward and reverse breadth-first searches. Add the index elements formed by v_1 and its path labels to the two-hop index of the remaining vertices. It's worth noting that although v_1 encounters

v_5 during the forward breadth-first search, since $(v_5, ABC) \in L_{out}(v_1)$ according to pruning rule 1, there's no need to record (v_1, ABC) in $L_{in}(v_5)$. Similarly, when v_1 reaches v_7 and v_8 during the forward breadth-first search, the visited path labels are all BCD. However, because $(v_5, BC) \in L_{out}(v_1)$, $(v_5, D) \in L_{in}(v_7)$, and $(v_5, D) \in L_{in}(v_8)$, according to pruning rule 2, there's no need to record (v_1, BCD) in $L_{in}(v_7)$ and $L_{in}(v_8)$. Therefore, 3 index entries are pruned. The index structure after processing v_1 is shown in Table 9.

Table 9. Shows the index structure after processing v1.

Vertex ID	L_{in}	L_{out}
v_0	ϕ	$(v_5, ABC), (v_1, A)$
v_1	ϕ	(v_5, BC)
v_2	ϕ	ϕ
v_3	(v_1, B)	(v_5, C)
v_4	(v_1, B)	ϕ
v_5	ϕ	ϕ
v_6	(v_1, BC)	ϕ
v_7	(v_5, D)	ϕ
v_8	(v_5, D)	ϕ
v_9	ϕ	(v_5, BF)
v_{10}	ϕ	(v_5, B)
v_{11}	ϕ	ϕ

Repeating the above steps, the resulting label-constrained two-hop index is shown in Table 10.

Table 10. Label-constrained Two-hop Index

Vertex ID	L_{in}	L_{out}
v_0	ϕ	$(v_5, ABC), (v_1, A)$
v_1	ϕ	(v_5, BC)
v_2	(v_0, A)	ϕ
v_3	(v_1, B)	(v_5, C)
v_4	(v_1, B)	ϕ
v_5	ϕ	ϕ
v_6	$(v_1, BC), (v_4, C)$	ϕ
v_7	$(v_5, D), (v_1, BCD)$	ϕ

(continued)

Table 10. (*continued*)

Vertex ID	L_{in}	L_{out}
v_8	$(v_5, D), (v_1, BCD)$	ϕ
v_9	ϕ	$(v_5, BF), (v_{10}, F)$
v_{10}	ϕ	(v_5, B)
v_{11}	ϕ	(v_7, D)

We use the two-hop index for the following queries.

Query 1: Query(v_1, v_8, $\mathcal{L} = \{B, C, D\}$). Since $(v_5, BC) \in L_{out}(v_1)$ and $(v_5, D) \in L_{in}(v_8)$, we have that $L_{out}(v_1) \cap L_{in}(v_8) = \{v_5\}$. Thus, the label constraint is satisfied and the query returns True.

Query 2: Query($v_1, v_6, \mathcal{L} = \{B, C, D\}$). Since $(v_1, BC) \in L_{in}(v_6)$, the label constraint is therefore satisfied and the query returns True.

Query 3: Query($v_9, v_7, \mathcal{L} = \{B, C, D\}$). Since $(v_5, BF) \in L_{out}(v_9)$ and $(v_5, D) \in L_{in}(v_7)$, hence $L_{out}(v_1) \cap L_{in}(v_8) = \{v_5\}$. However, the path labels do not meet the constraint, so the query returns False.

4.3 Label-Based Subgraph Query of MDATA

When the Steiner Tree is the optimization function, the label-based subgraph query is an NP-complete problem. The BANKS-I [11] algorithm is inefficient when dealing with large-scale graph data, especially graphs with many labeled vertices. To handle large-scale graph data, we applied a heuristic-based KeyKG algorithm [16] to address the efficiency issues. Below, we first present the main idea of the algorithm and then elaborate the specific steps.

4.3.1 Main Idea of KeyKG

KeyKG first uses a heuristic strategy to select a set U_x of mutually close label vertices, where each query label U_x contains and only contains one label vertex. Then, a Steiner Tree GST is constructed for U_x using a heuristic strategy. Since it requires frequent distance calculations between vertices, the KeyKG algorithm employs a two-hop indexing structure to quickly obtain the distances between vertices.

4.3.2 Computation Steps of KeyKG

To better introduce the specific steps of the algorithm, we first introduce some basic variables.

$l(v)$: The label of vertex v, and v is also called a label vertex.

$hit(l)$: The set of vertices with label l, also known as the candidate vertex set for label l.

U_x: For a vertex x in $hit(l_1)$, v_i is the vertex in $hit(l_i)$ that has the shortest distance from x. U_x is the set of all such v_i vertices, including x itself.

W_x: The sum of distances from vertex x to all vertices in U_x.

T_u: The Steiner Tree covers the query label set, which is expanded from the seed vertex u.

The specific steps of the algorithm are as follows:

Step 1: Identify the candidate vertex sets $hit(l_i)$ for each label in the query label set $Q = \{l_1, \ldots, l_k\}$.

Step 2: For each vertex v_1 in $hit(l_1)$, find the vertex v_i in $hit(l_i)$ that has the shortest distance from v_1. Let U_{v_1} be the set of all such v_i vertices, including v_1 itself. Let W_{v_1} be the sum of distances from v_1 to all vertices in U_{v_1}. Thus, each vertex v_1 in $hit(l_1)$ has a corresponding W_{v_1}.

Step 3: Select the vertex x from $hit(l_1)$ that has the smallest W_{v_1} value. Therefore, U_x covers all query labels and the distances between the vertices it contains are short.

Step 4: Starting from a vertex u in U_x, use a greedy strategy to expand and construct the Steiner Tree T_u of U_x.

Step 5: Select the T_u with the smallest weight and use it as the final output result.

To help readers better understand the application of this algorithm, we illustrate it using the example in Fig. 2. Suppose the query label set $Q = \{$Phishing Email, Data Exfiltration$\}$. The detailed steps of the algorithm are as follows:

Step 1: Initially, the candidate vertex sets corresponding to all labels are $hit($Phishing Email$) = \{v_0\}$, $hit($Data Exfiltration$) = \{v_7\}$.

Step 2: Since the distance from v_0 to v_7 is 4 and each query label's candidate set has only one vertex, $U_x = \{v_0, v_7\}$.

Step 3: Construct the Steiner Tree from U_x, resulting in a tree with v_0 as the root node and v_7 as the leaf node. The query result is $\{v_0, v_1, v_3, v_5, v_7\}$.

It is evident that the KeyKG algorithm has a smaller search space than the BANKS-I algorithm and does not backtrack to unrelated vertices.

4.4 Distributed Collaborative Knowledge Utilization Method in MDATA

When utilizing knowledge, computational tasks are often executed concurrently as multiple tasks. Additionally, knowledge storage may be hierarchical. Therefore, the distributed collaborative knowledge utilization technology based on MDATA is of great significance. This section will first introduce the fog-cloud computing architecture, and then explain how to extend the knowledge utilization methods introduced earlier in this chapter to achieve distributed collaborative knowledge utilization.

4.4.1 Fog-Cloud Computing Architecture

To implement distributed system computing for knowledge utilization, we propose an generalize cyberspace big data fog-cloud computing architecture [17], as illustrated in Fig. 8. Based on multi-knowledge bodies and their collaborative reasoning, this architecture comprises fog knowledge bodies, intermediate knowledge bodies, and cloud knowledge bodies.

(1) Fog Knowledge Bodies

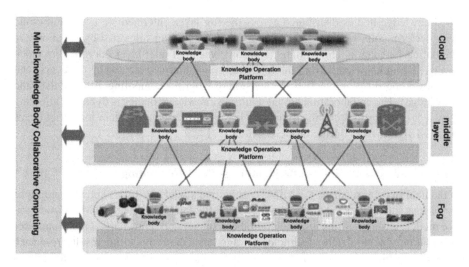

Fig. 8. Fog-Cloud Computing Architecture

The massive fog edge nodes are the direct sources of data. These nodes include cyberspace security devices, sensors in sensor networks, smart home devices, and apps in the mobile internet. Many of these edge nodes also possess certain computing capabilities, which can be used to deploy local real-time computing, data, and knowledge acquisition knowledge bodies. This makes them a part of the big data computing in cyberspace.

(2) Intermediate Knowledge Bodies

The intermediate knowledge bodies, located between the fog layer and the cloud layer, are typically deployed on servers close to the edge nodes. Sometimes, they are also deployed on aggregation nodes such as gateways, routers, and communication base stations. Intermediate knowledge bodies generally run on servers with strong computing and storage capabilities. Compared to the cloud nodes, intermediate knowledge bodies are closer to the fog edge nodes and data sources, serving as the center for comprehensive computing of local edge knowledge bodies.

(3) Cloud Knowledge Bodies

Cloud knowledge bodies usually serve as the remote backend processing centers in fog-cloud computing. They aggregate knowledge from edge IoT nodes, web applications, mobile apps, and intermediate internet nodes distributed worldwide. They also consolidate the content from numerous fog and intermediate knowledge bodies. Cloud knowledge bodies are contextually and spatially sensitive to the operations of fog and intermediate knowledge bodies, acting as the global center of fog-cloud computing. They usually store non-private global and contextual data and perform global knowledge reasoning.

(4) Collaborative Computing Among Multiple Knowledge Bodies

The knowledge bodies distributed across the fog layer, intermediate layer, and cloud layer perform collaborative computing and task scheduling supported by collaborative computing languages. This collaboration involves both inter-layer coordination (such as aggregating knowledge from the fog layer to the intermediate and cloud layers) and intra-layer coordination (such as the division of labor for computing different data and knowledge). The collaboration among multiple knowledge bodies is dynamic, allowing knowledge bodies to dynamically join or leave tasks based on system load or changes in knowledge sources during task execution.

4.4.2 Knowledge Utilization Based on Fog-Cloud Computing

In the field of cybersecurity, the MDATA cognitive model constructs knowledge graphs for various subnetworks at the fog layer. When utilizing knowledge, the MDATA cognitive model runs algorithms in parallel on these subnetwork knowledge graphs and uses information synchronization technology to aggregate the computation results from each subnetwork knowledge graph to form a global result. Here, we take reachability queries as an example to illustrate knowledge utilization based on fog-cloud computing.

Distributed reachability queries also involve the construction of two-hop indices. The challenge lies in the fact that vertices are distributed across different subnetworks, and the previously introduced two-hop index construction technology requires maintaining a global vertex order, which is not feasible in a distributed data scenario. Additionally, to minimize index size, the two-hop index construction algorithm needs to compute the index set for each vertex sequentially according to this vertex order, limiting parallelization.

To address this, Zhang et al. [18] proposed a two-hop label index construction technique for distributed graphs, implemented on a vertex-centric distributed computing framework [19]. We propose using multi-round supersteps for message synchronization to achieve a streamlined breadth-first search. In each superstep, each vertex uses the "compute" function provided by the framework to update its label state and distributes

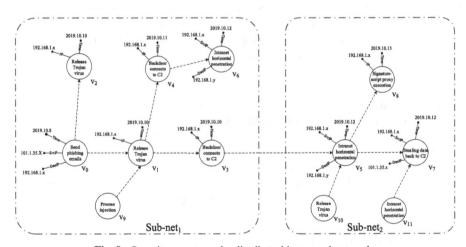

Fig. 9. Security event graphs distributed in two subnetworks

the updated state to its neighboring vertices. After multiple rounds of superstep computation, when the state of each vertex no longer changes, the algorithm terminates and finishes he construction of the distributed two-hop index labels. The process of distributed reachability queries is similar to the reachability queries introduced earlier.

As shown in Fig. 9, for the security events graphs of two subnetworks, in the first superstep, all vertices send their vertex IDs and vertex order information to neighboring vertices. In subsequent supersteps, they compute the received information from neighboring vertices to determine the reachability of vertices and the vertices that can reach the current vertex, ultimately constructing the two-hop index structure in a parallel manner.

5 Conclusion for the Chapter

In the MDATA cognitive model, knowledge utilization is the final and crucial step to accurately assess network attacks. Due to the massive scale of the knowledge graph in MDATA, this chapter introduces three key techniques that support knowledge utilization, including subgraph matching, reachability queries, and label-based subgraph query techniques. These methods are characterized by their real-time computational capability, support for knowledge updates, and integration of spatiotemporal correlations. Additionally, we propose a distributed collaborative knowledge utilization framework based on fog computing to further enhance the computational efficiency of knowledge utilization.

References

1. Milajerdi, S.M., Eshete, B., Gjomemo, R., et al.: Poirot: aligning attack behavior with kernel audit records for cyber threat hunting. In: Proceedings of the 2019 ACM SIGSAC Conference on Computer and Communications Security, pp. 1795–1812 (2019)
2. Garey, M.R., Johnson, D.S.: Computers and Intractability: A Guide to the Theory of NP-Completeness. W. H. Freeman, New York (1979)
3. Sun, Z., Wang, H.Z., WANG, H.X., et al.: Efficient subgraph matching on billion node graphs. In: Proceedings of the VLDB Endowment. ACM, New York, pp. 788–799 (2022)
4. Cordella, L.P., Foggia, P., Sansone, C., et al.: A (sub) graph isomorphism algorithm for matching large graphs. Trans. Pattern Anal. Mach. Intell. **26**(10), 1367–1372 (2004)
5. Bi, F., Chang, L.J., Lin, X.M., et al.: Efficient subgraph matching by postponing cartesian products. In: Proceedings of the 2016 International Conference on Management of Data. ACM, New York, pp. 1199–1214 (2016)
6. Han, M., Kim, H., Gu, G., et al.: Efficient subgraph matching: harmonizing dynamic programming, adaptive matching order, and failing set together. In: SIGMOD'19: Proceedings of the 2019 International Conference on Management of Data. ACM, New York, pp. 1429–1446 (2019)
7. Bhattarai, B., Liu, H., Huang, H.H.: CECI: compact embedding cluster index for scalable subgraph matching. In: SIGMOD'19: Proceedings of the 2019 International Conference on Management of Data. ACM, New York, pp. 1447–1462 (2019)
8. He, H.H., Singh, A.K.: Query language and access methods for graph databases. Manag. Min. Graph Data **2010**(40), 125–160 (2010)
9. Cohen, E., Halperin, E., Kaplan, H., et al.: Reachability and distance queries via 2-hop labels. SIAM J. Comput. **32**(5), 1338–1355 (2003)

10. Cheng, J., Huang, S.L., Wu, H.H., et al.: TF-Label: a topological-folding labeling scheme for reachability querying in a large graph. In: SIGMOD'13: Proceedings of the 2013 ACM SIGMOD International Conference on Management of Data. ACM, New York, pp. 193–204 (2013)

11. Bhalotia, G., Hulgeri, A., Nakhe, C., et al.: Keyword searching and browsing in databases using BANKS. In: ICDE'02: Proceedings of the 18th International Conference on Data Engineering, pp. 431–440 (2002)

12. Kim, K., Seo, I., Han, W.S., et al.: Turboflux: a fast continuous subgraph matching system for streaming graph data. In: SIGMOD'18: Proceedings of the 2018 International Conference on Management of Data. ACM, New York, pp. 411–426 (2018)

13. Min, S., Park, S.G., Park, K., et al.: Symmetric continuous subgraph matching with bidirectional dynamic programming. Proceedings of the VLDB Endowment. ACM, New York, vol. 14, no. 8, pp. 1298–1310 (2021)

14. Sun, X.B., Sun, S.X., Luo, Q., et al.: An in-depth study of continuous subgraph matching. In: Proceedings of the VLDB Endowment. ACM, New York, vol. 15, no. 7, pp. 1403–1416 (2022)

15. Peng, Y., Zhang, Y., Lin, X.M., et al.: Answering billion-scale label-constrained reachability queries within microsecond. In: Proceedings of the VLDB Endowment. ACM, New York, vol. 13, no. 6, pp. 812–825 (2020)

16. Shi, Y.X., Cheng, G., Kharlamov, E.: Keyword search over knowledge graphs via static and dynamic hub labelings. In: WWW'20: Proceedings of the Web Conference 2020. ACM, New York, pp. 235–245 (2020)

17. Jia, Y., Fang, B.X., Wang, X., et al.: Fog computing software architecture for ubiquitous network space big data. Chin. Eng. Sci. 21(6), 114–119 (2019)

18. Zhang, J.H., Li, W.T., Qin, L., et al.: Reachability labeling for distributed graphs. In: Proceedings of the 38th IEEE International Conference on Data Engineering. IEEE, Piscataway, pp. 686–698 (2022)

19. Valiant, L.G.: A bridging model for parallel computation. Commun. ACM 33(8), 103–111 (1990)

Application of the MDATA Cognitive Model in Cyber Attack Assessment

Zhaoquan Gu[1,2(✉)] and Yan Jia[3]

[1] Harbin Institute of Technology Shenzhen, Shenzhen 518055, China
guzhaoquan@hit.edu.cn
[2] Pengcheng Laboratory, Shenzhen 518066, China
[3] National University of Defense Technology, Changsha 410073, China
jiayanjy@vip.sina.com

Since the turn of the 20th century, cybersecurity incidents have become increasingly frequent, and the number of such incidents continues to grow. These incidents are marked by numerous highly covert, targeted, and persistent multi-step attacks that pose severe threats to users, enterprises, and even national security. To achieve a comprehensive, accurate, and real-time assessment of cybersecurity incidents, this chapter introduces how the MDATA cognitive model can be applied to cyber attack assessment.

The structure of this chapter is as follows. Section 1 introduces existing methods for cyber attack detection and assessment, further analyzing their advantages and limitations. Section 2 discusses the problems and challenges faced in cyber attack assessment. Section 3 describes in detail the MDATA cognitive modeling based cyber attack assessment method and its detection effectiveness. Section 4 presents the architecture, functions, and typical applications of the YHSAS system, which was developed based on the MDATA cognitive model. Section 5 summarizes the content of this chapter.

1 Existing Technologies for Cyber Attack Detection and Assessment

Cyber attack detection refers to the analysis and detection of network traffic or host operational behaviors to discover and identify potential malicious attacks or threat behaviors. It supports comprehensive, accurate, and real-time assessment of cyber attacks. Cyber attack assessment based on collected cyberspace data and abnormal alert information, by utilizes cybersecurity knowledge to comprehensively, accurately, and in real-time detect cybersecurity incidents. It involves conducting a comprehensive analysis of attack techniques, trends, and the potential impact associated with these events. Cyber attack detection is the foundation of cyber attack assessment.

According to the national standard "Information Security Technology—Specification of definition and description for network attack" (GB/T 37027—2018) [1] and other publicly available information, cyber attacks can be classified into various dimensions.

Cyber attacks can be categorized into effective and ineffective attacks based on their impact. Effective attacks refer to incidents where the attacker uses specific methods or techniques to cause substantial damage to a computer network, system, or the data within the system, thereby affecting the integrity, confidentiality, and availability of the computer network or system. Ineffective attacks, on the other hand, are those where the attacker's actions have not yet caused any substantial damage to the computer network, system, or the data within the system.

Cyber attacks can be divided into known attacks and unknown attacks based on the methods utilized in the attack. Known attacks refer to actions that exploit publicly disclosed software vulnerabilities and their exploitation methods or security flaws to target the hardware, software, or data within a computer network or system. Unknown attacks, on the other hand, involve exploiting undisclosed vulnerabilities or security flaws in computer networks or system software to launch cyber attacks, such as zero-day attacks.

Based on the complexity of the attack, cyber attacks can be classified into single-step attacks, multi-step attacks, and cross-domain attacks. A single-step attack, as the smallest and indivisible operational behavior unit, refers to an independently executed attack operation. A multi-step attack is a complex cyber attack composed of a series of single-step attacks combined according to a particular logical relationship or spatiotemporal dependency. An example of this is an Advanced Persistent Threat (APT) attack, which is a typical multi-step attack characterized by robust targeting, high concealment, and long duration. A cross-domain attack refers to cyber attacks collaboratively launched by attackers within different local area networks. This is also a typical form of multi-step attack.

1.1 Feature-Based Single-Step Attack Detection Methods

The core idea behind feature-based single-step attack detection methods is to match the current network's data packets or behavioral patterns against a database of known attack rules (signatures) and system vulnerability characteristics to detect intrusion activities. In practical scenarios, Snort, a widely used network intrusion detection system, exemplifies this method. Snort utilizes the Libpcap packet capture library to collect real-time network traffic data. After preprocessing the network traffic, it matches patterns against predefined detection rules for feature matching, thereby generating alerts. To improve the efficiency of feature matching, Snort parses all detection rules in the signature database at startup and constructs a rule syntax tree. The feature matching process involves matching rule headers and rule option keywords, with the specific steps as follows:

Step 1: Sequentially traverses the rule subtrees of the rule syntax tree, where each subtree corresponds to different operational behaviors.

Step 2: Search for the corresponding rule header in the rule subtree based on the IP address and port number of the network packet. If found, continue searching and matching within the rule subtree; otherwise, exit the matching process.

Step 3: Begin matching the first rule option. If the match is successful, proceed to match the remaining rule options in sequence; otherwise, perform pattern matching for the following rule.

Step 4: If the current rule is successfully matched, execute the actions defined by the matched rule and exit the matching process.

Step 5: Repeat steps 1 to 4 until the network packet has been matched against all detection rules in the rule syntax tree. If no alerts are generated during this process, it indicates that the network packet is not an intrusion.

Using the Snort detection rule illustrated in Fig. 1 as an example, we explain the feature-matching process with Snort rules. This detection rule corresponds to the "alert" operation subtree. It checks whether the captured network packets with a quintuple < protocol, source IP address, destination IP address, source port, destination port > match the detection rule header < TCP, $EXTERNAL_NET, any, $HOME_NET, $HTTP_PORTS > (where $ denotes system variables) and uses the content of the network packet to match the option keywords in the detection rule. For example, the keyword "flow" is used to determine if a session has been established and whether the session direction is from client to server initiating a request. The keyword "http_header" indicates whether the corresponding content in the option keywords appears in the session. The keyword "pcre" specifies using regular expressions to perform feature matching on the contents of the Payload. If all these criteria are meet, the detection rule is considered successfully matched, triggering the system to execute the corresponding alert operation; otherwise, the match is unsuccessful.

```
alert tcp $EXTERNAL_NET any -> $HOME_NET $HTTP_PORTS
( msg:"SERVER-APACHE Apache Tika crafted HTTP header command injection attempt";
flow:to_server,established;
http_header; content:"X-Tika-OCRtesseractPath"; content:"|00|",within 200;
pcre:"/X-Tika-OCRtesseractPath:[^\r\n]+?\x00/i";
metadata:policy max-detect-ips drop,policy security-ips drop; service:http; reference:cve,2018-1335;
classtype:attempted-user; sid:47615; rev:1; )
```

Fig. 1. Snort Detection Rule

Feature-based detection methods primarily include three types: state modeling, string matching, and expert systems. State modeling encodes attacks into different states within a finite automaton and observes them in traffic profiles to detect attack behaviors [2]. String matching uses string pattern matching to identify attack rules in network traffic packets, thereby determining the presence of intrusions [3]. Expert systems describe detection rules or procedures derived from system-known attacks to classify audit data for attack detection [4]. Manually generating signature rules for known attack behaviors is both time-consuming and error-prone. As a solution, some scholars have proposed automated methods for generating detection rules for known attacks. Syrius automatically generates detection rules for Suricata through deep packet inspection technology [5], while MQTT uses Bayesian methods to generate if-then detection rules automatically [6].

Feature-based detection methods typically employ pattern matching because this method is easy to implement and offers high detection accuracy. However, this method heavily relies on existing signature or rule characteristic knowledge bases, making it challenging to detect unknown attacks and adapt to new attack behaviors and variants of existing attacks.

1.2 Machine Learning-Based Single-Step Attack Detection Methods

The core idea behind machine learning-based single-step attack detection methods is to analyze network traffic data, logs, and other data using machine learning techniques to construct classifiers that can identify abnormal behavior. Training a machine learning model for single-step attack detection generally involves the following steps: data collection and preprocessing, feature extraction, division of the dataset into training and testing sets, model training, model evaluation, and optimization.

Sinclair et al. [7] proposed using the Iterative Dichotomiser 3 (ID3) algorithm to construct decision trees for single-step attack detection. Although this algorithm uses only a few network intrusion features, its core remains unchanged. A decision tree performs branching decisions based on a tree structure. The root node represents the entire dataset, non-leaf nodes indicate decisions based on a specific attribute, branches represent the outcomes of those decisions, and leaf nodes indicate the predicted classification results. The ID3 algorithm selects attributes based on information gain and divides the data accordingly. The calculation of information gain is denoted $InfoGain(D|A) = Entorpy(D) - Entorpy(D|A)$, where, D represents the entire dataset, A represents the data attribute, and the function $Entorpy = -\sum_{i=1}^{N} p(x_i) \cdot lb \, p(x_i)$ is used to calculate the amount of information. The greater the amount of information, the higher the uncertainty. The steps of the ID3 algorithm are as follows:

Step 1: Start at the root node, calculate the information gain InfoGain for all attributes, and select the attribute with the highest information gain for splitting.

Step 2: Create child nodes based on the different values of the selected attribute.

Step 3: Recursively apply steps 1 and 2 to the child nodes to complete the decision tree's construction.

Step 4: Stop when there are no more attributes to choose from or when the classes of the attributes are entirely homogeneous, resulting in the final decision tree.

Below, we use the decision tree algorithm as an example to introduce machine learning-based single-step attack detection methods, as shown in Fig. 2. A classification model based on a decision tree can predict whether specific cyber activity is "benign" behavior or an "intrusion" and makes decisions at each node of the tree until reaching a leaf node. The label of the data point (benign or intrusion) is determined at the leaf node. In other words, each node of the tree represents a feature, each branch represents a decision made based on the information obtained from each feature, and each leaf represents a predicted class. For instance, a sample (IP port 000010, system name Apollo) matching with a pruned decision tree may successfully match the root node but fail to match the branches of the IP port node, indicating that the sample does not belong to an intrusion behavior.

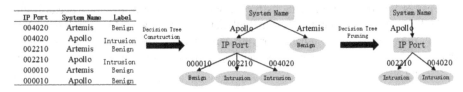

Fig. 2. An example of Machine Learning-based Single-Step Attack Detection Methods

Machine learning-based single-step attack detection methods can be divided into supervised and unsupervised machine learning algorithms. Standard supervised machine learning algorithms include the Naive Bayes model [8], Hidden Markov Model (HMM) [9], decision trees, logistic regression, and others [10]. Standard unsupervised machine learning algorithms include k-means clustering [11], hierarchical clustering [12], Gaussian Mixture Model (GMM) [13], and others。

Machine learning-based single-step attack detection methods typically require manual feature selection and significant expertise from practitioners. Supervised machine learning algorithms can fully utilize prior knowledge to accurately classify unknown sample data. However, the selection, evaluation, and labeling of training data demand considerable human effort and time. In contrast, unsupervised machine learning algorithms do not require manual labeling of data categories, reducing human error, but necessitate extensive manual analysis of unsupervised processing results.

1.3 Deep Learning-Based Single-Step Attack Detection Methods

The core idea of single-step attack detection methods based on deep learning is to utilize deep neural networks to automatically learn the intrinsic patterns and feature representations of sample data, thereby detecting cyber attacks. Deep learning-based attack detection methods generally adopt an end-to-end method, eliminating the need for manual feature extraction. The processing flow includes data preprocessing and normalization, automatic feature extraction, model training, model testing, and optimization. Below, we introduce a representative method based on deep learning, Kitsune [14], whose core algorithm is KitNET. Kitsune is a plug-and-play network intrusion detection system capable of real-time anomaly detection in network traffic. The specific steps for attack detection using the KitNET algorithm are as follows:

Step 1: Train an autoencoder network using benign network traffic data, with features extracted from the network traffic as the input for the network model.

Step 2: Use the ensemble of autoencoder networks to reconstruct the input samples, treating the reconstructed new samples as the output of the autoencoder network.

Step 3: Calculate the reconstruction error score between the input samples and the reconstructed new samples using the Root Mean Squared Error (RMSE) function and integrate the results of multiple autoencoders to obtain the final anomaly detection score.

Step 4: Update the parameters of the autoencoder network using the backpropagation algorithm.

Step 5: Repeat Steps 2 through 4 until the required number of training iterations is reached or the model performance no longer improves.

Step 6: Input test samples into the trained ensemble autoencoder network model to query the error scores. If the score exceeds a specified threshold, an alert is triggered; otherwise, no alert is generated.

As an example, the single-step attack detection process based on deep learning is introduced with the single-step attack detection of the Kitsune system shown in Fig. 3. First, the system automatically extracts features from the captured raw network traffic (packets) and inputs them into the integrated self-encoder network model. Then, the system reconstructs the input sample features using the self-encoder model and calculates the error between the input features and the reconstructed features using the RMSE function. Finally, the system passes the output of the RMSE function to the integrated self-encoder for nonlinear voting and calculates the score after voting by weighting. If the score is more significant than a set threshold, it indicates that the input traffic is anomalous network traffic.

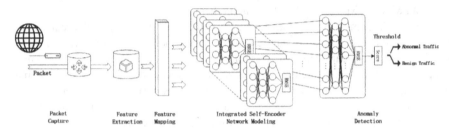

Packet   Feature   Feature   Integrated Self-Encoder   Anomaly
Capture   Extraction   Mapping   Network Modeling   Detection

Fig. 3. An example of Single-step Attack Detection in Kitsune System

There have been many results on single-step attack detection based on deep learning, and the main network architectures used include autoencoders [15], deep Boltzmann machines [16], deep belief networks [17], recurrent neural networks [18], convolutional neural networks [19], and generative adversarial networks [20].

Deep learning techniques are able to integrate feature extractors and classifiers into a single framework for end-to-end training without manual feature extraction, which has higher training inference efficiency and detection accuracy. In addition, compared with traditional machine learning methods, deep learning-based single-step attack detection methods have better adaptability and robustness and can handle large-scale and high-dimensional data. However, the training process of the method is more complex, the model interpretability could be better, and it relies heavily on large-scale labeled training data.

1.4 Multi-step Attack Detection Method Based on Attack Graph

Multi-step attack detection methods based on traceability graphs utilize graph mining and analysis techniques to discover the attacker's path of attack. This enables staff to more easily understand the security events and their relevance that occurred during the attack on the user. Such methods typically record interactions between system entities through traceability graphs and perform multi-step attack detection based on contextual data and operational interaction information. Multi-step attack detection based on a traceability graph includes the following steps.

Step 1: Extract field information from a system audit log by parsing.

Step 2: Construct a system traceability graph using the field information. The nodes in the graph represent either subjects or objects. Subjects are mainly manipulated objects, such as processes; objects are mainly manipulated objects, such as users, IP addresses, and files. The edges in the graph represent the interrelationships between nodes and data traffic.

Step 3: Detect multi-step attacks by matching with attack events to form attack paths and analyzing the relationship between different attack events.

We take the browser intrusion traceability shown in Fig. 4 as an example to introduce the traceability diagram of the intrusion using this browser vulnerability. The attacker launches the attack from X.X.X.X:80, creates and launches the Mozilla nightly plugin by exploiting the browser vulnerability, the plugin executes commands and obtains sensitive information through the command execution environment, and then sends it back to X.X.X.X:443, creates burnout.bat to remove all traces of the intrusion (the direction of the arrow indicates the direction of data flow or the direction of control flow).

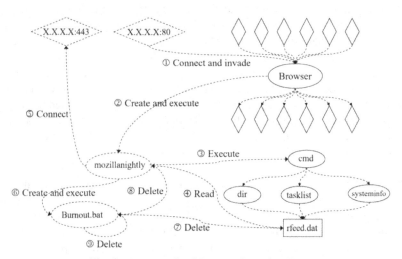

Fig. 4. An example of Browser Intrusion Trace

In a follow-up study, SLEUTH [21] proposed an attack reconstruction method that utilizes labels for multi-step attack detection on traceability graphs while meeting real-time requirements. ZePro [22] implemented a prototype system that adds the probabilistic formation of Bayesian networks to traceability graphs to identify zero-day attack paths. Holmes combined traceability graphs and kill chains [23, 24] to map low-level syslog information to high-level icons to help administrators more easily understand the status of current attacks. RapSheet [25] combines endpoint detection EDR with traceability graphs, employing tactical traceability graphs to characterize the lowest-level attack patterns. Alsaheel et al. [26] point out that different attacks may share similar abstract attack tactics and, therefore, combine natural language processing techniques with traceability graphs to propose a sequence model for representing attack semantics.

Traceability graph-based methods mainly rely on host logs, and it is difficult to detect traffic-based attacks effectively. Knowledge representation models (e.g., knowledge graphs) have good interpretability. Still, existing attack detection frameworks or methods based on knowledge representation models are less generalized and cannot meet the continuous dynamic updating of knowledge about assets, vulnerabilities, and so on.

1.5   Multi-step Attack Detection Method Based on Correlation

The core idea of the multi-step attack detection method based on correlation is to use multi-dimensional information for comprehensive analysis to find all the attack steps to form an attack path and reveal the attacker's intention. This method generally performs correlation analysis on the alarm events generated by the single-step attack detection algorithm and the security equipment to reduce noise and false alarms, aggregate similar alarms, and finally discover the attack path.

Shawly et al. [27] proposed an attack detection framework based on the hidden Markov model (HMM). The hidden Markov model is a statistical model used to model sequence data. Its main idea is to use Markov chains to describe the state transition in the sequence and use observations to represent the observation results in the state transition process. These observations are often difficult to observe or measure directly and are called "hidden variables". The basic assumption here is that the current state is only related to the state of the previous moment but not to other moments. Therefore, when modeling sequence data, the hidden Markov model can effectively capture the sequence's local correlation and perform well in prediction and recognition tasks. The general processing steps of the multi-step attack detection method based on correlation are as follows.

Step 1: Determine the type and number of hidden states according to the actual situation of the problem.

Step 2: Using the known data set, calculate the model's initial state probability distribution, state transition matrix, and observation probability matrix.

Step 3: Use the forward and backward algorithms to calculate the probability of the given observation sequence.

Step 4: Use the Viterbi algorithm to solve the state sequence with the highest probability under the current observation sequence.

Step 5: Use the Baum-Welch algorithm to optimize the model parameters iteratively, gradually improving the model's prediction accuracy.

Step 6: The trained hidden Markov model is used to classify or predict the new observation sequence.

Figure 5 shows the attack detection framework based on the hidden Markov model. The framework designs K hidden Markov model templates to deal with the complex interlaced coordination between multiple single-step attacks, that is, multi-stage attacks. Through such a design, the framework can identify warning information of length T and, at most, identify mixed attacks of K types.

The execution process of the framework is as follows. First, the Snort-based intrusion detection system (IDS) is used to obtain attack alarm information from the network/system, sort this alarm information by timestamp, and preprocess them into a suitable format; then, the alarm information is transferred to a database with multiple sets of hidden Markov model templates. The local information in the alarm sequence is captured by calculating the hidden variables of the information, and the correlation between these single-step attacks is analyzed to obtain some similar attack paths and generate corresponding alarms. For alarm information, the multi-step attack detection method based on the hidden Markov model will extract seven features (timestamp, ID, source IP address, source port, destination IP address, destination port, and priority), extract T alarm information each time, and form them into information streams, which are converted into input data that the hidden Markov model can use after preprocessing. Each hidden Markov model template calculates the most likely attack sequence through the Viterbi algorithm and gives a risk warning.

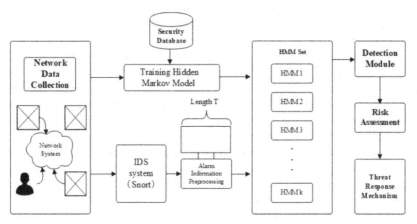

Fig. 5. Attack Detection Framework Based on Hidden Markov Model

The multi-step attack detection method based on correlation involves a variety of security defense measures and analysis methods, mainly including alarm generation, correlation analysis, and attack path discovery. According to different analysis methods, multi-step attack detection can be further divided into similarity-based detection [28], causality-based detection [29], structure-based detection [30] and instance-based detection [31].

The multi-step attack detection method based on correlation can fully use multi-dimensional attack information and explore the correlation between different attack information. Compared with the process based on machine learning, the multi-step attack detection method based on correlation does not need to rely on the rule knowledge of a particular attack field. It has obvious advantages when dealing with new attacks. However, since the correlation between attack information may be partially specific, this method will produce false positives or false negatives. In addition, the multi-step attack detection method based on correlation must extract features from a large amount of cyberspace data and perform model training when modeling, which requires a long training time and high computing and storage resource overhead.

2 Problems in Cyber Attack Analysis and Judgment

Cybersecurity incidents are characterized by large-scale evolution and correlation. To achieve the goal of comprehensive, accurate, and real-time analysis of cybersecurity incidents, many vital technical problems need to be solved. We summarize the issues faced by cyber attack analysis as follows.

Difficulty in correlation analysis. Cyberspace is boundless, and the means of attack are becoming more and more advanced and complex. The cyber attacks detected in each subnet will likely be just one step in a multi-step attack. Discovering the attacker's intentions and technical means is difficult by analyzing only the attacks detected in a single subnet. Even within the perceptible and detectable cyberspace, each subnet often has a high degree of independence. Therefore, the first problem that attack analysis faces is associating cyber attack events in different subnets for comprehensive analysis.

Many false positives and false negatives. The existing attack detection system has a large number of false positives and false negatives in the detection of single-step attacks and multi-step attacks. There will undoubtedly be more false positives and negatives after the subnets are associated, making it challenging to detect effective attacks. Based on comprehensive analysis, reducing the false positives and false negatives of the attack detection system and improving the accuracy of attack detection are the second problems faced by cyber attack analysis.

Real-time calculation is complex. The vast scale and real-time evolution of cyber-security incidents make it difficult to accurately and real-time analyze cross-domain attacks, and the computational complexity increases exponentially with the expansion of the scale of the MDATA cognitive model knowledge graph. How to achieve real-time response and support the evolving and developing attack detection is the third problem faced by cyber attack analysis. Only by solving the above three issues can it be possible to efficiently use cybersecurity knowledge and realize comprehensive, accurate, and real-time analysis of cybersecurity incidents. The analysis in the previous section shows that the existing detection methods for single- and multi-step attacks can only partially solve these three problems.

3   Cyber Attack Analysis Technology Based on MDATA Cognitive Model

The cyber attack judgment technology of the MDATA cognitive model can effectively solve the three problems of cyber attack judgment: difficulty in correlation analysis, many false positives and omissions, and difficulty in real-time calculation. Specifically, in response to the problem of difficulty in correlation analysis, the cyber attack judgment technology of the MDATA cognitive model to be introduced in this section can solve the problems of many false positives and omissions, as well as difficulty in correlation analysis and real-time calculation. Precisely, in response to the issue of many false positives and omissions, the effective attack judgment method of the MDATA cognitive model to be introduced in this section can remove false positives and complete omissions to achieve practical attack judgment in response to the problem of difficulty in correlation analysis and real-time calculation, the cross-domain attack judgment method of the MDATA cognitive model to be introduced in this section can combine cyber attack events with different time and space distributions for judgment. The attack judgment technology based on fog cloud computing can divide the MDATA cognitive model large-scale graph calculation into three levels: fog end, middle layer, and cloud, and realize the real-time calculation of attack judgment through the collaboration of these three levels. Furthermore, in order to deal with possible unknown attacks, this section will introduce the unknown attack judgment method of the self-evolution of the MDATA cognitive model to deal with potential risks and challenges in cyberspace.

3.1 Effective Attack Analysis Method Based on MDATA Cognitive Model

The effective attack analysis method of the MDATA cognitive model is as follows: First, a cybersecurity knowledge base for known attacks is established to cover known cyber attack knowledge comprehensively. Targeted data collection is carried out according to the characteristics of the protection system, and data related to effective attacks is collected according to the distribution of assets and vulnerabilities to remove a large number of false positives; finally, multi-step attacks are matched through the constructed attack detection subgraph to achieve adequate detection of cyber attacks.

3.1.1 Cybersecurity Knowledge Base

The cybersecurity knowledge base refers to all current asset information, including hardware models and software versions, as well as various known system security vulnerabilities and attack patterns. It is a fundamental knowledge base for cyber attack research and judgment. The cybersecurity knowledge base usually contains many known attack patterns, vulnerabilities, malware, and other information, which helps identify known attacks and is the basis for deploying defense systems in advance. In addition, the rules and algorithms in the cybersecurity knowledge base can be used to discover unknown attacks. For example, the analysis of network traffic and logs can detect some abnormal behaviors, and then, combined with the attack patterns in the knowledge base for reasoning, new attack behaviors that are different from the past can be discovered. In practical applications, the cybersecurity knowledge base must be updated according to the latest threat intelligence to respond promptly to new attack behaviors and improve real-time detection accuracy. The cybersecurity knowledge base can provide essential knowledge support for cyber attack research and judgment.

The knowledge acquisition, knowledge representation, and management introduced in the previous article lay the foundation for the construction of the cybersecurity knowledge base. Their key technologies can help us build a multi-dimensionally associated cybersecurity knowledge base. For example, the multi-dimensional association and unified representation of cyber attack events, vulnerabilities involved in the attack process, and assets can avoid the problem of complex data formats and provide a basis for comprehensive, accurate, and real-time analysis of cyber attacks.

The cybersecurity knowledge base includes three layers: attack event layer, vulnerability layer, and asset layer, as shown in Fig. 6. The attack event layer uses the attack event as the entity node, the time of occurrence of the attack event, and the IP address involved as the time attribute and space attribute. The vulnerability layer includes the vulnerabilities exploited by the attack behavior, among which the vulnerability attributes include information such as the time of publication and the publishing organization. The asset layer consists of the attacked assets, such as file servers, Web servers, etc.

124   Z. Gu and Y. Jia

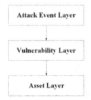

Fig. 6. Cybersecurity knowledge base structure

We use the OceanLotus attack incident as an example to construct the cybersecurity knowledge base of the incident, as shown in Fig. 7. The construction of the OceanLotus attack incident can be broken down into five steps.

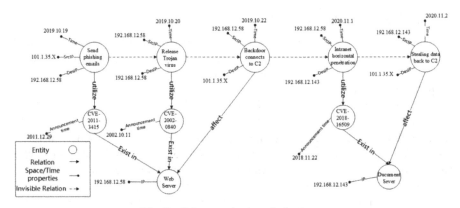

Fig. 7. Cybersecurity knowledge base

Step 1: At the attack event layer, the attacker 101.1.35.X sent a phishing email to the "victim" 192.168.12.58 on October 19, 2019, and used the vulnerability entity CVE-2011–3415 of the vulnerability layer to attack the Web server of the asset layer.

Step 2: At the attack event layer, the attacker released a remote control Trojan and used the vulnerability entity CVE-2002–0840 of the vulnerability layer to control the Web server of the asset layer.

Step 3: At the attack event layer, the attacker controls the asset layer's web server through the backdoor program installed by the Trojan virus and connects the server to the attacker's server. This step does not involve the entity of the vulnerability layer.

Step 4: At the attack event layer, after lurking for more than a year, the attacker conducted a lateral penetration of the intranet on November 1, 2020, and used the vulnerability entity CVE-2018–16509 of the vulnerability layer to gain control of the file server of the asset layer.

Step 5: At the attack event layer, the attacker steals data and sends it back. This step does not involve the entity at the vulnerability layer. Still, it will impact the file server at the asset layer.

After building the cybersecurity knowledge base, we can deduce the association between attacker behaviors through deductive operators, the invisible relationship in Fig. 7 (the part connected by the dotted arrow).

Unlike the existing representation method, which uses IP addresses as nodes, the cybersecurity knowledge base uses single-step attack behaviors/security events as entity nodes. It performs association analysis on each attack behavior's time and spatial attributes. It deduces the temporal relationship of the attack behavior. Subgraph matching, reachable path calculation, and other methods are then used to detect multi-step attacks in the network system.

3.1.2 Targeted Data Collection

Faced with the massive scale of cyberspace and the multi-source heterogeneity of data, aimless data collection will generate a lot of useless time overhead. Targeted data collection can solve this problem.

Targeted data collection is a customized method that can purposefully and specifically collect data on specific attack events, assets, vulnerabilities, alarms, and other indicators in cybersecurity scenarios. The purpose of targeted data collection is mainly to help security analysts quickly and accurately obtain representative cybersecurity data for more efficient data mining and security analysis. Through targeted data collection, security analysts can more quickly understand the security risks in the network and make timely decisions.

Targeted data collection is crucial to analyzing cybersecurity status, as reflected in the following aspects.

Accurately grasp the security status of cyberspace. Targeted data collection can collect specific security data according to the actual needs of security analysts, which helps security analysts to more accurately analyze the security status of cyberspace, quickly discover security vulnerabilities and threat behaviors in cyberspace, and make timely security responses.

Support cybersecurity decisions. Targeted data collection can collect data related to specific cybersecurity issues, which can help security analysts better understand cyberspace risks and vulnerabilities and formulate security strategies and plans.

Improve security protection capabilities. Targeted data collection can help security analysts gain a more comprehensive understanding of cybersecurity threats and vulnerabilities, improving the system's security protection and response capabilities. Based on the collected data, security analysts can analyze security threats' characteristics and behavior patterns and take effective security protection measures.

Improve security response efficiency. Targeted data collection can collect specific cybersecurity data, enabling security analysts to respond quickly. By collecting particular data, security analysts can locate security issues more quickly, identify potential risks, and formulate corresponding security measures, thereby improving security response efficiency.

Then, we introduce targeted data collection for a typical cybersecurity scenario, and its overall framework is shown in Fig. 8. The framework covers the entire process, from assets to vulnerabilities to attacks, as well as targeted data collection on the traffic and terminal sides.

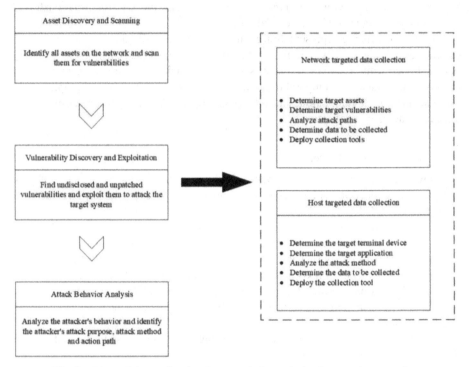

Fig. 8. Targeted data collection framework for typical cybersecurity scenarios

(1) Asset discovery and scanning

Asset discovery mainly refers to identifying all hosts, network devices, applications, etc., in the target network, including IP addresses, open ports, operating system versions, application versions, running services, etc. Standard asset detection tools include Nmap, Masscan, Zmap, etc.

Asset scanning involves performing vulnerability scanning on the discovered hosts to identify existing vulnerabilities. Standard vulnerability scanning tools include Nessus, OpenVAS, Qualys, etc. These tools can help us identify system vulnerabilities and weaknesses and determine collection targets.

(2) Vulnerability mining and exploitation

Vulnerability mining refers to finding undisclosed and unpatched security vulnerabilities. Standard methods include fuzz testing and disassembly.

Vulnerability exploitation involves using known vulnerabilities to attack the target system. This can be done by querying and analyzing the public vulnerability library and combining it with hacker attack tools. We can use tools like Metasploit, CANVAS, Core Impact, etc., to simulate attack behavior and determine the required information and data.

(3) Attack behavior analysis

Attack behavior analysis mainly identifies the attacker's purpose, means, action trajectory, etc., by analyzing the attacker's operating behavior on the target system. Standard attack behavior analysis tools include Snort, Suricata, Bro, etc.

(4) Targeted Data Collection on the Traffic Side

Targeted data collection on the traffic side primarily involves monitoring network traffic to acquire attackers' behavioral data. The process comprises the following steps:

Step 1: Identify Target Assets. Determine the target assets requiring data collection, including servers, network devices, and others.

Step 2: Identify Target Vulnerabilities. Based on known vulnerability databases or vulnerability scanning results, identify vulnerabilities present in the target assets.

Step 3: Analyze Attack Paths. Analyze potential attack paths that attackers may take, considering the target assets and vulnerability information.

Step 4: Determine the Data to Collect. Based on the attack methods, decide on the data to be collected, including process monitoring information, system logs, file modification records, and more.

Step 5: Deploy Collection Tools Based on Data Needs. Deploy appropriate collection tools, such as intrusion detection systems, intrusion prevention systems (IPS), and traffic analyzers, according to the defined data collection requirements.

During the targeted data collection process on the traffic side, attention should be paid to the scope and depth of collection to ensure meaningful data is captured. For instance, filters can be set to capture only traffic related to the target host or specific protocols.

(5) Targeted Data Collection on the Endpoint Side

Targeted data collection on the endpoint side primarily involves monitoring processes, files, registry information, and other details on the target host to acquire behavioral data of attackers. The process comprises the following steps:

Step 1: Identify Target Endpoint Devices. Determine the target endpoint devices requiring data collection, including computers, mobile phones, servers, and others.

Step 2: Identify Target Applications. Based on known vulnerability databases or security threat intelligence, identify high-risk applications or operating system vulnerabilities present on the target endpoint devices.

Step 3: Analyze Attack Methods. Analyze potential attack methods that attackers may employ, considering the target applications and vulnerability information.

Step 4: Determine Data to Collect. Decide on the data to be collected based on the attack methods, including process monitoring information, system logs, file modification records, and more.

Step 5: Deploy Collection Tools Based on Data Needs. Deploy appropriate collection tools, such as endpoint monitoring tools and file auditing tools, according to the defined data collection requirements.

In the process of targeted data collection on the endpoint side, attention should be paid to the accuracy and integrity of the collection to ensure that the collected data can provide useful clues. For instance, monitoring rules can be set to capture only data related to the target process or changes in key files.

For the OceanLotus attack incident, the targeted data collection process on the endpoint side is as follows:

Firstly, utilize Nmap to scan existing assets, such as web servers (IP address 192.168.12.58), file servers (IP address 192.168.12.143), and their application services (e.g., email systems), to identify the target entities that require protection.

Secondly, we need to collect potential vulnerabilities and their exploitation methods on the protected targets. For example, we need to collect vulnerability information related to the Microsoft.NET Framework used by web services (such as vulnerability CVE-2011–3415).

Thirdly, based on the combination of assets and vulnerabilities, analyze the possible attack methods that OceanLotus attacks might use with the aid of a cybersecurity knowledge base, such as phishing attacks using forged official notification Word documents.

Finally, monitor traffic on network-side IDS/IPS devices, analyze web server logs (such as the/public/games directory), correlate the collected targeted data, and analyze and detect attack behaviors.

3.1.3 Effective Attack Detection Based on Subgraph Matching

To better conduct multi-step effective attack detection, we require various auxiliary methods such as false alarm filtering, knowledge inference, and attack subgraphs. On the one hand, the complex network environment may lead to the misjudgment of some normal network behaviors as attacks. At the same time, some genuine threats are overlooked, and some irrelevant events are mistakenly labeled as threats. Therefore, methods based on feature matching are not suitable for multi-step attack detection. On the other hand, with the continuous emergence of new attack methods, traditional single-step attack detection methods may not effectively cope with complex threats, such as APT attacks.

In multi-step attacks, attackers achieve their ultimate goals through multiple steps. These steps may be challenging to detect or deceptive, and effective attack detection based on subgraph matching can better address such threats. The framework is illustrated in Fig. 9.

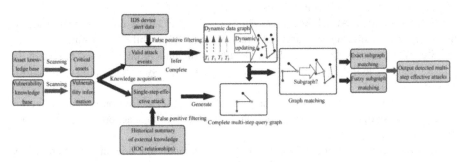

Fig. 9. Effective Attack Detection Framework Based on Subgraph Matching

The specific steps for effective attack detection based on subgraph matching are as follows.

Step 1: Discover critical assets and vulnerability information by scanning the asset knowledge base and vulnerability knowledge base.

Step 2: Generate a dynamic data graph.

① Alert data is generated by devices such as IDS, which are used to monitor malicious activities or unauthorized usage in networks or systems. After generating alert data, irrelevant alerts can be filtered out to reduce false alarms, a process called false alarm filtering, which aims to eliminate alerts that mistakenly label normal events as threats.

② By combining critical asset and vulnerability information, effective attack events can be obtained, and knowledge related to attack behaviors can be extracted from the alert data to achieve knowledge acquisition.

③ During the detection process, missed alarms may occur. Undetected attack behaviors can be discovered through inference supplementation, a process called knowledge inference, which refers to using existing knowledge and information to infer new conclusions or make predictions. For instance, when two detected attacks apparently lack a specific associative relationship, knowledge inference can be utilized to complement undetected attacks. Knowledge inference helps address missed alarms, enabling security analysts to understand attack situations better and take appropriate measures to prevent potential threats. Subsequently, based on time information, a dynamic data graph is obtained.

Step 3: Generate a multi-step query graph.

① Form single-step influential attack events based on external knowledge and historical knowledge, where external knowledge includes information about specific security vulnerabilities such as Indicators of Compromise (IOC), which helps security teams determine whether an attack has occurred.

② Obtain critical asset and vulnerability information through knowledge acquisition to form a complete multi-step query graph.

Step 4: Given the existence of two elements, data graphs and query graphs, in this scenario, we can utilize subgraph matching methods to find parts in the data graph that match the query graph, thus enabling effective attack detection. In the matching process, we can adopt both precise subgraph matching and fuzzy subgraph matching.

① Precise subgraph matching: This method searches for subgraphs in the data graph that perfectly match the query graph. It can be used for effective attack detection in the entire network topology.

② Fuzzy subgraph matching: Searches for subgraphs in the data graph that approximately match the query graph. When attack strategies change, fuzzy subgraph matching can detect suspected multi-step attacks. Fuzzy subgraph matching can involve manually setting a threshold for the degree of matching. If the actual degree of matching exceeds this threshold, it indicates a successful match with a multi-step attack, enabling effective attack detection in complex network topologies.

In summary, security analysts only need to focus on real-time alert data related to attack subgraphs. When a certain type of attack subgraph alert frequently appears, security analysts can determine that there is an effective attack behavior targeting critical system assets.

In effective attack detection based on subgraph matching, the key is to prepare descriptions representing the dynamic data graph and multi-step query graph. Next, we describe the specific process of generating the query graph, i.e., the attack subgraph.

The dynamic data graph is constructed based on alert information from security devices, dynamically generated through alert data filtering, attack knowledge acquisition, and inference. As the number of alerts increases, the scale of the dynamic data graph will expand. The query graph is used to describe the multi-step attack patterns to be detected, such as Fig. 10, which shows a multi-step query graph for detecting the OceanLotus attack. By matching the presence of this query graph in the dynamic data graph, accurate detection of the OceanLotus multi-step attack can be achieved. Detection templates, i.e., query graphs, are constructed for each known multi-step attack, and subgraph matching is performed in parallel in the data graph to achieve accurate detection of multiple known multi-step attacks.

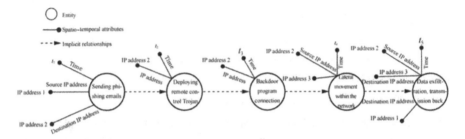

Fig. 10. Detecting the Multi-Step Query Graph of OceanLotus Attacks

Note: t_1 to t_5 represent time periods.

To enhance the detection rate of effective attacks, we optimize the dynamic data graph based on the status of assets and vulnerabilities, thereby reducing irrelevant attack behaviors. The specific process is as follows:

Firstly, we collect and organize alert data from sources such as IDS devices.

Secondly, we conduct asset scanning to determine which assets exist in the network. Following that, vulnerability scanning is performed to ascertain the vulnerabilities present in those assets.

Thirdly, based on the results of asset and vulnerability scanning, we filter out irrelevant alert data and query relevant attack patterns in the network space security knowledge base.

Finally, using the query results, information on critical assets, and vulnerability details, we generate a dynamic data graph, specifically an attack subgraph, for the detection of practical attacks.

3.2 Cross-Domain Attack Evaluation Methodology Utilizing the MDATA Cognitive Model

Subnetworks possess a certain degree of independence, and cybersecurity data often involves sensitive information such as internal assets and internal network structures. Multi-step attacks are often composed of multiple single-step attacks originating from different subnetworks. Only by connecting the various subnetworks can we detect multi-step attacks. To achieve cross-domain attack assessment in practical application scenarios, we must first address the key issue of how to correlate the data from various subnetworks. Once the subnetworks are connected, they form an immensely vast system, and utilizing the vast amount of data within the system for real-time calculations will be a significant challenge.

To address the challenges of difficulty in data correlation analysis and real-time calculation for cross-domain attack assessments, we introduce a cross-domain attack assessment method based on the MDATA cognitive model within a fog computing architecture. The core idea is to divide the large-scale computing of the MDATA cognitive model into distributed subgraphs (also known as knowledge entities) that comprise a fog layer, an intermediate layer, and a cloud layer. This method constructs a multi-knowledge entity distributed hierarchical collaborative computing system. It achieves real-time calculations for attack assessments through the coordinated hybrid scheduling of data flow and control flow, as illustrated in Fig. 11. The specific steps of the cross-domain attack assessment method using the MDATA cognitive model are outlined as follows.

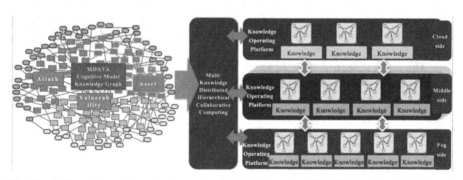

Fig. 11. A Cross-Domain Attack Assessment Methodology for MDATA Cognitive Model Based on Fog Computing Architecture

Step 1: Establish a knowledge entity architecture in each subnet to lay the foundation for the assembly and collaborative computation of multiple knowledge entities. The knowledge entity consists of a data acquirer, a knowledge inference engine, a task coordinator, and other components. It manages knowledge through the data acquirer and the knowledge inference engine. The knowledge entities are assembled and coordinated through task input interfaces. The internal architecture of the knowledge entity is shown in Fig. 12.

Step 2: Establish a remote online assembly system for knowledge entities based on distributed component technology. This system will facilitate the assembly of knowledge

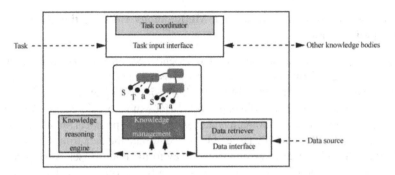

Fig. 12. Internal Architecture of Knowledge System

entities within different subnets, enabling the flexible segmentation and assembly of MDATA cognitive model knowledge graphs tailored to different network structures and assets.

Step 3: Design a collaborative hybrid scheduling method that integrates data flow and control flow. This method will enable coordinated computation of large-scale knowledge entities across fog endpoints, intermediate layers, and the cloud, thus achieving real-time computation for attack analysis and judgment.

Step 4: After establishing the fog-cloud computing architecture, corresponding MDATA cognitive model subgraphs will be formed based on the composition and distribution of subnet assets and vulnerabilities. These subgraphs will detect local attack events in each subnet. Parallel and collaborative computation for cross-domain attacks will be conducted within the fog-cloud computing architecture, enabling comprehensive, accurate, and real-time analysis and judgment of multi-step attacks across the entire network. The system for cross-domain attack analysis and judgment based on the MDATA cognitive model is illustrated in Fig. 13.

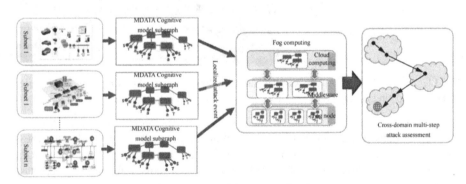

Fig. 13. A Cross-Domain Attack Analysis Methodology Based on the MDATA Cognitive Model

The cross-domain attack assessment methodology based on the MDATA cognitive model leverages the fog computing architecture to support the collaborative application of distributed MDATA cognitive model knowledge bases. This enhances the sharing, interaction, and correlation of dynamic knowledge with spatiotemporal characteristics, fostering a knowledge synergy effect. It addresses the challenge of complex data correlation across subnets in the cybersecurity domain and can be applied to cross-domain attack assessment scenarios with spatiotemporal sensitivity. Ultimately, the cross-domain attack assessment system based on the MDATA cognitive model can process ultra-large-scale datasets of billions of entries, stabilizing the response time for conventional computations such as reachable path, subgraph matching, and subgraph querying to the millisecond level. This resolves the difficulty of real-time computation with massive data in cyberspace. In terms of computational scale, this system achieves vertex-related computations at the 100 million and billion-scale levels for the first time, surpassing large graph computing systems like Neo4J and TigerGraph.

3.3 Self-evolving Unknown Attack Evaluation Methodology Based on the MDATA Cognitive Model

As information technology upgrades accelerate and the number of various vulnerabilities continues to grow, attackers' techniques are also evolving and developing, with new attack methods and strategies emerging constantly. Existing attack detection methods struggle to detect novel and unknown cyber attacks, posing a challenge for cyber attack analysis and judgment.

To address the ever-increasing unknown attacks, we introduce an MDATA cognitive model-based self-evolving method for unknown attack analysis. This method comprises the following two functions:

Real-time knowledge extraction and update based on the MDATA cognitive model.

Cybersecurity knowledge exists in structured and semi-structured data from blogs, forums, and other sources. As new vulnerabilities and cyber attacks are disclosed, various unknown cybersecurity knowledge emerges. Our MDATA cognitive model-based self-evolving method can continuously extract knowledge from newly disclosed vulnerabilities and attacks, and complement the knowledge through the MDATA model's knowledge acquisition methods. Meanwhile, with the organization of numerous cyber offensive and defensive exercises and competitions, the related data provides a new data source for acquiring cybersecurity knowledge. Analyzing these data can effectively uncover the offensive and defensive strategies of both parties, extract unknown knowledge related to offensive and defensive behaviors, and enrich the cybersecurity knowledge base, supporting the detection of more types of cyber attacks.

Reasoning-based adaptive attack strategy generation using the MDATA cognitive model.

Since attack steps often have a specific temporal sequence, unknown attacks may be variants of existing attack methods, employing different strategies to achieve their objectives. Therefore, we utilize a temporal knowledge graph reasoning method based on the MDATA cognitive model to continuously deduce unknown attack strategies. The specific process is as follows:

First, a series of single-step attacks extracted are sorted in the order of occurrence, forming an attack sequence M of length n.

Next, candidate sequences with lengths between 2 and n are constructed, where each candidate sequence is a subsequence of the attack sequence M.

Then, temporal knowledge graph reasoning is performed based on the MDATA cognitive model to derive potential new attack chains.

Finally, the deduced attack chains and strategies are reproduced on a network simulation validation platform. If the attack objectives are achieved and the strategy is not present in the knowledge base, the cybersecurity knowledge base is updated accordingly, thus enhancing the detection capabilities against unknown cyber attacks.

The overall process of generating attack chains based on the MDATA cognitive model's reasoning adaptive attack strategy is illustrated in Fig. 14.

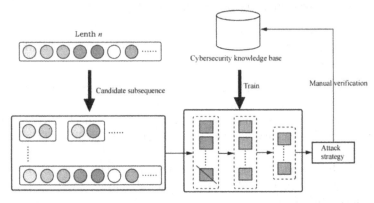

Fig. 14. Overall Process of Generating Attack Chains with Reasoning and Adaptive Attack Strategies Based on the MDATA Cognitive Model

Through continuous extraction and inference of cybersecurity knowledge, the MDATA cognitive model's self-evolving method for identifying unknown attacks has enriched and refined the cybersecurity knowledge base, enhanced the ability to respond to unknown cyber attacks, and further improved the level of cybersecurity assurance.

3.4 Complexity Analysis

Cyber attack detection and assessment is a challenging task which costs much time. A traditional multi-step attack detection process consists of two stages: finding effective singe-step attacks among the collected network data in each time slot and detecting the multi-step attacks by associating these single-attacks during a time period. Supposing there are N_1 different single-step attacks in total (the number may increase as new attack may exist once new vulnerability or variant attack emerges) and N_2 network data collected in each time slot, it costs $T_1 = f_1(N_1, N_2) = O(N_1 * N_2)$ time to find these effective single-step attacks such as comparing each data with the attacks. For the second stage, supposing there are $N_{1t} \leq N_1$ attacks for each time slot t, the time complexity of detecting multi-step attacks by associating these single attacks are $T_2 = f_2(N_{11}, N_{12}, \ldots, N_{1t}) = O(N_1^t)$ which increases exponentially as time t increases. Hence, the time complexity of traditional multi-step attack detection and assessment is $T = tT_1 + T_2 = O(N_1^t + tN_1N_2) = O(N_1^t)$, which is a challenging tack that cannot be finished in real-time.

In this chapter, we introduce the attack detection and assessment method on the basis of the MDATA cognitive model. There are two parts for time complexity analysis: the pre-processing part and the attack detection part. Considering the pre-processing part, it first establishes a cybersecurity database which includes cybersecurity knowledge such as single-step attacks, vulnerabilities, assets, and their relationships. Supposing there are N_3 vulnerabilities and N_4 assets in total, the time complexity to establish the large cybersecurity database is $T_{p1}^M = g_1(N_1, N_3, N_4) = O(N_1 * N_3 * N_4)$. Then it establishes the multi-step attack graphs according to the known attack chains. Supposing there are K known multi-step attacks and each attack has at most m steps, the time complexity is $T_{p2}^M = g_2(N_1, K, m) = O(KN_1^m)$. Hence, the pre-processing of the method costs $T_p^M = T_{p1}^M + T_{p2}^M = O(N_1N_3N_4 + KN_1^m)$ time.

The multi-step attack detection part consists of three steps: 1) detecting effective single-step attacks in each time slot; 2) establishing a real-time data graph during the time period; 3) detecting the multi-step attacks by the subgraph matching methods. As the method has established the relationships among assets, vulnerabilities and single-step attacks, it can compare the network data in each time slot with the vulnerabilities, then map the relations to the assets and single-step attacks. Therefore, the time complexity is $T_{d1}^M = h_1(N_1, N_2, N_3, N_4) = O(N_1N_3 + N_2 + N_4)$ for each time slot. Supposing the original data graph is the constructed cybersecurity database in the pre-processing step, as there are $N_{1t} \leq N_1$ effective single-step attacks detected in time slot t, there are $3N_{1t}$ nodes added to the data graph as the temporal (time stamp) and spatial information (source address and destination address) are added to the attack node thanks to the MDATA model's effective representation method, hence the time complexity of adding these nodes is only $T_{d2}^M = h_2(N_{1t}) = O(N_1)$. For a time period t, there are at most $L_d = h(N_{11}, N_{12}, \ldots, N_{1t}) = O(tN_1)$ nodes in the data graph. As there are at most K known multi-step attacks and each attack has at most m steps, there are K query graphs and each graph has at most $L_q = 4m$ nodes (the attack node, temporal information node, and two spatial information nodes). The subgraph matching method costs time $T_{d3}^M = h_3(L_d, L_q, K) = O(KL_d^{L_q}) = O(K(tN_1)^{4m})$. Combining these three steps, the time complexity of the multi-step attack detection is $T_d^M = tT_{d1}^M + tT_{d2}^M + T_{d3}^M = O(tN_1N_3 + N_2 + N_4 + K(tN_1)^{4m})$. As K, m, N_1 and N_3 are constants (normally K and m are small, N_1, N_2, N_3 and N_4 are large), the time complexity can be considered as a polynomial function of time period t, which is possible to be finished in real-time.

Comparing the traditional multi-step attack detection method and the MDATA model based method, the MDATA cognitive model can transform the challenging task (time complexity increases exponentially) to a real-time computable problem.

4 YHSAS: Cyber Attack Research and Judgment System Based on MDATA Cognitive Model

In the preceding paragraphs, we have introduced the primary technologies employed in cyber attack research and judgment using the MDATA cognitive model. Now, we focus on the cyber attack research and judgment system known as YHSAS, which is built upon the MDATA cognitive model.

The YHSAS system offers a unified platform for network administrators to gain a comprehensive and detailed overview of the security situation within their cyber jurisdiction, including attacks, traffic, assets, vulnerabilities, comprehensive risks, and so on. By empowering security personnel to configure association analysis rules and the cybersecurity index, the YHSAS system enables the analysis of various cybersecurity incidents. Additionally, it calculates the cybersecurity index and presents an intuitive representation of the overall cybersecurity situation. This real-time analysis allows for the timely detection of cybersecurity incidents, facilitating adjustments to the security policies of cybersecurity products. As a result, the YHSAS system ensures a swift response to cybersecurity threats. Comprising several functional components, the YHSAS system can be tailored to meet the specific requirements of individual users.

4.1 Architecture and Function Introduction of the YHSAS System

The architecture of the YHSAS system is illustrated in Fig. 15, consisting of the following key modules: Data Collection Module, System Configuration Module, Cyber attack Detection Module, Cyber attack Analysis Module, Security Situational Index Calculation Module, and System Presentation Module. Each module provides specific functionalities, as outlined below.

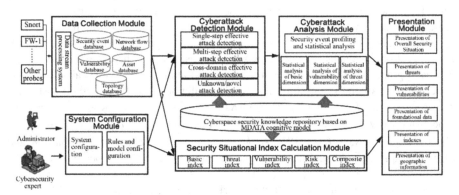

Fig. 15. Architecture of the YHSAS system

(1) Data Collection Module

The data collection module can be integrated with the existing cybersecurity tools, which can detect the cybersecurity incidents in real-time, and can also be used as a plugin of the system to expand the system dynamically, such as targeted data collection of the target network, detection and management of the operating state of each security tool (perform the operation of starting/closing the plugin). The data collection module provides a log-based passive data collector, which collects cybersecurity incidents by actively monitoring the log information generated by cybersecurity devices. It encapsulates the collected cybersecurity incidents into predefined data objects and sends them to the central database server for storage and preprocessing. This is served as the foundational data for subsequent analysis of cybersecurity incidents and situational calculations. Additionally, the data collection module offers an active query-based information collector, where the core server invokes remote security tools to scan remote cyberspace and retrieve the scan results actively. The scanned information primarily includes inherent network data, such as basic traffic information, network topology, and vulnerability information. By leveraging the data collection module, the system can seamlessly integrate with existing cybersecurity infrastructure, enabling real-time monitoring of the cybersecurity status. It allows for targeted data collection and active scanning, providing essential data for association analysis of cybersecurity incidents and situational calculations.

(2) System Configuration Module

The system configuration module provides users with a user-friendly interface encompassing probe configuration, network and host configuration, server configuration, user configuration, and index configuration. The probe configuration primarily includes traffic configuration and vulnerability scanning configuration. The network and host configuration offers users an interface to configure critical assets within the network, including hosts, subnets, host groups, subnet groups, as well as port and port group configuration. The server configuration allows network administrators to configure the system, which is divided into framework configuration (mainly configuring parameter values for system presentation), front-end plugin configuration (including front-end plugin grouping configuration and default value configuration), and server-side configuration. The user configuration supports network administrators in managing system users, including user management, user group management, and permission definition. The index configuration enables users to configure the cybersecurity index system according to their specific needs. Once the configuration is completed, the YHSAS system can perform cybersecurity situational calculations and presentations based on the newly defined cybersecurity index system. By utilizing the system configuration module, the YHSAS system offers a user-friendly interface for users to configure various aspects of the system, including probes, networks, hosts, servers, users, and indices. This flexibility allows administrators to tailor the system to their requirements, facilitating effective cybersecurity situational calculations and presentations.

(3) Cyber attack Detection Module

Given the characteristics of cyber attacks, such as their massive scale, stealthiness, and real-time nature, the cyber attack detection module is capable of rapidly detecting real-time attack behaviors within the target cyberspace. It also explores internal cyber attack paths, providing data support for security event association analysis and security situational assessment.

The YHSAS system has built a large-scale multi-dimensional association cybersecurity knowledge database using the MDATA cognitive model. By leveraging real-time traffic data, asset information, vulnerabilities, network topology, and other data sources, the system utilizes the temporal and spatial correlations among threat data generated by different security devices to guide the detection of single-step and multi-step attacks within subnets. The cyber attack detection module employs subgraph matching techniques based on the MDATA cognitive model to infer and explore attack paths within subnets, supporting cross-domain attack analysis. Additionally, this module combines external threat intelligence and integrates threat intelligence within different subnet domains to detect cross-domain attack paths, enabling effective detection of cross-domain attacks and unknown/novel attacks. The Cyber attack Detection Module is capable of detecting known single-step effective attacks, multi-step effective attacks, cross-domain effective attacks, and unknown/novel cyber attacks. It significantly reduces false positives and avoids false alarms in practical applications, thus minimizing the occurrence of false alerts.

(4) Cyber attack Analysis Module

The cyber attack analysis module conducts multidimensional association analysis on cybersecurity alerts from different locations, time periods, and levels. This analysis aims to uncover cybersecurity incidents and identify real cybersecurity risks. The YHSAS system's association analysis encompasses various event sources, including network-based intrusion detection engines (e.g., Snort), host-based intrusion detection engines (e.g., Snare), statistical packet anomaly detection engines (e.g., Spade), vulnerability scanning tools (e.g., Nessus), network traffic monitoring tools (e.g., Ntop), active probing tools (e.g., Arpwatch, POf, Pads), network scanners (e.g., Nmap), and open-source vulnerability databases. The association analysis process consists of the following steps.

Step 1: data preprocessing is performed, and the merging process is completed at the detection end to alleviate the performance burden on the engines. Event categorization is carried out to enhance the targeted analysis of alerts. For events originating from heterogeneous security devices with different formats, normalization is applied, taking into accounts descriptive standards such as the Incident Object Description Exchange Format (IODEF) [32] and the Intrusion Detection Message Exchange Format (IDMEF).

Step 2: read the configuration policy, which includes defining asset importance, the handling method for specific event types (required association types), and the event processing method (redirecting to other servers or local storage).

Step 3: associate events with vulnerabilities, assets and perform statistical analysis on existing data according to user requirements. For example, statistical analysis can be conducted from the event dimension on event profiles and raw packet data. Statistical analysis can also be performed from the fundamental operational dimension on traffic data, service information data, and network structure. Additionally, statistical analysis can be carried out from the vulnerability and threat dimensions on vulnerability names, occurrence frequency, priority, risk level, and more, providing data support for index calculation.

(5) Security Situational Index Calculation Module

The security situation index calculation module performs quantitative analysis and visualization of the cybersecurity situation from five aspects: Basic Index, Threat Index, Vulnerability Index, Risk Index, and Composite Index. These indices provide insights into the severity and dynamics of the security landscape. The indices are presented using a two-dimensional coordinate system, with time represented on the horizontal axis and index values on the vertical axis. A higher index value indicates a more critical situation. Below, we describe the four indices excluding the Risk Index.

The Basic Index is primarily used to showcase the security status of the network's fundamental operations. Network administrators can view real-time and historical Basic Indices for specific regions. For example, when the Basic Index ranges from 0 to 2, the basic network operations are functioning normally, and users have minimal awareness of cybersecurity issues. On the other hand, when the Basic Index ranges from 8 to 10, it signifies that the basic network operations are severely impacted by widespread network outages, and users have a significant awareness of cybersecurity issues.

The Threat Index is primarily used to showcase the network's exposure to cyber attacks. To meet the diverse perception needs of different users regarding network threats, the Threat Index is presented across three dimensions: confidentiality, integrity, and availability. It provides the functionality to view real-time and historical threat indices for specific regions. When the Threat Index ranges from 0 to 2, it indicates an excellent security state where network services operate normally, all users can use the network without issues, and the network maintains integrity with no unauthorized data modification events. On the other hand, when the Threat Index ranges from 8 to 10, it signifies a critical security state where the network's availability, integrity, and confidentiality are severely threatened. This implies that network services are completely unavailable, most of data has been modified without authorization, and users' private information faces significant risks.

The Vulnerability Index is primarily used to showcase the potential risk situation of cyberspace and provides the functionality to view real-time and historical vulnerability indices. When the Vulnerability Index ranges from 0 to 2, it indicates an excellent security state in the cyberspace. Conversely, when the Vulnerability Index ranges from 8 to 10, it signifies a critical security state where the network's core devices have exceptionally severe vulnerabilities. These vulnerabilities pose a significant threat to the network's availability, integrity, and confidentiality.

The Composite Index assesses the interrelations between system threats, vulnerabilities, and assets, providing an evaluation of the current risks faced by the cyberspace. When the Composite Index ranges from 0 to 2, it indicates an excellent security state in the cyberspace. The cyberspace has experienced minimal attacks, and their impact on users' normal network usage is negligible. Any losses incurred can be easily compensated for through simple measures. On the other hand, when the Composite Index ranges from 8 to 10, it signifies a critical security state in the cyberspace. The cyberspace is confronted with a high volume of cyber attacks, significantly impacting the network's functionality and hindering users' ability to use the network normally. At this point, only substantial costs can mitigate the losses caused by these detrimental effects.

(6) System Presentation Module

The cybersecurity situation can be effectively presented through a variety of visual modes, such as graphs, tables, and other visual representations. These visualizations encompass diverse aspects, including regional security situations, cyberspace situation assessments, available cybersecurity resources, as well as scenario-specific construction of a cybersecurity knowledge graph.

The macro-level Regional Security Situation visual interface maps the occurrence of cybersecurity incidents into a graph. It visually displays real-time threats detected, including the regions of attackers, attacked vulnerabilities, basic attack types, and targeted IP addresses of victims. This provides users with an intuitive understanding of the cybersecurity status across different locations. On the other hand, the micro-level Situation Visualization interface presents complex multi-step attacks in a list format, as shown in Fig. 16. It sequentially displays the attack source, target, and steps involved in sophisticated attacks. It also allows users to view the distribution of attacks and provides the functionality to search for attacks based on the source and target of the attack.

Fig. 16. Micro-level situation visualization interface

The visual interface for cyberspace situation assessment showcases the cybersecurity indices calculated based on a comprehensive set of indicators. These indices encompass various dimensions about the cybersecurity, including the Composite Risk Index, Basic Index, Vulnerability Index, and Threat Index. By observing the fluctuations of the curves, users can gain an intuitive understanding of the current cyberspace status, as illustrated in Fig. 17.

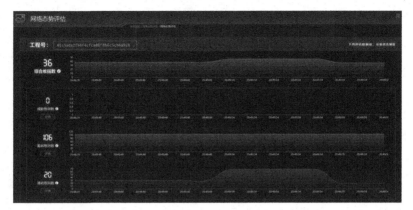

Fig. 17. Visualization Interface for Cyberspace Situation Assessment

The visualization interface for cybersecurity vulnerability resources presents information from four resource database: Vulnerabilities, Weaknesses, Basic Attacks, and Complex Attacks. It serves as a platform for managing knowledge related to cybersecurity vulnerabilities and attack techniques, facilitating the subsequent construction of cybersecurity knowledge graphs. These visual interfaces are illustrated from Fig. 18, 19, 20 and 21.

Fig. 18. Visualization interface for cybersecurity vulnerability resources

The visualization of the cybersecurity knowledge database showcases a multidimensional and context-specific cybersecurity knowledge database constructed based on the MDATA cognitive model. It provides support for subsequent asset, vulnerability, and attack correlation analysis, as well as effective detection of complex attacks. As depicted in Fig. 22 and Fig. 23, the visualization interface for basic attacks displays the interrelations between vulnerabilities, assets, weaknesses, and basic attacks. Similarly, the

Fig. 19. Visualization interface for cybersecurity weakness resources

Fig. 20. Visualization interface for cybersecurity basic attack resources

visualization interface for complex attacks illustrates the interconnections between basic attacks, vulnerabilities, assets, and weaknesses.

4.2 Typical Application and Effect of the YHSAS System

The YHSAS system has been successfully deployed in various industries, including government, public security, military, telecommunications, finance, etc., playing a significant role in safeguarding the cyberspace of our country. The system has demonstrated its capabilities in several applications. In a particular Internet center, it accurately detects and predicts attacks originating from overseas sources. In a specific information center, it achieves a removal rate of over 99.9% for false alarms and false positives, while providing real-time insights into the overall cybersecurity situation, supporting efficient and secure cyberspace management. In multiple public security bureaus and internet information offices, it effectively identifies cybersecurity incidents, providing robust security

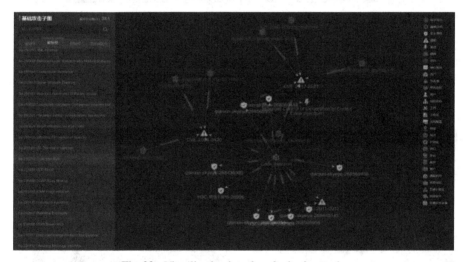

Fig. 21. Visualization interface for cybersecurity complex attack resources

Fig. 22. Visualization interface for basic attacks

assurance for the smooth operation of our country's information systems and critical infrastructure.

The YHSAS system is also utilized in activities related to national security, such as security protection for major tasks, attack-defense exercises, and cybersecurity competitions. Taking the application of the YHSAS system in a cybersecurity competition as an example, we can illustrate its real-time attack detection capabilities and effectiveness. In the cybersecurity competition, the cyber attack detection module of YHSAS system can detect single-step and multi-step attacks in specific scenarios, providing real-time visualization of the overall attack situation. Figure 24 demonstrates the detection of a multi-step attack, where the "Complex Attack List" on the left side of the visualization interface sequentially displays all the multi-step attacks that occurred in the scenario,

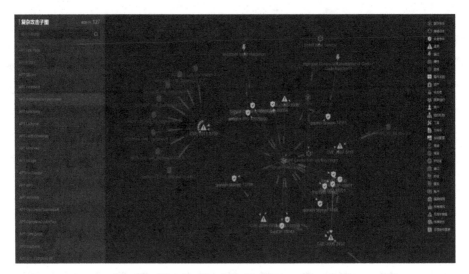

Fig. 23. Visualization interface for complex attacks

along with their corresponding timestamps. By clicking on a specific multi-step attack, the individual attack steps, represented by their corresponding single-step attack types, are displayed in the "Attack Steps" section below.

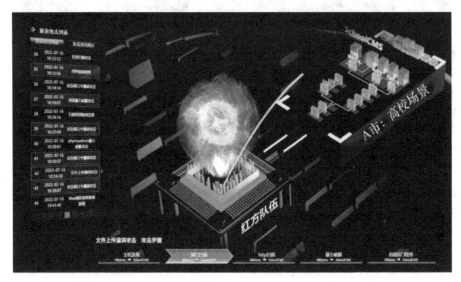

Fig. 24. Visualization interface for multi-step attack detection results

The YHSAS system also offers a more detailed visualization of attack detection results. In the micro-level visualization interface depicted in Fig. 25, the left side presents the comprehensive results of multi-step attacks in the cyberspace, including information about the attack source, target, complex attack name, and occurrence time. The right side provides specific details of each complex attack, displaying the individual attack steps, which correspond to single-step attacks. The detection results for single-step attacks include the source IP address, destination IP address, destination port, detecting device, and descriptive information about the attack behavior.

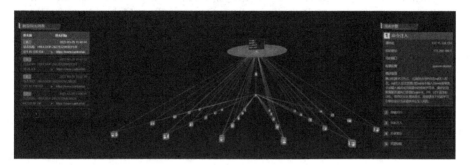

Fig. 25. Micro-level visualization interface

5 Chapter Summary

This chapter provides an overview of the application of the MDATA cognitive model in cyber attack research and judgment. Starting from the three characteristics of cybersecurity incidents: massive scale, evolutionary nature, and inter-connectivity, it analyzes the challenges faced in cyber attack research and judgment, including difficulties in correlation analysis, high rates of false positives and false negatives, and real-time computation. To address these challenges, we examine the advantages and limitations of existing cyber attack detection and assessment technologies in this chapter, and proposes a cyber attack detection and assessment method based on the MDATA cognitive model. Our proposed method includes effective attack assessment, cross-domain attack assessment, and unknown attack assessment. This chapter also introduces the YHSAS cyber attack research and judgment system based on the MDATA cognitive model.

References

1. Ministry of Industry and Information Technology of the People's Republic of China. Information Security Technology - Network Attack Definition and Description Specification: GB/T 37027—2018 [S]. (2018). Accessed 30 Apr 2023
2. Porras, P.A., Kemmerer, R.A.: Penetration state transition analysis: a rule-based intrusion detection approach. In: Proceedings Eighth Annual Computer Security Application Conference, pp. 220–229. IEEE, Piscataway (1992)
3. Sheu, T.F., Huang, N.F., Lee, H.P.: NIS04-6: a time- and memory-efficient string matching algorithm for intrusion detection systems. In: IEEE GLOBECOM 2006, pp. 1–5. IEEE, Piscataway (2006)

4. Shuai, C.Y., Jiang, J.H., Ouyang, X.: A multi-stage network attack model and detection algorithm based on state machine. In: Proceedings of the Sixth China Testing Academic Conference. Beijing: China Computer Federation, pp. 503–509 (2010)
5. Alcantara, L., Padilha, G., Abreu, R., et al.: Syrius: synthesis of rules for intrusion detectors. IEEE Trans. Reliab. **71**(01), 370–381 (2022)
6. Liu, Q., Keller, H.B., Hagenmeyer, V.: A Bayesian rule learning based intrusion detection system for the MQTT communication protocol. In: Proceedings of the 16th International Conference on Availability, Reliability and Security, pp. 1–10. ACM, New York (2021)
7. Sinclair, C., Pierce, L., Matzner, S.: An application of machine learning to network intrusion detection. In: Proceedings 15th Annual Computer Security Applications Conference, pp. 371–377. IEEE, Piscataway (1999)
8. Yu, N.: A novel selection method of network intrusion optimal route detection based on naive Bayesian. Int. J. Appl. Decis. Sci. **11**(01), 1–17 (2018)
9. Xu, J., Shelton, C.R.: Intrusion detection using continuous time Bayesian networks. J. Artif. Intell. Res. **39**(01), 745–774 (2010)
10. Liu, Y.F., Pi, D.C.: A novel kernel SVM algorithm with game theory for network intrusion detection. Trans. Internet Inf. Syst. **11**(08), 4043–4060 (2017)
11. Al-Yaseen, W.L., Othman, Z.A., Nazri, M.Z.A.: Multi-level hybrid support vector machine and extreme learning machine based on modified k-means for intrusion detection system. Expert Syst. Appl. **67**, 296–303 (2017)
12. Aung, Y.Y., Min, M.M., et al.: A collaborative intrusion detection based on K-means and projective adaptive resonance theory. In: International Conference on Natural Computation, Fuzzy Systems and Knowledge Discovery (ICNC-FSKD), pp. 1575–1579. IEEE, Piscataway (2017)
13. Butun, I., Ra, I.H., Sankar, R.: An intrusion detection system based on multi-level clustering for hierarchical wireless sensor networks. Sensors **15**(11), 28960–28978 (2015)
14. Mirsky, Y., Tshman, T., Elovici, Y., et al.: Kitsune: an ensemble of autoencoders for online network intrusion detection [DB/OL]. (2018−05−27) [2023−04−30]. arXiv: arXiv. 1802.09089
15. Kamalov, F., Zgheib, R., Leung, H., et al.: Autoencoder-based intrusion detection system. In: 2021 International Conference on Engineering and Emerging Technologies (ICEET). IEEE, Piscataway (2021)
16. Yao, R., Liu, C.D., Zhang, L.X., et al.: Unsupervised anomaly detection using variational auto-encoder based feature extraction. In: 2019 IEEE International Conference on Prognostics and Health Management (ICPHM), pp. 1–7. IEEE, Piscataway (2019)
17. Gao, N., Gao, L., Gao, Q.L., et al.: An intrusion detection model based on deep belief networks. In: 2014 Second International Conference on Advanced Cloud and Big Data, pp. 247–252. IEEE, Piscataway (2014)
18. Yan, B.H., Han, G.D.: LA-GRU: building combined intrusion detection model based on imbalanced learning and gated recurrent unit neural network. Security and Communication Networks (2018). 30 Apr 2023. 10.1155.2018.6026878
19. Cui, Y., Sun, Y.P., Hu, J.L., et al.: A convolutional auto-encoder method for anomaly detection on system logs. In: 2018 IEEE International Conference on Systems, Man, and Cybernetics (SMC), pp. 3057–3062. IEEE, Piscataway (2018)
20. Zhang, S.C., Xie, X.Y., Xu, Y.: Intrusion detection method based on a deep convolutional neural network. J. Tsinghua Univ. (Sci. Technol.) **59**(01), 44–52 (2019)
21. Hossain, M.N., Milajerdi, S.M., Wang, J.A., et al.: SLEUTH: real-time attack scenario reconstruction from COTS audit data. In: Proceedings of the 26th USENIX Security Symposium, pp. 487–504. USENIX Association, Berkeley (2017)
22. Sun, X.Y., Dai, J., Liu, P., et al.: Using Bayesian networks for probabilistic identification of zero-day attack paths. IEEE Trans. Inf. Forensics Secur. **13**(10), 2506–2521 (2018)

23. Milajerdi, S.M., Gjomemo, R., Eshete, B., et al.: HOLMES: real-time APT detection through correlation of suspicious information flows. In: 2019 IEEE Symposium on Security and Privacy (SP), pp. 1137–1152. IEEE, Piscataway (2019)
24. Hutchins, E.M., Cloppert, M.J., Amin, R.M. Intelligence-driven computer network defense informed by analysis of adversary campaigns and intrusion kill chains. In: Leading Issues in Information Warfare & Security Research. Reading, pp. 78–104. Academic Publishing International Ltd (2011)
25. Hassan, W.U., Bates, A., Marino, D.: Tactical provenance analysis for endpoint detection and response systems. In: 2020 IEEE Symposium on Security and Privacy (SP), pp. 1172–7789. IEEE, Piscataway (2020)
26. Alsaheel, A., Nan, Y.H., Ma, S.Q., et al.: ATLAS: a sequence-based learning approach for attack investigation. In: Proceedings of the 30th USENIX Security Symposium, pp. 3005–3022. USENIX Association, Berkeley (2021)
27. Shawly, T., Elghariani, A., Kobes, J., et al.: Architectures for detecting interleaved multi-stage network attacks using hidden Markov models. IEEE Trans. Dependable Secure Comput. 18(05), 2316–2330 (2021)
28. Wang, C.H., Chiou, Y.C.: Alert correlation system with automatic extraction of attack strategies by using dynamic feature weights. Int. J. Comput. Commun. Eng. 5(01), 1–10 (2016)
29. Kholidy, H.A., Erradi, A., Abdelwahed, S., et al.: A finite state hidden Markov model for predicting multistage attacks in cloud systems. In: 2014 IEEE 12th International Conference on Dependable, Autonomic and Secure Computing, pp. 14–19. IEEE, Piscataway (2014)
30. Zhang, S.J., Li, J.H., Chen, X.Z., et al.: Building network attack graph for alert causal correlation. Comput. Secur. 27(5–6), 188–196 (2008)
31. Panichprecha, S., Zimmermann, J., Mohay, G.M., et al.: Multi-step scenario matching based on unification. In: Proceedings 5th Australian Digital Forensics Conference, pp. 87–96. Edith Cowan University, Perth Western Australia (2007)
32. Takahashi, T., Landfield, K., Millar, T., et al.: IODEF-Extension to support structured cyber security information: draft-takahashi-mile-sci-02 [DB/OL] (2011). Accessed 30 Apr 2023

The Application of the MDATA Cognitive Model in Open Source Intelligence Analysis

Bin Zhou[1](✉), Binxing Fang[2,3], and Ye Wang[1]

[1] National University of Defense Technology, Changsha 410073, China
{binzhou,ye.wang}@nudt.edu.cn
[2] Guangzhou University, Guangzhou 510066, China
fangbx@cae.cn
[3] Pengcheng Laboratory, Shenzhen 518066, China

Open source intelligence (OSINT) refers to information that is collected, identified, refined, and utilized from any publicly available sources to meet intelligence needs. With the advent of the internet, particularly the widespread use of social media, OSINT information in many fields is distributed across various online platforms, fundamentally altering its value, status, and impact. Generally, OSINT has characteristics such as low value density (a small proportion of valuable intelligence relative to total data), frequent spatiotemporal evolution (the content and connections of the information can change over time), and complex multidimensional relationships (intelligence and its related information can be embedded in any dimension and appear in any form).

The structure of this chapter is as follows. Section 1 introduces intelligence analysis techniques using the MDATA cognitive model in the context of OSINT analysis. Section 2 analyzes the difficulties and challenges faced in OSINT analysis. Section 3 provides a detailed explanation of OSINT analysis techniques based on the MDATA cognitive model, illustrated with a case study in scientific and technological intelligence analysis. Section 4 presents an OSINT analysis system based on the MDATA cognitive model. Section 5 summarizes the contents of this chapter.

1 Overview of OSINT Analysis

OSINT analysis is primarily reflected in major national strategic decisions. For example, achieving the carbon peak and carbon neutrality (referred to as the 'dual carbon' goals) requires comprehensive interaction in various fields such as science and technology, law, and institutional frameworks. To fully realize the 'dual carbon' goals, the government and the market need a clear understanding of existing technologies to make forward-looking predictions about emerging technologies, thereby optimizing the implementation and development path of the 'dual carbon' goals. Open source scientific and technological intelligence can provide direction and support for the realization and planning of the 'dual carbon' goals from the perspectives of scientific and technological development strategies, legal system construction, and institutional policy planning. Open source scientific and technological intelligence focuses on open source information as its main research

Y. Jia et al. (Eds.): *MDATA Cognitive Model: Theory and Applications*, LNCS 15470, pp. 148–180, 2025.
https://doi.org/10.1007/978-981-96-3528-3_6

object and uses intelligence monitoring and analysis methods to identify technologies related to the 'dual carbon' goals or potential new technologies, promptly discovering and nurturing relevant technologies. It scientifically evaluates the capabilities for scientific and technological innovation at the national or regional level under the 'dual carbon' goals, providing references and suggestions for high-quality development. Additionally, it assists relevant parties in formulating policies and plans in areas such as low-carbon technology standards and other policy innovations, promoting the industrialization of low-carbon technologies [1].

The important role of OSINT analysis in serving scientific and technological development, supporting commercial competition, aiding social governance, and maintaining national security is beyond doubt. It has also promoted the formation of a series of technologies and tools. These technologies and tools encompass multi-source collection of open source information and data, extraction of intelligence elements in OSINT analysis, and knowledge association and reasoning in OSINT analysis.

1.1 Multi-source Collection Techniques for Open Source Information and Data

Multi-source collection of open source information and data is the foundation of OSINT analysis. Open source data and information are found in public intelligence sources and can be obtained through legal means. Open source information refers to information acquired from public network resources and other publicly available sources, collected and mined using relevant technologies. The commonly used collection technologies for OSINT include web crawling framework technology, multimedia application programming interface (API) collection technology, geographic information data collection technology, and meta-search technology based on search engines.

1.1.1 Web Crawling Framework Technology

Web crawling frameworks are tools that automatically extract data from web pages. Its core task is to parse the source code of pages, such as HTML and XML, and extract useful information from them. Web data extraction tools can simulate browser behavior, such as entering keywords, clicking buttons, scrolling through pages, etc., to obtain the complete page content. On this basis, web crawling framework technology processes the page content by using data extraction tools or writing code to extract the required data, such as text, images, videos, links, and more. Selenium.

Commonly used crawling frameworks include Selenium and Scrapy. Many web testing tools, due to their ability to simulate browser behavior, are also used for web extraction, such as Microsoft's Playwright. Users must comply with relevant laws, regulations, and website usage agreements when extracting web data to avoid infringing on others' intellectual property or privacy rights. Additionally, using web crawlers to scrape web data can impose a burden on the target website. Therefore, users should minimize the impact on the server when scraping data by reducing the crawling frequency, setting appropriate delays, and so on. Users should also adhere to the crawling access restrictions specified in the website's robots.txt file.

1. **Multilingual Web Scraping Tool Selenium.**

Selenium automates browser interactions by simulating user actions, enabling web automation testing. This tool is open-source and supports test scripts written in various programming languages, such as Java, Python, and C#. From the perspective of OSINT search, Selenium can be used to automate web data crawling. By writing programs, it can automatically open a browser and simulate user actions, such as entering keywords and clicking the search button, to obtain the HTML source code of the search results page, and then extract the information from it.

Selenium also has an important feature: the ability to handle content generated by JavaScript. When crawling certain websites, the web page data might be dynamically generated by JavaScript. In such cases, simply parsing the HTML code is insufficient to obtain the data. Selenium can simulate the browser executing JavaScript code, thereby retrieving the complete page content.

Selenium can be deployed on operating systems such as Windows, Linux, Solaris, and macOS. Additionally, it supports mobile operating systems such as iOS, Windows Mobile, and Android.

2. **Python Web Scraping Framework Scrapy.**

Scrapy is a Python-based crawling framework that can be used to scrape website data and extract structured data. It can function as a general web crawler tool and also use Web Services and other APIs to extract and parse data, perform data monitoring, and automate testing. Scrapy supports complex operations such as concurrent requests, login-free access, and URL deduplication. It also supports configuring anti-crawling measures. Overall, Scrapy adopts an asynchronous model, which helps improve programming efficiency, enabling high-performance data crawling. It offers advantages such as strong concurrency capabilities, ease of writing and maintenance.

3. **Microsoft's Automation Testing Tool Playwright**

Playwright is an automation testing tool released by Microsoft. It is based on the Chrome DevTools protocol and supports multiple browsers such as Chrome, Microsoft Edge, and Firefox. Playwright can simulate browser actions such as inputting, clicking, scrolling, and dragging, and it supports taking screenshots and recording videos of browser elements. As an automation testing tool designed for the Python language, Playwright provides better automation effects in regression testing.

Playwright has the following characteristics.

① Supports multiple browsers without the need for additional configuration or installation.

② Supports cross-platform deployment and can run on operating systems such as Windows, Linux, and macOS.

③ Does not rely on third-party libraries like Selenium or WebDriver; instead, it executes tests through the Chrome DevTools protocol and browser internal APIs.

④ Supports multiple programming languages including JavaScript, TypeScript, Python, Java, and C#, making it convenient for developers to choose their preferred programming language for development.

1.1.2 Multimedia API Collection Technology

Multimedia API collection technology is a technique that utilizes programming languages or software development tools to collect multimedia data from the internet or local devices through multimedia APIs. Multimedia APIs encompass various types of data interfaces, such as audio, video, images, etc., allowing developers to retrieve corresponding types of data by invoking these interfaces. Multimedia API collection technology can be applied in various fields, including audio-video capture, image recognition, virtual reality, etc. We'll take the Facebook Graph API as an example to illustrate how to obtain multimedia information from the Facebook website (referred to as Facebook hereafter).

The Facebook Graph API is a set of web services APIs provided by Facebook, which can be used to access and manipulate various objects within the Facebook Social Graph. By utilizing the Facebook Graph API, developers can easily access and manipulate objects such as Facebook users and their preferences, photo albums, etc., and retrieve associated information between these objects, such as friend connections, tags, shared content, and other relationships.

The Facebook Graph API employs the OAuth 2.0 protocol to handle authentication and authorization. Developers acquire corresponding credentials (application ID and application key) by registering their application, which are then used for API calls. Data returned by the Facebook Graph API is formatted in JSON, allowing access and manipulation through RESTful HTTP requests.

The Facebook Graph API provides various types of data, with some of the more typical ones including:

User data: Accessing and manipulating users' basic information, profiles, friend lists, etc.

Web Page data: Accessing and manipulating posts, comments, etc., on Facebook pages.

Application data: Accessing and manipulating application data, settings, advertisements, etc.

Message data: Accessing and manipulating messages, conversations, etc., in Facebook Messenger.

Advertisement data: Accessing and manipulating data, settings, etc., for Facebook advertisements.

1.1.3 Geographical Information Data Collection Technology

(1) Google Maps API

Geographical Information Data Collection Technology refers to the techniques used to gather geographic information from the Earth's surface through various means and tools. This geographic information can include topography and landforms, geological structures, climate conditions, land use, transportation routes, hydrological resources, population distribution, and other aspects.

(1) Google Maps API

Google Maps API is a set of APIs provided by Google for accessing and manipulating map data on Google Maps. With the Google Maps API, developers can embed Google Maps into their applications to implement map-related functionalities such as location lookup, route planning, and place search.

Google Maps API offers various services, including:

Map Services: Providing functions like map tiles, map styles, geocoding, etc., allowing developers to embed Google Maps into their applications.

Directions Services: Providing functions for finding routes, calculating route distances and travel times, retrieving traffic conditions, etc., enabling route planning and navigation.

Places Services: Providing functions for obtaining location information, searching nearby places, searching for specific places, etc., enabling developers to create location-based applications.

Maps Data Services: Providing functions for obtaining map data, map layers, satellite images, etc., allowing developers to achieve customized map display effects.

Business Services: Providing functions for obtaining business information, user reviews, real-time public transportation information, etc., enabling developers to create various location-based commercial applications.

(2) Amap Web Services API

The Amap Web Services API is a set of Web APIs based on the HTTP/HTTPS protocol, providing developers with HTTP interfaces to access various types of geographic data services. Developers can use these interfaces to access geographic data services, and the returned results (data) support JSON and XML formats. These geographic data services include map data queries, route planning, geocoding/reverse geocoding, administrative area queries, traffic event queries, coordinate conversion, traffic conditions, static maps, weather queries, etc.

Map Data Query Service: Provides queries for point of interest (POI) information, road information, traffic flow, and other map service data within specified areas.

Route Planning Service: Calculates the optimal route based on the start and end points' location information and provides multiple travel modes (such as walking, driving, public transit, etc.).

Geocoding/Reverse Geocoding Service: Provides mutual conversion between structured addresses and latitude/longitude coordinates for map display and route planning convenience.

Administrative Area Query Service: Provides detailed information such as area codes, city codes, central points, administrative area boundaries, subordinate areas, etc., to support map functions based on administrative areas.

Traffic Event Query Service: Retrieves valid events in authorized cities, such as traffic accidents, road construction, traffic control, etc., to provide users with more reasonable travel options.

Coordinate Conversion Service: Converts non-Amap map coordinates (GPS coordinates, Mapbar coordinates, Baidu coordinates) into Amap map coordinates.

Traffic Conditions Service: Returns corresponding traffic conditions based on user input.

Static Map Service: Responds to HTTP requests by returning a map image, allowing users to embed Amap maps into their web pages in image form.

Weather Query Service: Provides weather information for specified cities based on data provided by the China Meteorological Administration, including temperature, humidity, wind force, etc.

1.1.4 Search Engine-Based Metasearch Technology

Search Engine-Based Metasearch Technology is a technique that utilizes programming languages and software development tools to collect and integrate information from multiple search engines and websites. With this technology, users can simultaneously query multiple search engines and websites, obtaining more comprehensive and accurate search results. The implementation of meta-search technology based on search engines requires developers to write specific programs or software. By accessing the APIs of multiple search engines and websites, search requests are sent to these search engines and websites, and the returned results are integrated to form the final search results.

(1) Google Search API

The Google Search API, developed by Google, allows developers to programmatically use Google search services to obtain results for specific search queries. With the Google Search API, developers can programmatically search and retrieve metadata about query results, such as titles, descriptions, URLs, and thumbnails. Additionally, developers can use filters in queries to specify the type of results, such as images, news, videos, etc.

The Google Search API also enables customized search results. Developers can use their own search engines to search specific websites. These websites can be created and configured in the Google Custom Search Engine (CSE), and then accessed through the Google Search API.

The Google Search API is a paid service, and developers need to register and obtain an API key on the Google Cloud Platform (GCP).

(2) Bing API

The Bing API, provided by Microsoft, allows developers to integrate Bing search functionality into their applications. Bing API offers APIs for image search, news search, video search, web search, etc., enabling developers to access search results returned by the Bing search engine.

Bing API functionalities are similar to those of Google Search API. Developers can programmatically search and retrieve metadata about search results, such as titles, descriptions, URLs, and thumbnails. Additionally, Bing API provides special searches like map search and entity search to support different types of applications. Furthermore, Bing API offers voice and translation APIs, which developers can use to implement functionalities such as voice recognition and translation, for building applications like voice assistants, voice search, translation, etc.

Bing API is a paid service, and developers need to register on the Azure website and obtain an API key.

(3) Baidu Search API

The Baidu Search API, provided by Baidu Inc., allows developers to integrate Baidu search functionality into their applications. Baidu Search API offers various APIs, including web search API, image search API, news search API, knowledge graph API, etc., enabling developers to access search results returned by the Baidu search engine.

1.2 Information Element Extraction Techniques in OSINT Analysis

In OSINT analysis, information element extraction refers to identifying essential components such as entities, relationships, and attributes from multi-source raw data, and performing deduplication and disambiguation. From a operations perspective, information elements can be commonly understood as the time, location, individuals (or organizations), events, reasons, and results reflected in intelligence, hence also referred to as "5W1H", namely When, Where, Who, What, Why, and How. The extraction technology of information elements has made significant progress in recent years, particularly in enhancing the acquisition capabilities of factual and existent intelligence due to the development of identification and disambiguation technologies. However, methods for extracting potential intelligence information are still under continuous research and maturation. Intelligence subjects and key character (or organizations) are two important categories of potential intelligence information.

1.2.1 Identification and Disambiguation Techniques of Information Elements

Faced with low-density heterogeneous data from different sources, converting them into usable intelligence information is a fundamental issue in OSINT analysis. OSINT applications typically require the identification and disambiguation of information elements from multi-source raw data. Information elements refer to key information that can reveal or aid in understanding certain intelligence subjects or issues. For example, in counterterrorism intelligence analysis, information elements [2] may include the identity of terrorists, organizational hierarchies, and the timing and location of plans. Information element identification [3, 4] from multi-source raw data involves automatically or semi-automatically identifying meaningful information elements through computer programs or artificial intelligence algorithms to support intelligence analysis and decision-making. The process of identifying information elements from multi-source raw data typically includes data collection and preprocessing, entity identification and classification, relationship extraction, event identification and classification, and attribute identification.

Results of open source information element identification may present ambiguity such as Same name but not the same meaning, same meaning but not the same name. Entity ambiguity, for instance, refers to a single entity mention that can correspond to multiple real-world entities. For example, "Michael Jordan" may refer to a basketball player, a computer scientist who received the 2020 von Neumann Award, or other individuals. Resolving the real-world entities referred to by an entity mention is entity disambiguation. Entity disambiguation algorithms can be classified into several types based on the features they rely on, including entity salience-based disambiguation, context similarity-based disambiguation, entity association-based disambiguation, and deep learning-based disambiguation [5].

In recent years, deep learning-based extraction methods have gradually become the mainstream approach for information element identification and entity disambiguation. Their advantage lies in its ability to automatically identify and extract information elements from massive unstructured data such as text, images, and speech, as well as efficiently integrate these information elements. This method can be applied in fields such as natural language processing, computer vision, and speech recognition. Deep learning-based extraction methods have been widely used in person and organization discovery, aiding in better identification of entities and relationships in text data, thereby enhancing the accuracy and efficiency of text analysis.

1.2.2 Topic Modeling and Tracking Technology

Topic modeling and tracking technology mainly address the issue of how to model topics for text data. Current applications utilize topic modeling and tracking technology to uncover deep associations behind open-source data, thereby obtaining high-value intelligence. Topic modeling for multi-source [6] data is a technique in the field of text mining that automatically identifies topics from multi-source data objects and discovers hidden patterns, thereby aiding in better decision-making. Existing topic modeling techniques mainly fall into two categories: non-probabilistic topic modeling techniques and probabilistic topic modeling techniques. Non-probabilistic topic modeling techniques use various statistical measures to describe topics in text data, such as word frequency, clustering, principal components, etc. Probabilistic topic modeling techniques, on the other hand, describe topics in text data based on probability models, with common models including Latent Semantic Analysis (LSA) [7] and Latent Dirichlet Allocation (LDA) [8, 9].

LSA is a model based on matrix factorization, which represents text data as a dense low-dimensional matrix, making it easier to discover and understand the meaning and topics of the text. LDA is a generative model that assumes the text data generation process involves randomly selecting words from some latent topics to generate the text data, and inferring the distribution of topics by observing the distribution of the text data. Hierarchical Dirichlet Process (HDP) [10, 11] is a non-parametric Bayesian model that can automatically discover the number and distribution of topics from text data, and track and analyze topics through hierarchical Dirichlet processes.

In the context of intelligence analysis tasks in the internet environment, data often undergo dynamic changes. Therefore, topic modeling techniques are used not only for static text but also for dynamic topic tracking, enabling automatic identification of new topics in the news media information flow and continuous tracking of known topics. Topic Detection and Tracking (TDT) [12] originated from early Event Detection and Tracking (EDT). Unlike EDT, TDT extends its tracking objects from specific events to topics with more related information. TDT can be divided into methods based on probabilistic models and methods based on representation learning. Dynamic Topic Modeling (DTM) [13, 14] is a commonly used model, an extension of the LDA model, which can be used to model and track topics in time series text data. The basic assumption of DTM is that the topics and distributions of text data change dynamically over time, requiring consideration of temporal factors for modeling and tracking topics. Specifically, DTM assumes that text data consist of several static and dynamic topics, where static topics do not change over time, and dynamic topics vary over time. To achieve this goal, DTM introduces a time latent variable to represent the changes in topic distribution over time. In DTM, each time point has a topic distribution vector to represent the topic distribution of the text data at that time point. These vectors can describe the trend of topic changes and reflect the distribution and variation of topics through statistical methods. Additionally, DTM can utilize deep learning methods for representation learning to extract high-level features from text data, thus better capturing the relationships and evolution trends between topics, addressing the frequent spatio-temporal evolution of intelligence information in open-source data.

1.2.3 Discovery Techniques for Key Character and Organizations

In the extraction of intelligence elements from open-source data, a critical technique employed is the discovery of key character and organizations. Essentially, this technique is a form of entity discovery that involves identifying, tracking, and studying important individuals or organizations through the analysis of social media data and other sources. It utilizes various methods such as data extraction, multidimensional analysis, social network analysis, and pattern recognition to achieve the discovery of key character and organizations.

The discovery of key character and organizations originated in the 1980s when rule-based entity discovery techniques were first used to identify prominent individuals or organizations in cyberspace data. Rule-based entity discovery methods typically employ rule templates constructed by linguistic experts, utilizing features such as statistical information, punctuation marks, keywords, indicators, direction words, positional words (e.g., tail words), and central words, primarily relying on string matching, and often depending on the establishment of knowledge bases and dictionaries. Generally, rule-based entity discovery methods outperform statistically based methods when the extracted rules accurately reflect linguistic phenomena. However, these rules often depend on specific languages, domains, and text styles, making it challenging to cover all language phenomena and time-consuming in the rule-making process. Additionally, the portability of rules in this technique is poor, as different problems require linguistic experts to formulate rules anew.

With technological advancements, the discovery techniques for key character and organizations have become increasingly complex. Natural language processing, machine learning, and other artificial intelligence technologies can assist in better extracting the behaviors of important individuals and organizations from social settings, leading to the emergence of machine learning-based statistical methods, such as Hidden Markov Models, Maximum Entropy (ME), Support Vector Machines, Conditional Random Fields (CRF), and other algorithms. Statistically based entity discovery methods have high requirements for feature selection, necessitating the selection of influential features from the text for the task and incorporating these features into feature vectors. The primary approach involves statistical analysis of the linguistic information contained in the training corpus to extract features from it. Relevant features may include word features, context features, dictionary and part-of-speech features, stop-word features, core word features, semantic features, etc. Statistically based entity discovery methods rely heavily on corpora, but there are relatively few large-scale general corpora available for building and evaluating named entity recognition systems.

Since natural language processing is not a random process, solely using statistically based entity discovery methods would result in a very large state search space. Therefore, it is necessary to filter and prune the search space in advance using rule knowledge. Currently, there are hardly any named entity recognition systems that solely utilize statistical models without employing rule knowledge. In many cases, a hybrid approach is used, incorporating methods such as rules, dictionaries, and machine learning.

1.3 Knowledge Association and Inference Technology in OSINT Analysis

Knowledge association refers to the various connections that exist between elements constituting knowledge. Revealing and utilizing the associations in OSINT is the starting point for knowledge organization, management, and discovery. In OSINT analysis, the main function of knowledge inference is to derive unknown knowledge from known knowledge based on the representation of intelligence knowledge through inference rules or operators. This section takes OSINT processing as an example to introduce knowledge association technology based on knowledge bases, inference technology based on intelligence knowledge, and user profiling technology based on OSINT, which is an important application in OSINT analysis.

1.3.1 Knowledge Association Technology Based on Knowledge Bases

The relationships between pieces of knowledge mainly include containment relationships, parallel relationships, proof relationships, opposition relationships, common underlying logical relationships, and common surface phenomenon relationships. Compared to fragmented knowledge, establishing connections between pieces of knowledge to form an organic knowledge system is an important foundation for constructing knowledge bases.

Knowledge association technology based on knowledge bases includes classification and spatiotemporal knowledge association representation methods based on graph structures, as well as graph representation methods for agnostic knowledge information and statistical knowledge association [15].

(1) Classification and Spatiotemporal Knowledge Association Representation Methods Based on Graph Structures

The representation of classification knowledge association is based on the knowledge graph structure. Through deep learning methods, it captures recognized aggregation relationships between target entities represented by specific concepts, thereby describing classification knowledge of the category relationships between target entities. The representation of spatiotemporal knowledge association can capture the spatiotemporal attribute information of intelligence knowledge, thus describing the spatiotemporal evolution characteristics of target entities.

(2) Graph Representation Methods for Agnostic Knowledge Information and Statistical Knowledge Association

The discovery and analysis of the value of big data rely on the statistical and probabilistic judgment of data characteristics. This probability-based computation requires the underlying knowledge association representation model to support uncertainty information. In graph representation methods, research specifically models the expression forms and computational characteristics of agnostic information in the knowledge structure, designing appropriate descriptions for uncertain knowledge to support the graph representation and computation of statistical knowledge association.

1.3.2 Inference Technology Based on Intelligence Knowledge

In the context of OSINT analysis, OSINT often contains valuable information or hides important relationships. As an essential means to complete missing knowledge and infer unknown knowledge, knowledge inference technology can discover new intelligence clues or hidden relationships between intelligence clues. This process helps form a complete chain of intelligence clues or extract critical intelligence information. Here, intelligence clues refer to the associative information between targets (entities).

Inference technology based on intelligence knowledge utilizes existing target (entity) attribute information and their relationships with other targets (entities) to perform knowledge inference. This technology applies in two scenarios: interpolation and extrapolation. Considering an intelligence knowledge graph with incomplete information within the time range $[t_0, t_T]$, interpolation predicts missing information (such as entities and relationships) in the knowledge graph at a specific time t ($t_0 \leq t \leq t_T$), while extrapolation makes predictions for a time t ($t > t_T$). Simply put, extrapolation predicts the future based on the past, and it is usually more challenging than interpolation.

Regarding inference methods, inference technology based on intelligence knowledge mainly includes the following:

Knowledge Inference Methods Based on Logical Reasoning: These methods directly use first-order predicate logic, description logic, etc., to represent and deduce rules formulated by intelligence analysis experts. These methods are characterized by high accuracy and strong interpretability.

Knowledge Inference Methods Based on Production Rules: Based on the existing intelligence knowledge base and the rule base formulated by intelligence analysis experts, these methods derive new intelligence knowledge by matching the preconditions of rules, thereby completing the inference process.

Knowledge Inference Methods Based on Deep Learning: This involves using deep learning algorithms to automatically infer and learn intelligence knowledge. The main idea is to use the distributed representation and deep architecture of deep learning to construct triples or quintuplets in the intelligence knowledge graph.

Knowledge Inference Methods Based on Knowledge Graphs: This involves using the information of entities, attributes, relationships, and rules in the intelligence knowledge graph to discover new knowledge and relationships through deduction and logical inference.

In terms of intelligence elements, inference technology based on intelligence knowledge mainly includes entity-oriented inference technology, relationship-oriented inference technology, attribute-oriented inference technology, and time/space-oriented inference technology. These technologies infer unknown or missing targets (entities), clues (relationships) between targets, intelligence (attribute information) of targets, and the temporal/spatial information of targets based on existing intelligence clues.

The application scenarios for inference technology based on intelligence knowledge are very rich. In the fields of social networks, finance, natural disasters, and other OSINT information, knowledge inference technology enables the system to automatically learn from a vast amount of intelligence clues, mine public opinion information, predict future developments, update threat intelligence, and guide decision-making and action planning to avoid risks.

1.3.3   User Profiling Technology Based on OSINT

User profiling is one of the significant applications of big data technology, aiming to construct descriptive label attributes of users in multiple dimensions. These label attributes depict and outline various real personal characteristics of users, describing their related interests, traits, behaviors, and preferences. This section introduces user profiling technology based on OSINT using researchers as an example.

The common construction of user profiles involves three steps: user data collection, data analysis and user segmentation, and profile refinement. User profiling technology for researchers needs to consider more professional attributes, hence requiring a multi-dimensional coverage and multi-technology integration approach to construct a comprehensive profile of the researcher community. Specifically, in the profile label system, two dimensions are established: personnel attributes and research attributes. The research attribute dimension includes three sub-dimensions: research ability, relationship network, and research credit. Additionally, machine learning and other technologies can be introduced to create models for personnel attribute labels, research ability calculation, relationship network construction, and research credit analysis. These models analyze the original data of researchers to predict deeper information, thereby enhancing the practical value of the profiling system. The overall architecture of the researcher community profile model is shown in Fig. 1.

The concept of community profiling originates from user profiling, and related technologies have flourished in various fields. User profiling uses real user data to establish user models, which can be viewed as the labeling of user information. In some areas (such as online social network analysis), to simplify complex relationships to be processed, a virtual overall image can be mined to label and describe user group information.

First, to construct researcher community profiles, researchers are grouped based on the similarity of their research interests. Grouping researchers with similar research interests most effectively reflects the internal homogeneity and external heterogeneity of the group. Internal communication within the group can deepen field research, while inter-group communication can promote cross-innovation.

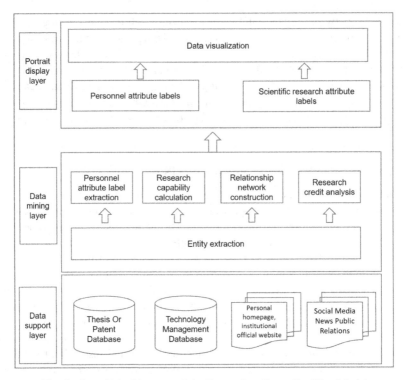

Fig. 1. Overall Architecture of the Researcher Group Profiling Model

Second, constructing researcher community profiles can draw from the construction ideas of user profiles. Cooper's seven-step persona method and Nielsen's ten-step persona method are classic user profile construction methods, both of which include four stages: identifying target users, acquiring user information, recognizing behavior patterns, and constructing virtual personas. Community profiling focuses more on how to segment similar users to obtain multiple distinctive groups. By integrating the persona method from user profiling, the definition of researcher community profiling, and construction methods from other fields, the construction method for researcher community profiles mainly involves five steps: designing the profile label system, building the basic information database, constructing the research interest model, segmenting researcher communities, and storing and presenting profiles.

Finally, keyword co-occurrence analysis and community division methods are used to construct researcher community profiles. Keyword co-occurrence analysis involves using keywords and their relevance to extract the research interests of researchers. The more frequently keywords co-occur, the stronger the thematic relevance, and the more similar the research interests. The network formed by these co-occurring keywords is called the keyword co-occurrence network. In the keyword co-occurrence network, there are community structures with dense internal connections and sparse external connections, suitable for community division algorithms. Hence, the keyword co-occurrence network can be divided into multiple closely connected sub-communities, representing multiple researcher groups. Each sub-community contains multiple semantically related keywords, indicating similar research interests [17]. Researcher community profiles can be divided according to sub-communities and presented through these semantically related keywords.

2 Challenges and Difficulties in OSINT Analysis

The diverse sources of OSINT and its constantly evolving nature over time present numerous challenges and difficulties for OSINT analysis, as detailed below:

Frequent Temporal and Spatial Evolution: Knowledge in cyberspace exhibits temporal and spatial characteristics and undergoes continuous changes. Traditional knowledge representation models struggle to effectively represent these temporal and spatial aspects. Knowledge is not static; as it changes over time and space, traditional models fail to represent and reflect the dynamic process of knowledge evolution. Integrating task-specific and demand-driven computational and efficient representations of intelligence knowledge in accordance with temporal and spatial constraints is the first pressing issue in intelligence analysis.

Low Value Density: The continuous growth of OSINT data due to advancements in collection technologies exacerbates the challenge of low knowledge value density. Simultaneously, the covert interrelations between intelligence elements become increasingly difficult to uncover. Existing knowledge processing techniques within knowledge graphs and user profiling technologies struggle to meet the demands of large-scale and diverse knowledge requirements. Analyzing and processing massive data sets in a timely and precise manner to extract key elements and relationships, and to unearth potentially valuable information, constitutes the second critical issue in OSINT analysis.

Complex Multidimensional Clue Association: As the volume of OSINT explodes, the complexity of intelligence knowledge associations intensifies. Existing knowledge graph-based on triple structures struggle to adapt to the complexity of multiple paths of association and inference. Faced with challenges posed by complex semantic relationships and scenario associations, efficiently utilizing knowledge for inference and accurately understanding the development trends and motivations behind intelligence events stands as the third pressing issue in intelligence analysis.

Only by addressing these three challenges can individuals efficiently utilize network intelligence information, achieve modeling and analysis of OSINT, and achieve comprehensive, accurate, and real-time assessment of intelligence clues.

3 MDATA Cognitive Model for OSINT Analysis Techniques

To address challenges such as frequent temporal and spatial evolution, low value density, and complex multidimensional relationships in OSINT, this section utilizes the MDATA cognitive model elaborated in the previous sections to analyze typical cases of OSINT analysis. Regarding the issue of frequent temporal and spatial evolution of intelligence, the knowledge representation technology of the MDATA cognitive model supports the accurate acquisition of OSINT elements and their corresponding temporal and spatial characteristics. To tackle the problem of low value density in OSINT, the knowledge extraction and computation technology of the MDATA cognitive model further accurately extracts intelligence elements and represents them as embedded intelligence knowledge with temporal and spatial constraints, enabling efficient computation of complex intelligence. In addressing the complex multidimensional association of clues, the inference and utilization technology of the MDATA cognitive model can unearth more valuable intelligence clues, facilitating intelligence clue analysis and expansion of OSINT. Figure 2 illustrates the architecture of OSINT analysis based on the MDATA cognitive model.

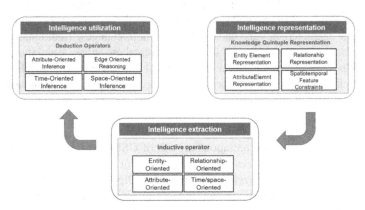

Fig. 2. The architecture of OSINT analysis based on the MDATA cognitive model, as depicted.

3.1 Knowledge Representation Technology of the MDATA Cognitive Model for OSINT Temporal and Spatial Evolution

The rapid emergence and dynamic uncertainty presented by the frequent temporal and spatial evolution of OSINT knowledge pose challenges for OSINT analysis. Traditional triple-based representations of intelligence knowledge struggle to depict the dynamic process of intelligence knowledge evolution. Therefore, there is a need for intelligence knowledge representation techniques that can integrate temporal and spatial constraints. We propose the MDATA cognitive model knowledge representation method to support OSINT temporal and spatial evolution. Taking technological intelligence related to Musk as an example, we briefly introduce how this method represents the three major elements of intelligence knowledge and integrates temporal and spatial constraints.

Entity Element Representation: The entity elements of the MDATA cognitive model refer to the individuals and organizations involved in OSINT knowledge. For example, in the intelligence knowledge "Musk's nationality is American", "Musk" is the entity element.

Attribute Element Representation: Attribute elements describe the attributes of entities, such as the value of the attribute "Musk's nationality" being "America".

The representation of entity and attribute elements in the MDATA cognitive model knowledge representation method is illustrated in Fig. 3.

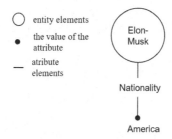

Fig. 3. Representation of Entity and Attribute Elements in the MDATA Cognitive Model Knowledge Representation Method

The relationship representation: A relationship describes the connection between entities. For example, in the knowledge "Musk founded OpenAI", the relationship <Musk, founded, OpenAI> depicts the relationship element "founded" between the two entities "Musk" and "OpenAI". The representation of relationship elements in the MDATA cognitive model knowledge representation is shown in Fig. 4.

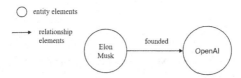

Fig. 4. The representation of relationship elements in the MDATA cognitive model knowledge representation.

Spatiotemporal feature constraints: To incorporate spatiotemporal information into intelligence knowledge, the MDATA cognitive model knowledge representation extends the traditional triple representation by adding time and space attributes, expanding the triples into quintuples of <head entity, relation, tail entity, time, space>.

Taking the relationship between Musk and OpenAI shown in Fig. 5(a) as an example, we can derive two quintuples: one is <Musk, founded, OpenAI, 2015–12-11, San Francisco>, and the other is <Musk, exited, OpenAI, 2018–02-20, NaN>. As can be seen, this quintuple representation adds time information (2015-12-11, 2018–02-20) and spatial information (San Francisco) to the traditional triple representation, accurately describing the facts that "Musk founded OpenAI in San Francisco on December 11, 2015", and "Musk exited OpenAI on February 20, 2018". Without the constraints of spatiotemporal relationships, these two quintuples would conflict with each other regarding the aforementioned facts.

Similarly, entities can also have spatiotemporal features. For example, in the quintuple <BYD, competes with, Tesla, NaN, NaN> representing the fact that "BYD and Tesla are in competition", the entity "BYD" has a spatial attribute, with its location being "China", and the entity "Tesla" also has a spatial attribute, with its location being "USA", as shown in Fig. 5(b). This demonstrates that the MDATA cognitive model knowledge representation can effectively model the dynamic changes and spatial evolution of intelligence knowledge.

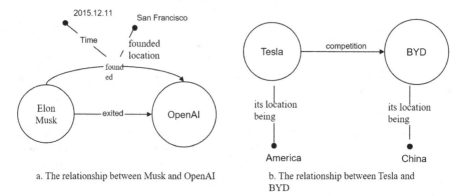

a. The relationship between Musk and OpenAI   b. The relationship between Tesla and BYD

Fig. 5. Spatiotemporal Constraint Features in the MDATA Cognitive Model Intelligence Knowledge Representation Method

3.2 MDATA Cognitive Model Extraction and Computing Techniques for Large-Scale OSINT

3.2.1 Extraction of Intelligence Elements

Open source data is characterized by its large scale and low value density. How to analyze and process a vast amount of data timely and accurately, extract key elements and potential correlations, and uncover valuable intelligence information is an urgent problem in OSINT analysis. The MDATA cognitive model was proposed precisely to address this issue. Using the OSINT analysis process "How natural language processing technologies such as large language models impact the development of the intelligent automotive industry" as an example, we briefly explain how to use the MDATA cognitive model to automatically extract OSINT elements.

Assuming the OSINT analysis task "How natural language processing technologies such as large language models impact the development of the intelligent automotive industry", we have obtained the following public data:

- On December 11, 2015, the famous tech entrepreneur Musk, as one of the initiators and funders, founded OpenAI and co-chaired the board with Altman.
- Altman and OpenAI's other founders rejected Musk's proposal. In turn, Musk walked away from the company, leading to the announcement of Musk's departure on February 20, 2018.
- In mid-2019, Bill Gates announced that Microsoft invested $1 billion, becoming OpenAI's most important strategic investor.
- Since 2019, Musk has frequently expressed his dissatisfaction with OpenAI's transition to a for-profit organization on social media.

- Starting from February 2023, Musk has been closely interacting with several engineers from DeepMind on social media.
- In April 2023, Musk admitted that Twitter purchased 10,000 Nvidia graphics cards.

As relevant information is continuously collected into the intelligence data resource library, the analysis system will face the problem of data overload. The MDATA cognitive model can quickly identify and integrate relevant core intelligence elements and efficiently complete the automatic extraction of relevant intelligence elements through induction operators such as entity recognition, relationship extraction, attribute extraction, and spatiotemporal feature recognition. The specific steps are as follows:

Step 1: Entity Extraction.
Using the entity recognition operators provided by the MDATA cognitive model, the analysis system can identify relevant entities in the public corpus and assign each entity a unique identifier. For example, using neural network-based named entity recognition methods to identify words related to these entities in the public corpus, thus accurately obtaining intelligence entity elements related to "How natural language processing technologies such as large language models impact the development of the intelligent automotive industry", such as Musk and OpenAI, see Example 1.

Example 1: From "On December 11, 2015, the famous tech entrepreneur Musk, as one of the initiators and funders, founded OpenAI", the induction operator can extract the intelligence entity elements "Musk" and "OpenAI".
Step 2: Attribute and Relationship Extraction.
Using attribute extraction operators and relationship extraction operators, extract the intelligence attribute elements and relationship elements related to "How natural language processing technologies such as large language models impact the development of the intelligent automotive industry." In Example 2, we use feature selection and other methods to screen out research intelligence attribute elements related to Musk, such as Musk's "tech entrepreneur" attribute and OpenAI's "founding date" and other research intelligence attribute elements. In Example 3, we can extract the "Musk—founded—OpenAI" relationship.

Example 2: From "On December 11, 2015, the famous tech entrepreneur Musk, as one of the initiators and funders, founded OpenAI", extract Musk's "tech entrepreneur" attribute and OpenAI's "founding date" attribute.

Example 3: From "On December 11, 2015, the famous tech entrepreneur Musk, as one of the initiators and funders, founded OpenAI and co-chaired the board with Altman," the relationship "Musk—founded—OpenAI" can be extracted.
Step 3: Intelligence Entity Disambiguation.
Through the extraction of the above entities, relationships, and attributes, the MDATA cognitive model extracts intelligence elements from different data sources and associates them in multiple dimensions through spatiotemporal feature operators. To further obtain accurate intelligence information, the MDATA cognitive model uses entity disambiguation techniques to unify the representation of intelligence elements. In Example 4, "马斯克" and "Musk" are equivalent entities from different intelligence sources and are unified into "Musk" through entity disambiguation.

Example 4: Starting from February 2023, Musk has been closely interacting with several engineers from DeepMind on social media. In April 2023, Musk admitted that Twitter purchased 10,000 Nvidia graphics cards.

Through the above steps, the MDATA cognitive model's extraction and computing techniques complete the extraction of OSINT information entities, attributes, relationships, and other elements, providing data support for the construction of MDATA cognitive model quintuples. By repeatedly performing the above extraction process, the MDATA cognitive model quintuple set can be automatically generated, thereby constructing the MDATA cognitive model knowledge graph. A partial representation of the MDATA cognitive model's knowledge representation is shown in Fig. 6.

3.2.2 Computing Techniques Based on the MDATA Cognitive Model Knowledge Representation

The computing techniques based on the MDATA cognitive model knowledge representation are grounded in representation learning theory. They retain graph relational structures, attributes, and spatiotemporal features while learning continuous embedding representations of knowledge, thereby supporting the application of the MDATA cognitive model intelligence knowledge graph in downstream intelligence analysis tasks.

We use a joint embedding method based on spatiotemporal information to transform the quintuples in Fig. 6 into embedding representations, representing intelligence knowledge with spatiotemporal feature constraints. Using two quintuples, <Musk, purchased, graphics cards, 2023-04, Null> and <Tesla, adopted, graphics cards, 2021-06, Null>, as examples, we illustrate the embedding steps of the intelligence knowledge graph as follows.

Step 1: Entity and Relationship Embedding. The ConvE neural network [18] encodes each entity and relationship into embedding vectors. For instance, "Musk" and "OpenAI" are represented as fixed embedding vectors.

Step 2: Spatial Embedding. The joint embedding method based on spatiotemporal information can represent spatial information as embedding vectors. Spatial information can be described using coordinates, regions, directions, etc., to indicate the spatial attributes of quintuples. For example, San Francisco and New York both belong to the USA, so their initial embedding vectors are the same.

Step 3: Temporal Embedding. The joint embedding method based on spatiotemporal information encodes temporal information as embedding vectors, which can be concatenated with entity, relationship, and spatial embeddings for training. Since temporal information is sequential, each timestamp is encoded as an ordered low-dimensional vector to represent the temporal sequence of quintuple information, guiding the model's training. Using the traditional triple model, it is impossible to determine the chronological order of the events <Musk, purchased, graphics cards> and <Tesla, adopted, graphics cards>, which would affect the accuracy of subsequent intelligence reasoning.

Through these steps, we can build computable embedding representations for different quintuples, which is crucial for subsequent intelligence analysis tasks.

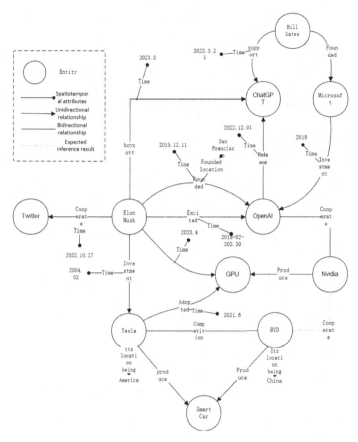

Fig. 6. Knowledge Representation Based on the MDATA Cognitive Model (partial)

3.3 MDATA Cognitive Model Knowledge Inference and Utilization Techniques for Complex Intelligence Clue Associations

Through the content of the previous two sections, we have completed the extraction of intelligence elements, the construction of intelligence knowledge quintuples, and obtained the embedded representations of the intelligence knowledge graph through computation. However, with the exponential growth of OSINT data, the complexity of intelligence associations is continuously increasing. Therefore, to address the issue of complex intelligence clue associations, and to achieve the completion and inference of intelligence clues, as well as the search and discovery of intelligence knowledge, we propose MDATA cognitive model intelligence clue analysis techniques and MDATA cognitive model OSINT extension techniques based on the knowledge inference and utilization technologies of the MDATA cognitive model.

3.3.1 MDATA Cognitive Model Intelligence Clue Analysis Techniques

In the previous sections, we introduced the MDATA cognitive model knowledge inference techniques, which involve completing and inferring quintuples based on attributes, edges, time, and space for elements related to cyberspace security relationships, entities, and spatiotemporal attributes. In the context of OSINT analysis, the MDATA cognitive model intelligence clue analysis techniques are used to discover new intelligence clues or important hidden relationships between intelligence clues through knowledge inference based on existing clues.

Specifically, the task of MDATA cognitive model intelligence clue analysis techniques is to predict the missing parts of quintuples using the embedded representations of intelligence elements (entities, attributes, relationships, etc.) through MDATA cognitive model deduction operators. This enables the completion and inference of intelligence clues based on specific user needs, such as entity inference, relationship inference, and temporal/spatial attribute inference. The inference process generally includes the following three steps:

Step 1: Represent the target entities of the MDATA cognitive model intelligence knowledge base as three concatenated vectors—static feature vector, temporal feature vector, and spatial feature vector—representing the attribute information of the entity.
Step 2: Embed the relationships in the MDATA cognitive model intelligence knowledge base.
Step 3: Calculate based on the entity vectors and relationship vectors to infer unknown knowledge.

Let's explore a typical case of missing tail entity inference in OSINT analysis. Given a quintuple $<v, r, ?, t, s>$, where the head entity v, relationship r, and temporal attribute t, and spatial attribute s are known, the goal is to predict the missing tail entity (?).
News Corpus:
As artificial intelligence technology continues to advance, the development of the intelligent automotive sector is becoming increasingly rapid. Which graphics card manufacturing company might BYD, one of China's more successful new energy vehicle companies, consider establishing a partnership with?

According to existing news, several intelligent automotive companies such as Tesla, NIO, and Xpeng have already introduced large models into their vehicle products and started building their own supercomputing centers. The training of large models requires a vast amount of graphics card resources. Therefore, companies like Tesla, NIO, and Xpeng have established partnerships with the renowned graphics card company Nvidia. Based on this trend, we can infer a high likelihood of a partnership between BYD and Nvidia.

This brief news corpus involves numerous intelligence elements. Extractable entities include "Tesla", "Xpeng", "BYD", "Nvidia", among others, as shown in Fig. 7. The relationships between these intelligence elements are complex. When attributes are added, the multidimensional associative relationships involved in broader OSINT information become even more intricate.

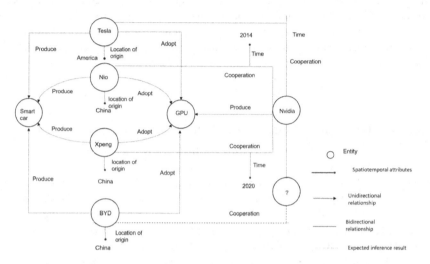

Fig. 7. Knowledge Inference of the MDATA Cognitive Model

To comprehensively and efficiently solve the above problem, the MDATA cognitive model intelligence clue analysis technique is required. This technique formalizes the problem as an entity inference task, namely <BYD, cooperate, ?, t, s>. We use the ConvTransE algorithm [19], as shown in Fig. 8, to predict BYD's potential partners. The specific inference steps are as follows.

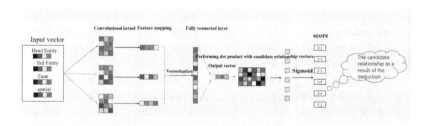

Fig. 8. ConvTransE algorithm

Step 1: Concatenate the given head entity vector (BYD), relationship vector (cooperate), time attribute vector, and spatial attribute vector to obtain a fused vector containing multidimensional information.

Step 2: Use the vector obtained in Step 1 as input, and sequentially pass it through a one-dimensional convolutional layer and pooling layer based on the ConvTransE algorithm (corresponding to convolutional kernels and feature mappings), and a fully connected layer to extract features and adjust dimensions. Output a vector of the same dimension as the tail entity embedding vector.

Step 3: Compute the dot product between the vector obtained in Step 2 and the relationship vectors of all entities in the candidate entity set to calculate the similarity between vectors. Use the similarity as the score for each candidate entity inference result.

Step 4: Among the scores of numerous candidate entities, select the candidate entity with the highest score (in this example, the candidate entity with the highest score is "Nvidia"), thereby obtaining the complete inferred knowledge quintuple <BYD, cooperate, Nvidia, t, s>.

3.3.2   MDATA Cognitive Model OSINT Extension Technology

In the previous sections, we have focused on the MDATA cognitive model knowledge utilization technology, specifically for cyberspace security event knowledge graphs. This involves using MDATA cognitive model computation operators = {QueryOps | SubG, RoadQ, EQ, PQ, TQ, ScopeQ, KNN, …}, which include functionalities such as subgraph matching, reachable path calculation, entity querying, attribute querying, temporal search, and spatial search to meet user-specific knowledge search needs. In the context of OSINT analysis, the MDATA cognitive model OSINT extension technology leverages existing intelligence knowledge graphs to extract crucial intelligence information or form complete intelligence clue chains through knowledge utilization.

Specifically, the main task of the MDATA cognitive model OSINT extension technology is to perform labeled semantic and spatiotemporal indexed query matching using a set of MDATA cognitive model graph computation operators based on intelligence knowledge graphs and their embedded representations. This involves calculating reachable paths in single/multi-hop bridge relationships between people and between people and organizations (projects or technologies) to fulfill user-specific intelligence knowledge search and mining needs. The primary applications of this technology include the following two aspects:

Intelligence Knowledge Quality Ranking: For the problem of intelligence knowledge quality ranking in OSINT analysis question-answering systems, a language model is constructed using combined neural networks, and relevance ranking of intelligence knowledge is achieved through learning-to-rank algorithms.

Clue Association Shortest Path Inference: By utilizing deep learning models such as the neural tensor network model, dimensionality reduction and shortest path scoring and ranking are performed to infer relationships between target entities and query the clue associations between target entities, achieving shortest path-based inference.

Case Study: Shortest Path Inference for Clue Associations in OSINT Analysis.Let's introduce the shortest path inference for clue associations through a case study in a typical OSINT analysis scenario. In this case, given the head entity v, the tail entity u, the time attribute t, and the spatial attribute s, the task is to predict the clue association relationship between the two intelligence entities, i.e., to predict the missing relationship $\langle v, ?, u, t, s \rangle$.

With the global surge of large language models (LLMs), we want to determine from the collected technological intelligence clues whether Twitter is considering training a large language model. According to the collected news corpus, Twitter's CEO Elon Musk has publicly called for a pause in AI development and openly opposed OpenAI's release of the large language model ChatGPT, while secretly purchasing 10,000 GPUs, which are often used by tech companies to train large AI models. Meanwhile, Musk has hired AI talent for Twitter, including AI engineers Igor Babuschkin and Manuel Kroiss from Alphabet's DeepMind. Additionally, Musk's desire to improve Twitter's search functionality and increase ad revenue makes the development of a large language model imperative, suggesting a high likelihood that Twitter is researching large language models.

In the above corpus, the intertwining of intelligence elements is complex and voluminous. We use the MDATA cognitive model OSINT extension technology to formalize the corpus into a relationship inference task, i.e., ⟨Twitter, ?, LLM, t, s⟩, predicting the missing relationship between Twitter and the large language model. The inference steps are as follows, with an example shown in Fig. 9:

Inference Steps

Step 1: Concatenate the vector representations of the given head entity (Twitter), the tail entity (large language model), the time attribute (t), and the spatial attribute (s).

Step 2: Use the result from Step 1 as input, passing it through a one-dimensional convolutional layer and pooling layer based on the ConvTransE algorithm (corresponding to convolution kernels and feature mapping), followed by a fully connected layer to extract features and adjust dimensions.

Step 3: Use the known intelligence knowledge quintuplets such as <Musk, acquire, Twitter, t, s>, <Musk, purchase, GPU, t, s>, <Musk, recruit, Igor Babuschkin and Manue Kroiss, t, s>, <Musk, exit, OpenAI, t, s>, and <Musk, boycott, ChatGPT, t, s> as inputs. Employing the fact that AI engineers, GPUs, ChatGPT, and large language models are all in single-hop relationships as auxiliary information, use deep learning models such as the Neural Tensor Network (NTN) to reduce the vector dimensionality from Step 2 and perform shortest path scoring and ranking. The output will be a vector of the same dimensionality as the relationship embedding vector.

Step 4: Compute the dot product between the vector obtained in Step 3 (i.e., the shortest reachable path) and the vectors of all candidate relationships in the candidate relationship set to determine the similarity between the vectors, using these similarities as the scores for each candidate relationship.

Step 5: Among the scores of the various candidate relationships, select the candidate relationship with the highest score (in this example, the highest-scoring candidate relationship is "develop"). This allows for the inference of the complete intelligence knowledge quintuplet <Twitter, develop, large language model, t, s>.

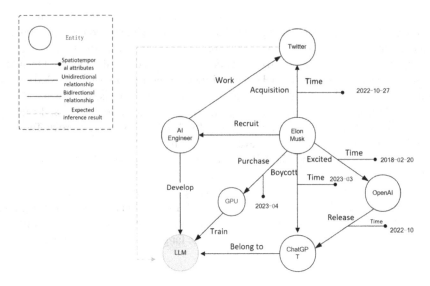

Fig. 9. MDATA Cognitive Model Entity Inference Example

4   MDATA Cognitive Model-Based OSINT Analysis System - TANGENT

4.1   Architecture and Functionality Overview of the TANGENT System

The architecture of the TANGENT system is illustrated in Fig. 10, which includes modules for intelligence knowledge acquisition and storage, system functionality, and system interface.

In terms of data collection, the TANGENT System is capable of collecting data from the entire web, including online social media, academic research reports, newspaper news, internet websites, open-source databases, subscription databases, and more.

For intelligence knowledge acquisition and storage, the TANGENT System processes the collected data through steps such as data cleaning, target virtual identity identification, entity relationship extraction, specific entity linking and disambiguation, spatiotemporal attribute extraction, intelligence knowledge graph construction, and intelligence target library storage. This process extracts intelligence knowledge from the data and stores it in the intelligence target library.

Regarding system functionality, the intelligence analysis process involves six functional modules: intelligence information acquisition, system configuration, intelligence knowledge graph construction, user information search and intent understanding, intelligence analysis, and system presentation. These modules are utilized to gather valuable OSINT.

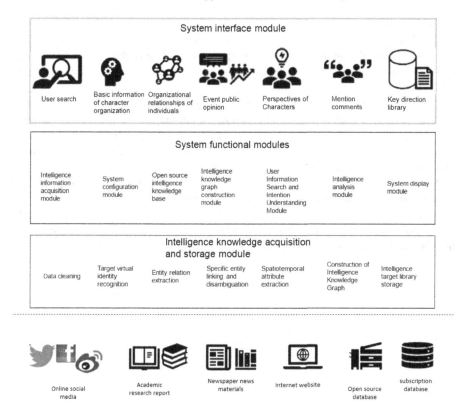

Fig. 10. Architecture of the TANGENT System.

Concerning the system interface, the TANGENT System can display multiple modules, such as user search, basic information about individuals and organizations, relationships between individuals and organizations, public opinion on events, personal opinions, mentioned comments, and key directional target libraries, providing users with a user-friendly interactive interface.

The functional modules of the TANGENT System are illustrated in Fig. 11, and the specific functions of each module are as follows:

User Information Search and Intent Understanding Module: This module understands the user's search intent by preprocessing the user's input, restating the query, analyzing user preferences, and semantically expanding the query. It converts the intent into a formalized query sequence (in the form of quintuples), laying the foundation for the intelligence information acquisition module.

Intelligence Information Acquisition Module: This module retrieves data from multiple sources and channels. Through data cleaning, entity recognition, user query entity linking, extraction of entity attribute values, extraction of intelligence event genes, virtual identity identification, and other sub-modules, it extracts intelligence knowledge from massive data, laying the foundation for the intelligence knowledge graph construction module.

Intelligence Knowledge Graph Construction Module: Based on the knowledge information obtained from the intelligence information acquisition module, this module constructs the knowledge graph through techniques such as knowledge fusion, knowledge verification, knowledge reasoning, and knowledge updating, providing technical support for the intelligence analysis module.

Intelligence Analysis Module: On the existing intelligence knowledge graph, this module performs operations such as relationship mining, network behavior analysis, spatiotemporal correlation analysis, and topic discovery, using techniques such as association analysis and knowledge reasoning, to obtain the intelligence clues needed by intelligence analysts and meet their business requirements.

System Presentation Module: This module presents important information obtained by the intelligence analysis module, such as relationships between individuals and organizations, public opinion on events, and personal opinions, to intelligence analysts.

System Configuration Module: This module mainly includes the personal center of intelligence analysts and the editing and modification of account attributes.

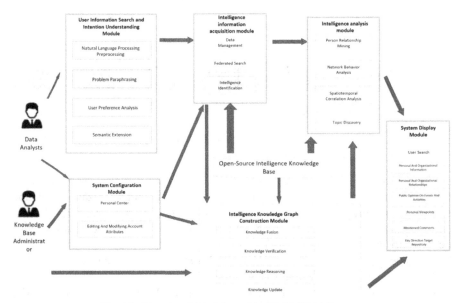

Fig. 11. Functional Modules of the TANGENT System.

4.2 Typical Applications and Effects of the TANGENT System

We take the example of how natural language processing models such as large language models affect the intelligent automotive smart car technology and industrial development intelligence related to the entity "Elon Musk" to illustrate how the TANGENT System achieves OSINT analysis.

The TANGENT System first analyzes user search intent through the User Information Search and Intent Understanding module, helping the Information Acquisition module to obtain intelligence knowledge from multiple channels. We searched for "Elon Musk" in the system, and after intelligent analysis, the system obtained multiple pieces of intelligence entity information related to "Elon Musk," as shown in Fig. 12. Users can merge relevant virtual accounts based on their own knowledge. User-oriented intelligence element fusion is shown in Fig. 13.

Fig. 12. Intelligence knowledge acquired from multi-channel sources by the Information Acquisition module.

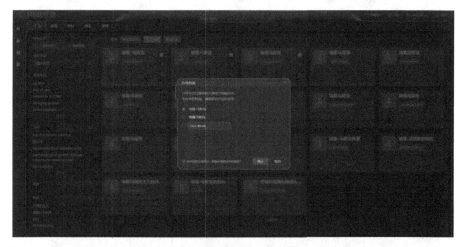

Fig. 13. Fusion of intelligence elements for users.

Faced with massive-scale OSINT data, the TANGENT System extracts and displays relevant information about intelligence elements, such as basic information, personal profiles, associated accounts, work experience, education history, and person-location trajectories, and provides users with the ability to view evidence for each piece of information. The information display page for intelligence elements is shown in Fig. 14. On this page, users can view evidence, manually correct erroneous information, or delete unnecessary information by moving the mouse pointer. After extracting intelligence elements, the TANGENT System integrates intelligence knowledge obtained from multiple channels through the Intelligence Knowledge Graph Construction Module, building a graph of institutions and personal relationships related to Musk, as shown in Fig. 15. By clicking on the central node 'Elon Musk', users can iteratively expand the graph to show more relationships and relevant individuals or organizations. The TANGENT System provides temporal knowledge filtering functionality; users can filter information based on time using the timeline below to quickly access graphs and intelligence for specific time periods.

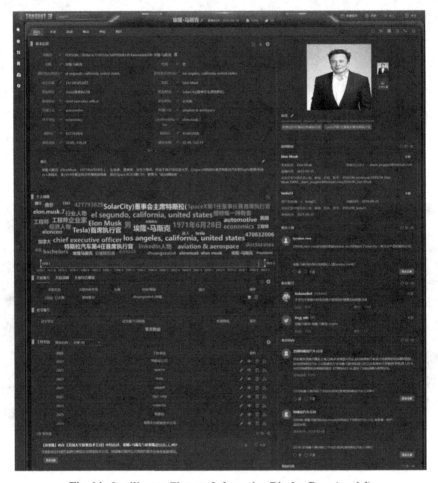

Fig. 14. Intelligence Element Information Display Page (partial)

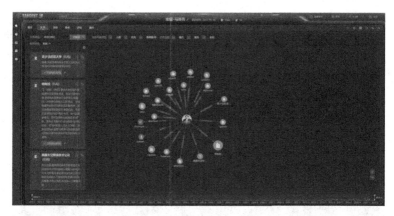

Fig. 15. Schematic of Organizational, Personal, and Account Relationships Related to Musk

On the established intelligence knowledge graph, the TANGENT System's intelligence analysis module can conduct further data analysis on the individuals related to the target intelligence. In Fig. 16, an analysis of 'Person Comments' regarding Musk reveals associated locations, such as 'Shanghai Factory'. If the time range is set to January 2017 and beyond, the page can display multiple pieces of evidence starting from January 2017, indicating Musk's keen interest in cooperating with Chinese companies.

Fig. 16. Illustration of Person Comments Analysis

For frequently evolving temporal and spatial intelligence, the TANGENT System provides users with fully automated rapid updates and deep involvement of data analysts in the update process, ensuring controlled data updates and computations for real-time representation in the open-source knowledge base and intelligence knowledge graph.

For massive global OSINT data, the TANGENT System provides users with the ability to rapidly and batch mine valuable intelligence clues. Through the button in the top right corner of the page, users can create new cases according to the requirements of the analysis event, add relevant individuals and organizations to the case target library, and export relevant data packets and reports, as shown in Fig. 17. Mining the group relationship characteristics of individuals related to Musk, the system proactively expands and discovers the interrelationships between accounts such as those with the same address or colleagues in the target group, and provides interactive display, as shown in Fig. 18.

Fig. 17. Case Creation for Specific Intelligence Event Analysis Requirements

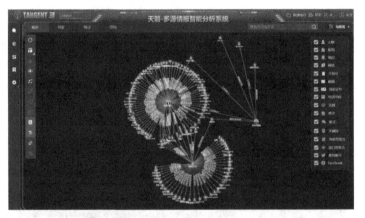

Fig. 18. Illustration of Group Expansion Analysis Capability Provided by the TANGENT System

Note: 'TANGENT - Multi-Source Intelligence Analysis System' in the interface refers to the TANGENT System.

5   Summary

This chapter mainly introduces the application of the MDATA cognitive model in OSINT analysis, provides a detailed overview of existing OSINT analysis technologies, and summarizes their advantages and disadvantages. Next, starting from the three characteristics of massive scale, evolution, and correlation of OSINT, this chapter analyzes the problems faced in OSINT analysis. In response to these issues, this chapter proposes OSINT analysis technologies based on the MDATA cognitive model, including

MDATA cognitive model knowledge representation technology for the spatiotemporal evolution of OSINT, MDATA cognitive model extraction and computation technology for massive scale OSINT, and MDATA cognitive model knowledge inference and utilization technology for the complex correlation of intelligence clues. This chapter also introduces the TANGENT System, an OSINT analysis system based on the MDATA cognitive model, which practically implements comprehensive, accurate, and real-time analysis of OSINT.

References

1. Zhao, Z., Zeng, W.: Analysis of scientific and technical intelligence services under the goals of 'carbon peaking and carbon neutrality.' China Soft Sci. **22**(1), 1–6 (2022)
2. Qin, R.: A brief discussion on intelligence elements. J. Intell. **10**(1), 94–95, 93 (1989)
3. Wei, W.: Design and implementation of public security intelligence information processing system based on element extraction technology. Unpublished doctoral dissertation, Southeast University, Nanjing (2021)
4. Fu, C.: Research and application of open source intelligence mining system for thematic applications. Unpublished doctoral dissertation, University of Electronic Science and Technology of China, Chengdu (2016)
5. Wen, P., Ye, Z., Ding, W., et al.: A comprehensive review of named entity disambiguation research progress. Data Anal. Knowl. Discov. **4**(9), 15–25 (2020)
6. Tang, S., Zhang, L., Zhao, J., et al.: A scalable topic modeling analysis framework for multi-source data. J. Comput. Sci. Explor. **13**(5), 742–752 (2019)
7. Deerwester, S., Dumais, S.T., Furnas, G.W., et al.: Indexing by latent semantic analysis. J. Am. Soc. Inf. Sci. **41**(06), 391–407 (1990)
8. Blei, D.M., Ng, A.Y., Jordan, M.I.: Latent Dirichlet allocation. J. Mach. Learn. Res. **3**(Jan), 993–1022 (2003)
9. Jelodar, H., Wang, Y.L., Yuan, C., et al.: Latent Dirichlet allocation (LDA) and topic modeling: models, applications, a survey. Multimed. Tools Appl. **78**(11), 15169–15211 (2019)
10. Zhou, J.Y., Wang, F.Y., Zeng, D.J.: Hierarchical Dirichlet processes and their applications: a survey. ACTA Autom. Sinica **37**, 389–407 (2011)
11. Li, D.C., Dadanch, S.Z., Zhang, J.Y., et al.: Integration of knowledge graph embedding into topic modeling with hierarchical Dirichlet process. In: Proceedings of NAACL-HLT2019. Stroudsburg: Association for Computational Linguistics, pp. 940–950 (2019)
12. Liu, W., Jiang, L., Wu, Y.S., et al.: Topic detection and tracking based on event ontology. IEEE Access **08**, 98044–98056 (2020)
13. Blei, D.M., Lafferty, J.D.: Dynamic topic models. In: Proceedings of the 23rd International Conference on Machine Learning, pp. 113–120. ICM, New York (2006)
14. Wu, X., Zhang, C.: Research on the method of public event topic evolution based on DTM-LPA: taking H7N9 microblog as an example. Libr. Inf. **3**, 9–16 (2015)
15. Li, X., Fan, M.: Knowledge association in big data. Theory Pract. Intell. **2**(68–73), 107 (2019)
16. Wang, D., Li, Q., Zhang, Z., et al.: Research on the construction method of scientific researcher portrait. J. Intell. Sci. **8**, 812–821 (2022)
17. Xu, W., Dou, Y., Li, W.: Research on the construction method of scientific researcher group portrait considering similar interests. Theory Pract. Intell. **11**(166–172), 142 (2021)

2

18. Jiang, X.T., Wang, Q., Wang, B.: Adaptive convolution for multi-relational learning. In: Proceedings of the 2019 Conference of the North American Chapter of the Association for Computational Linguistics: Human Language Technologies. Stroudsburg: Association for Computational Linguistics, pp. 978–987 (2019)
19. Shang, C., Tang, Y., Huang, J., et al.: End-to-end structure-aware convolutional networks for knowledge base completion. In: Proceedings of the 33rd AAAI Conference on Artificial Intelligence, the 31st Innovative Applications of Artificial Intelligence Conference, the 9th AAAI Symposium on Educational Advances in Artificial Intelligence, pp. 3060–3067. AAAI, Menlo Park (2019)

The Application of MDATA Cognitive Model in Network Public Opinion Analysis

Guandong Xu[1]([✉]) and Binxing Fang[2,3]

[1] The Education University of Hong Kong, Ting Kok, Hong Kong
gdxu@eduhk.hk
[2] Guangzhou University, Guangzhou 510066, China
fangbx@cae.cn
[3] Pengcheng Laboratory, Shenzhen 518066, China

In the era of we-media, there has been a significant change in the patterns of information dissemination. Social media and other digital channels have made it more convenient for people to share information and engage in mutual communication. This has made network public opinion analysis even more important. Network public opinion analysis is a method of collecting, analyzing, studying, and predicting social information, events, emotions, and attitudes in the online sphere. It requires an understanding of the entire public opinion process, including the sources of network public opinion event data, the discovery of public opinion events, and the trends in the evolution of public opinion.

The chapter is structured as follows. Section 1 introduces the concept and technical background of network public opinion analysis, including basic concepts and existing technologies. Section 2 presents network public opinion analysis technology based on the MDATA cognitive model, including the three-dimensional integrated model of the MDATA cognitive model in network public opinion analysis (i.e., network structure, network subject, and network object). Section 3 introduces a case study—the 'Eagle Strike' system—a network public opinion analysis system based on the MDATA cognitive model. Section 4 provides a summary of the chapter's content.

1 Concept and Technical Background of Network Public Opinion Analysis

1.1 Information Dissemination Patterns in the Era of We-Media

In the age of the internet and we-media, the speed and scope of information dissemination have significantly surpassed previous levels. Everyone can express their opinions and views through the internet, and these pieces of information can potentially garner widespread attention and discussion. In such an environment, the management and analysis of network public opinion become particularly crucial. In the era of we-media, information dissemination exhibits the following characteristics.

Socialization of the internet: In the era of we-media, information dissemination is no longer a one-way push of traditional media, but a socialized and interactive process. Users can create personal accounts on social media platforms in cyberspace, generate, publish, share, and retweet content, interact with other users, and exchange opinions and

Y. Jia et al. (Eds.): *MDATA Cognitive Model: Theory and Applications*, LNCS 15470, pp. 181–207, 2025.
https://doi.org/10.1007/978-981-96-3528-3_7

views, all of which have become part of information dissemination. The dissemination method of WeChat Official Accounts (referred to as WeChat OA) is a typical form of network socialization. WeChat OA allow users to establish their accounts, create and publish content, and interact with other users. This socialized dissemination method greatly enhances users' sense of participation and interactivity with information, thereby improving the efficiency of information dissemination.

Faster dissemination: The speed and efficiency of information dissemination are crucial characteristics of the we-media era. Users can generate and publish content anytime and anywhere through devices like smartphones and laptops. Due to this rapid updating, information can swiftly reflect societal hot topics and public sentiment. Taking Sina Weibo (referred to as Weibo) as an example, users can rapidly post various forms of information including text, images, and videos to express their opinions, facilitating the instant dissemination of information. Therefore, Weibo has become an integral part of the public discourse, influencing people's perceptions and attitudes.

Abundance of content: In the we-media era, high-quality content has become key to attracting users. While users can access information through search engines, social media, and other channels, content of superior quality holds greater appeal to them. Therefore, creating and sharing premium, valuable content has become a crucial aspect that we-media practitioners must emphasize. A prominent example of this is the online question-and-answer community, Zhihu. It serves as a social platform primarily focused on knowledge sharing and exchange, where users share their knowledge and experiences, or acquire valuable insights through asking and answering questions. The platform ensures the quality and value of content through rigorous review mechanisms.

Personalized dissemination method: User demands in the we-media era have become increasingly personalized. We-media practitioners must offer personalized services that cater to these demands in order to attract and retain users. Taking the video social app TikTok as an example, it utilizes algorithms to recommend video content that aligns with users' interests, thereby enhancing user engagement and retention. Additionally, TikTok encourages users to create original content, thereby attracting and retaining users through the cultivation of personalized content and styles.

Internet ideology: In the era of we-media, Internet ideology has become an essential tool for enterprises and practitioners. Enterprises need to adapt to the development trends of the Internet and utilize Internet ideology to explore, innovate, and develop their own businesses. Practitioners employ Internet ideology to operate their we-media accounts, promote their content, and better attract and serve users. A successful representative in this regard is Alibaba Group, a typical enterprise that adopts Internet ideology. Its range of Internet service products—including Taobao, Tmall, and Alipay—has profoundly changed people's consumption and lifestyles. Additionally, Alibaba Group also utilizes we-media platforms for brand promotion and marketing, enhancing brand awareness and reputation.

1.2   The Lifecycle of Public Opinion Events

Public opinion can be defined as the biased remarks and viewpoints held towards a certain event or topic. It is not merely an event or piece of news, but rather a comprehensive manifestation of the views, comments, and attitudes of people from all walks of society towards the event or news. Network public opinion typically goes through several stages.

Outbreak stage: The event occurs and attracts a certain level of attention.

Dissemination stage: Relevant information begins to broadcast on the internet, potentially leading to wider attention.

Formation stage of public opinion: The public begins to emotionally react to the event, forming a certain public opinion.

Evolution stage of public opinion: With the passage of time, public opinion undergoes new changes and developments, leading to shifts in the public's attitudes towards the event.

Extinction stage of public opinion: The event gradually loses its momentum, and public attention and discussion about it fade away.

Let's walk through the complete process of public opinion from start to finish using the example of the 'SpaceX Starship Explosion' that occurred on April 20, 2023. On that date, local time in Texas, USA, SpaceX conducted the inaugural test launch of their new heavy-lift rocket, the 'Starship'. Given that this rocket represented the most powerful rocket system to date and held the potential for Mars colonization, the event garnered widespread international attention. Topics related to this event began to broadcast widely across the internet. For instance, discussions emerged on platforms like Zhihu with trending topics such as "How to Interpret Elon Musk's New Heavy-Lift Rocket" and on Weibo with topics like "Breakthrough Technologies in Elon Musk's Heavy-Lift Rocket." These topics allowed the general public to gain a broader understanding of the event, leading to larger-scale discussions. Some netizens criticized Elon Musk's 'Starlink' project and its associated launches, thereby initiating a series of public opinions surrounding the 'Starship' launch.

During this test launch, the rocket became unstable and started to rotate after 2 min and 30 s of liftoff, ultimately disintegrating and exploding. As the event unfolded, public opinion began to shift. For instance, some netizens transitioned from initially supporting Elon Musk's space exploration to questioning whether the test launch was a money-making scheme. Additionally, another group of netizens began to doubt the level of advancement in SpaceX's technology. Several domestic media outlets also published editorials, expressing regret over the failure of the SpaceX Starship test launch and acknowledging the challenges and setbacks inherent in human space exploration. They praised SpaceX's technological innovation and spirit of exploration in space. Subsequently, the incident gradually faded from public view.

From this event, we can see that public opinion incidents often go through several stages: event outbreak, information dissemination, formation, evolution and extinction. As the event continues to unfold, many topics related to the event will emerge. Therefore, Network public opinion topics are an important part of public opinion incidents.

1.3   Concept and Existing Technologies of Network Public Opinion Analysis

Online social networks (referred to as social networks) are a type of social structure formed by the aggregation of individuals and the connections between them. They consist of three elements: relationship structures, network communities, and network information. Among these, the relationship structure provides the underlying platform for the interactive behaviors of network communities, serving as the carrier of social networks. Network communities directly drive the dissemination of network information, serving as the subject of social networks. Network information serves as both the stimulus for and the result of collective behaviors, functioning as the object of social networks.

1. **The carrier of social networks**

The relationship structure serves as the carrier of social networks and is also the fundamental data form that network public opinion analysis needs to utilize. Structural analysis examines the relationships between nodes in social networks to discover the structural characteristics and changes of virtual network communities.

(1) Community

Community: Refers to specific groups, which can be geographical communities or groups with common interests, occupations, etc. People in communities form their own interactive circles in cyberspace for information exchange and opinion expression. The role of communities in network public opinion analysis mainly manifests in the following two aspects.

On one hand, communities serve as crucial mediums for the dissemination of public opinion. Due to the shared values and backgrounds among community members, information circulated within communities is more likely to resonate and be accepted and broadcast easily. The close connections between members within communities expedite the broadcast of information, leading to a wider dissemination effect.

On the other hand, communities are important subjects of network public opinion analysis. By studying the topics, perspectives, and emotions within communities, we can gain a deep understanding of the formation and evolution of public opinion, and reveal the essence and root causes of societal hot-button issues.

(2) Community mining

Community mining is a network analysis technique that can be used to identify community structures within a network. In the context of network public opinion analysis, community mining can be employed to identify social relationships among users on social media, thereby enhancing our understanding of user communication and interaction.

2. **The subject of social networks**

The subject of social networks are network communities. Analysis of social network communities primarily investigates user behavior data, network sentiment data, etc., revealing individual influence, group activity mechanisms, and so on.

(1) Opinion leader mining

Opinion leaders are individuals who frequently provide information to others in interpersonal communication networks and exert influence over others. They play an important intermediary role in the process of mass communication, or act as filters to disseminate information to other users, leading to the further broadcast of information. Opinion leader mining is an important issue in social network analysis, and many scholars are devoted to discovering opinion leaders through the characteristics of social networks. For example, some researchers identify opinion leaders based on features such as the number of articles posted by a user, the number of responses received from others, and the number of followers. However, these methods may encounter information overlap issues due to the neglect of network structure. Information overlap means that discovered opinion leaders may have many common followers, and they may actually only influence a small fraction of people. Some scholars discover opinion leaders by observing network structure; however, this approach often requires a significant amount of time, especially when dealing with large social networks, and the computational performance of the model typically decreases sharply. Additionally, because social networks usually evolve over time, if it takes a week or a month to detect opinion leaders, the results obtained may already be outdated.

Zhai et al. proposed two methods based on interest domain and global measurement algorithms for identifying opinion leaders in BBS [6]. Miao et al. pointed out that opinion leaders often possess diverse expertise and interests, so considering features such as professional knowledge, interests, and number of followers could be beneficial for detecting them [7]. One algorithm utilizes various user features from the network to detect opinion leaders [4, 8, 9]. Li et al. developed a framework that uses information extracted from blog content, authors, readers, and friend relationships to identify opinion leaders [3]. Duan et al. combined clustering algorithms with sentiment analysis to find opinion leaders [8]. Li et al. proposed a hybrid framework for identifying opinion leaders in online learning communities using online learning communities [9].

(2) Sentiment analysis

Sentiment analysis is a text analysis technique used to identify the emotional tone expressed within text. In the realm of online sentiment analysis, it can be employed to discern users' emotional inclinations on social media platforms, thereby providing insights into their attitudes and viewpoints. In recent years, there has been extensive exploration of sentiment analysis in both academia and industry, with a focus on the sentiment classification techniques widely utilized in online sentiment analysis.

Pang et al. (2002) proposed a method for categorizing movie reviews into positive and negative classes using individual words or word combinations as features. Whether utilizing the Naive Bayes algorithm or Support Vector Machine (SVM), this method demonstrated quite satisfactory performance [10]. Additionally, researchers have introduced custom techniques tailored to sentiment classification, such as scoring functions based on words in positive and negative reviews, and aggregation methods using manually curated domain-specific words and phrases [11]. Studies have indicated that employing deep learning methods in sentiment analysis can enhance classification performance; for instance, utilizing Convolutional Neural Networks (CNNs) and Recurrent Neural Networks (RNNs) for sentiment analysis can yield improved classification results. Turney

(2002) proposed an unsupervised sentiment analysis approach that identifies opinion-expressing text through fixed syntactic patterns and conducts sentiment classification [12]. These syntactic patterns are formed based on combinations of part-of-speech tags.

(3) User profiling

User profiling refers to the process of collecting, aggregating, and analyzing personal information to analyze or predict an individual's personal characteristics, such as their occupation, economic status, health, education, preferences, credit, and behavior, forming their personal characteristic model. Significant progress has been made in the research of user profiling, with researchers using multiple data sources and technological methods to extract and analyze personal information. In terms of data collection and processing, researchers utilize multi-channel data (such as social media data, browsing history, purchase records, etc.) and employ data mining and machine learning techniques to extract personal characteristics. In feature selection and representation, researchers use various feature selection algorithms and representation methods, such as text mining, sentiment analysis, topic modeling, etc., to identify and extract important user features. In terms of user classification and modeling, researchers classify and analyze user data through clustering, dividing users into different groups, and establishing corresponding user models.

3. The object of social networking

The objects of social networking are the information shared within the network. Analysis of information dissemination in social networks primarily focuses on swiftly and accurately identifying topics within the network, as well as understanding how topics and information evolve and broadcast across the network. This analysis directly supports applications such as network marketing and network public opinion analysis.

(1) Network public opinion

Network public opinion, also known as internet public opinion, refers to the various viewpoints on social issues that circulate on the internet. It reflects people's perceptions, attitudes, emotions, and tendencies towards a particular public event. It is characterized by virtualization, speed, diversity, openness, anonymity, and interactivity. Network public opinion is typically triggered by sudden social public events, such as natural disasters, major accidents, public health issues, social security, local economy, social governance, official corruption, and other events.

(2) Public opinion event

Public opinion events are the causes of internet public opinion, referring to incidents that occur in specific events and locations in the physical world. Public opinion events mainly include event labels, event names, event descriptions, start/end times of events, locations where events occur, and other information.

(3) Network public opinion topic

Network public opinion topics are collections of relevant reports on a particular public opinion event and serve as the primary carrier for the evolution of internet public opinion. Network public opinion topics typically consist of basic information such as unique topic identifiers, topic names, topic descriptions, topic categories, start/end times of topics, topic popularity, related events, opinion leaders, related documents, parent topics, and child topics. In the analysis of internet public opinion, topic models are often used to quickly obtain the topic distribution of event-related public opinion, helping people conduct targeted analysis and responses based on the type of event. Topic models are mainly divided into latent semantic analysis and latent Dirichlet allocation (LDA). Specifically, latent semantic analysis is a technique used to extract topics from large amounts of text. It uses singular value decomposition (SVD) to reduce the dimensionality of textual data and represent text as vectors. These vectors can be used to compute the similarity between texts, thereby aiding in the understanding of textual data. Latent semantic analysis is typically used in fields such as information retrieval and natural language processing, representing public opinion topics as similar vectors, thus capable of handling synonyms and polysemous words, but not suitable for tasks involving word order and contextual information. LDA is a generative probabilistic model for a collection of texts. It assumes that each document is composed of multiple topics and each topic is composed of multiple words. Compared to latent semantic analysis, LDA can handle complex relationships between existing words and newly added words, but cannot deal with synonyms and polysemous words.

(4) Tracing the sources of public opinion

Public opinion tracing utilizes information retrieval and analysis techniques to trace the origins, dissemination pathways, and scope of public opinion events. The purpose is to understand the true circumstances and context behind these events. By tracing the sources of public opinion, we can gain deeper insights into the background and causes of these events, thereby providing more comprehensive information for network public opinion analysis.

In general, the outbreak of hot events often accompanies a plethora of information from unclear sources. These sources may lack reliability, thereby impacting the accuracy and reliability of social computation. Hence, there is a need for tracing and validating the sources of data. Obtaining complete data on the dissemination chain of such information is almost an impossible task. Therefore, in scenarios where partial observational data is missing, swiftly locating the origins of information can significantly enhance the level of public opinion governance. Several scholars have conducted valuable research on tracing the origins of social network public opinion events. For example, in the context of social computation, research has been conducted on how tracing information can improve people's collaborative work and on constructing topology-based tracing frameworks in decentralized social networks [13–15].

Tracing the sources of public opinion is an emerging research field in recent years. Although there have been some studies on tracing in communication networks, research on tracing in social networks is still very scarce. The main issues in this field currently revolve around how to more effectively conduct tracing analysis on multimodal data in social networks, and how to utilize techniques such as inference analysis to enhance the effectiveness of tracing.

Analysis of network public opinion requires the comprehensive application of various technologies and methods for research and analysis. With the continuous evolution of social media, analysis of network public opinion has become a complex and intricate process, necessitating the continuous updating and refinement of analytical techniques and methods to adapt to the changes and developments in public opinion events. The immense scale of big data from social networks, the multidimensional correlations among subjects, objects, and carriers, as well as the spatiotemporal evolution of public opinion events, all demand a more effective scientific analytical framework.

1.4   Difficulties and Challenges of Network Public Opinion Analysis

1. The '5V' characteristics of big data

The analysis of social public opinion often involves the mining of online data. Due to the practical nature of public opinion analysis, effectively analyzing large-scale online data has become a bottleneck issue. The data from social networks exhibit the '5V' characteristics of big data: First, there is a massive volume (Volume), for example, Weibo has over 500 million users; Second, there is a wide variety (Variety), including text, images, videos, and audio, among dozens of other data types; Third, the data is generated at high velocity (Velocity), such as the peak of 810 million interactions per minute during the WeChat shake feature on the 2015 CCTV Spring Festival Gala; Fourth, there is uncertainty in the data (Veracity), as the complexity and ambiguity of internet information lead to data ambiguity; Fifth, there is inherent value within the data (Value). Moreover, data generated by social media exhibits highly fragmented characteristics due to temporal changes. This means that while facing massive data, we must promptly and effectively filter out a large amount of irrelevant content from the fragmented information. Thus, the challenge lies in how to effectively analyze social public opinion from sparsely dense data with intrinsic value in such circumstances.

2. Multi-dimensional relation of subject, object and carrier

With the continuous emergence of various social media platforms with different functionalities, the development of social public opinion exhibits a decentralization and multi-source trend. These data show strong spatiotemporal correlations; Users post or comment on different social media platforms at different times. Even if the content of the posts or comments is similar, there may be varying levels of response across different platforms. These characteristics pose significant challenges to accurately calculating the influence of internet users. At the same time, it implies that the analysis of network public opinion needs to target different online communities and their information dissemination methods on various social media platforms. The dissemination of public opinion topics is closely related to network structures (through opinion leaders and communities). Different network structures can lead to different influences on public opinion, thereby resulting in varied subsequent responses to public opinion. Hence, the analysis of network public opinion needs to correlate multiple dimensions such as network structures (carriers), subjects, and objects for comprehensive analysis.

3. Spatiotemporal evolution of public opinion events

The focus of topics in public opinion events often changes with the progression of the event. For example, the 'Starship Explosion' incident involves various topics such as space technology, human exploration of space, innovation, entities, capital, culture, and commercial promotion. These characteristics pose significant challenges to the discovery and evolution analysis of topics within networks. The inability to rapidly and accurately understand the overall situation of events and the basic attitudes of public opinion is a major obstacle that drives related research towards mature applications. In such circumstances, rapidly and effectively analyzing the evolution of topics from fragmented, temporally changing short texts data becomes a highly promising approach to enhancing real-time responsiveness performance.

2 Network Public Opinion Analysis Technology Based on MDATA Cognitive Model

The analysis of network public opinion refers to the process of analyzing social networks, participant groups, and topic evolution. It faces challenges such as low effective information density, rapid topic evolution, and difficulty in real-time response.

Building upon the MDATA cognitive model, we deconstruct a typical case of network the analysis of public opinion. In addressing the spatiotemporal evolution of network public opinion, we utilize the knowledge representation method of the MDATA cognitive model to accurately capture the spatiotemporal features related to network public opinion. To tackle the challenge of massive social network data, we employ the knowledge acquisition method of the MDATA cognitive model to accurately extract the elements of public opinion topics and represent these elements as topic vectors through computation, laying the foundation for subsequent rapid and effective vector calculations. To address the complexity of the relationships during the evolution stages of public opinion, we utilize the knowledge utilization method of the MDATA cognitive model for efficient computation of network public opinion, enabling the analysis of community dissemination trends and providing data support for public opinion regulation. The structure of the network public opinion analysis model based on the MDATA cognitive model is illustrated in Fig. 1.

2.1 Knowledge Representation of MDATA Cognitive Model for Spatiotemporal Evolution of Network Public Opinion

Network public opinion is characterized by massive amounts of data and suddenness, which pose difficulties and challenges for the rapid response required in analysis of network public opinion. Traditional knowledge representation methods for network public opinion analysis are typically based on local network analysis and are unable to rapidly and effectively provide comprehensive feedback on the overall internet public opinion situation. In contrast, the MDATA cognitive model's knowledge representation method integrates spatiotemporal features and can represent key elements of network public opinion. Taking the 'Starship Explosion' incident as an example, we illustrate how the knowledge representation method of the MDATA cognitive model represents community relationships in network public opinion events.

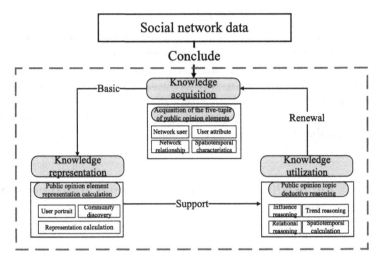

Fig. 1. Structure of network public opinion analysis model based on MDATA cognitive model

(1) Network user representation

In the MDATA cognitive model, network users refer to users who participate in the dissemination and broadcast of network public opinion events. For example, in the incident of Elon Musk speaking out after the 'Starship Explosion', Elon Musk's own social media account is considered a network user (referred to as 'Elon Musk' in this book). The representation of network users, user attributes, and attribute values in the knowledge representation method of the MDATA cognitive model is illustrated in Fig. 2.

(2) User attribute representation

User attributes mainly describe the interests, preferences, and characteristics of users. For example, when user Elon Musk expresses an opinion regarding the Starship explosion, it indicates that Elon Musk is interested in the topic of the Starship explosion. Therefore, the topic attribute value for user Elon Musk is 'Starship explosion'.

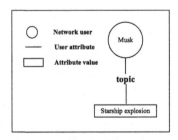

Fig. 2. The representation of network users, user attributes, and attribute values in the knowledge representation of MDATA cognitive model

(3) Network relation representation

Network relationships describe the interactions between network users. For example, users Elon Musk and Zuckerberg mutually follow each other on a social network. Their relationship can be represented as <Musk, follows, Zuckerberg, 2007-03-05, USA> and <Zuckerberg, follows, Musk, 2009-07-05, USA> in the MDATA cognitive model. These two users can be associated through relational elements, as shown in Fig. 3.

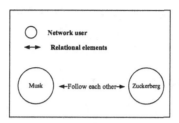

Fig. 3. MDATA cognitive model Knowledge representation in the network public opinion analysis of the relationship elements

(4) spatiotemporal characteristics of public opinion dissemination

Due to the dynamic spatiotemporal characteristics of social network behaviors generated by users, such as following other users, posting personal opinions, and modifying user attributes, the MDATA cognitive model's quintuples <head entity, relationship, tail entity, time, space> accurately represents user behaviors in network public opinion data. Taking the example of user CNTV retweeting (broadcast) Elon Musk's statement regarding the 'Starship Explosion' incident, we illustrate the process of network public opinion dissemination. The spatiotemporal dissemination of this example is depicted in Fig. 4.

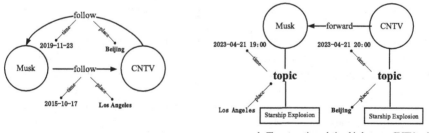

a. The attention relationship between Musk and CNTV

b. The retweeting relationship between CNTV and Musk's blog post on 'Starship Explosion'

Fig. 4. Spatiotemporal dissemination of public opinion

First, we establish the following relationship between users Elon Musk and CNTV, obtaining two quintuples <CNTV, follows, Musk, 2019-11-23, Beijing> and <Musk,

follows, CNTV, 2015-10-17, Los Angeles>. Figure 4(a) clearly depicts the relationship between these two users. After Elon Musk posts related statements about the 'Starship Explosion' incident, CNTV receives the statement and disseminates it in the form of news, leading to a wider broadcast. This process also has spatiotemporal characteristics and can be represented in the MDATA cognitive model by three quintuples: <Musk, topic, Starship Explosion, 2023-04-21 19:00, Los Angeles>, <CNTV, retweets, Musk, 2023-04-21 20:00, Beijing>, and <CNTV, topic, Starship Explosion, 2023-04-21 20:00, Beijing>, as shown in Fig. 4(b). In this representation, each edge signifies an association established. Through the knowledge representation of the MDATA cognitive model, we can effectively construct the dynamic spatiotemporal evolution process of public opinion event dissemination.

2.2 Knowledge Acquisition Method of MDATA Cognitive Model for Data Giant Community Groups

The preceding sections introduced the elements of network public opinion dissemination, proposing that public sentiment broadcasts through social networks as its carrier. However, with billions of pieces of information being posted by internet users every day, the challenge lies in how to accurately and promptly identify topics of public interest amidst this vast amount of data. This constitutes the most crucial and significant scientific issue in the analysis of network public sentiment. As previously discussed, the MDATA cognitive model offers advantages in swiftly and effectively addressing the challenges posed by massive spatiotemporal dynamics. Assuming that users' network communities and individual preferences remain relatively stable over short periods without significant changes, knowledge related to network communities and user profiling can be pre-learned and stored using the MDATA cognitive model. This approach not only enhances the responsiveness of network public sentiment analysis but also enables interpretability in community dissemination analysis.

1. Network user profiling technology

The user community is a key entity in the dissemination of public opinion. User profiling on social networks, as a form of knowledge, can help assess users' attitudes and emotions towards different public opinions, providing a rapid response for user analysis. Taking the analysis of key user profiling characteristics in the 'Starship Explosion' event as an example, let's briefly describe the automated extraction process of constructing user profiling using the knowledge acquisition method of the MDATA cognitive model. After the occurrence of the 'Starship Explosion' event, as key users and related information are continuously collected into the public opinion data repository, a network public opinion analysis system based on the MDATA cognitive model will continually establish knowledge quintuples of users, relationships, and topics. Assuming that historical statements made by user Elon Musk and relevant knowledge about users he has followed have been obtained through the knowledge representation method of the MDATA cognitive model, the next step involves accumulating user characteristics through knowledge acquisition processes such as entity extraction, relationship extraction, and attribute extraction. The specific process is as follows.

(1) Entity extraction

Extract entities from historical statements posted by user Elon Musk on Weibo to obtain relevant entities of interest to the user. For example, from the historical remarks of user Elon Musk shown in Fig. 5, we can use inductive operators to extract elements of public opinion topics such as 'China' and 'space program', thereby discovering Elon Musk's preference for space programs.

Fig. 5. Historical remarks of user Elon Musk posted on Weibo (part)

(2) Relation and attribute extraction

Utilizing the attribute extraction and relationship analysis operators of the MDATA cognitive model, construct user profiling elements related to Elon Musk. Attribute elements include Elon Musk's interests, hobbies, etc., while relationship elements include users followed by Elon Musk and circles with historical interactions. Figure 6 shows a partial list of Weibo friends of user Elon Musk.

Fig. 6. User Elon Musk's Weibo friends list (part)

Through the above case study, it can be observed that with the continuous increase in social network data, the profile of user Elon Musk becomes more comprehensive and specific. By iteratively repeating the knowledge acquisition process based on the MDATA cognitive model, we can automatically obtain and generate quintuple knowledge sets, thereby constructing knowledge graph of network public opinion data based on the MDATA cognitive model, as shown in Fig. 7. This knowledge graph can clearly express the adjacency relationships and interest preferences of user Elon Musk, providing a foundational data basis for determining whether topics will broadcast in the network community.

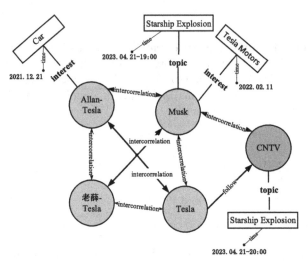

Fig. 7. Knowledge graph of network public opinion data based on MDATA cognitive model (part)

2. **Network community discovery technology**

Network communities are primarily built upon the relationships between internet users and serve as vehicles for the dissemination of network public opinion. The likelihood of public opinion broadcasting widely is inherently linked to the network communities where the opinion originates. The MDATA cognitive model possesses powerful knowledge processing capabilities. For relatively stable network community structures, existing technologies can be utilized to preemptively acquire the network community structures of user groups and incorporate them into the knowledge storage of the MDATA cognitive model. This provides a foundational background knowledge for rapidly responding to the dissemination of public opinion within communities. Essentially, network community discovery technology is computed through user relationship networks, typically modeling the connectivity of network nodes' topological structures using relevant algorithms. Traditional community analysis techniques include greedy optimization algorithms, spectrum analysis methods, and modularity-based analysis methods, among others. With the advancement of deep learning technologies, community analysis based on feature representation has achieved more accurate results. We will illustrate the specific process of network community partitioning using the example of the modularity-based greedy algorithm [16] within the network community where user Elon Musk is situated.

Assuming that for user Elon Musk, we have accumulated relatively comprehensive knowledge of user relationships and user attributes through knowledge acquisition methods, and have constructed a spatiotemporal user relationship network using node relationship extraction algorithms. Figure 8 illustrates user Elon Musk's (part) social network relationships (second-order neighbor).

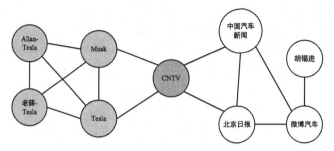

Fig. 8. User Elon Musk's (part) social network relationships (second-order neighbor)

We use Elon Musk as the node to calculate the community partitioning results of the network structure based on modularity using a greedy algorithm. Modularity [16] is a good indicator for measuring the community strength of the network partitioned community structure, and it is defined as:

$$Q = \frac{1}{2m} \sum_{ij} \left(A_{ij} - \frac{k_i k_j}{2m} \right) \delta(C_i, C_j) \tag{1}$$

wherein, A_{ij} represents an element of the adjacency matrix A of the complex network, k_i represents the degree of node i, m represents the total number of connections (number of edges) between all nodes. In a random graph, the probability of an edge's (i,j) existence is denoted by $\frac{k_i k_j}{2m}$, in which case A represents the number of edges in the network graph A; C_i represents the community to which node i belongs. The closer the value of modularity is to 1, the stronger the community structure partitioned from the network, indicating better partition quality. Therefore, we can obtain the optimal community partition of the network by maximizing the modularity Q. The steps for partitioning the community of the second-order neighbor social network relationships of user Elon Musk are as follows.

Step 1: Removing all edges in the network and treating each node as a separate network community, then Fig. 8 can be divided into 9 regions (a total of 9 nodes).

Step 2: Considering each node and its connected components in the network as a network community, and attempting to add edges that are not yet in the network. If a newly added edge connects two different network communities, which merges two network communities. it is necessary to recalculate the modularity increment of the merged network community partition and then merge the two network communities with the largest or smallest increment. Specifically, by substituting each of the 9 users in Fig. 8 into Eq. (1) for calculation. it is found that when the edge (胡锡进, 微博汽车) is added to the network, the resulting modularity increment of the new network community partition is the largest. Therefore, the network communities {胡锡进} and {微博汽车} are merged to form a new network community {胡锡进, 微博汽车}.

Step 3: If the number of network communities is greater than 1, return to Step 2 for further iterations; otherwise, proceed to Step 4. Specifically, continue to execute Step 2 for the new 8 nodes until all nodes in the network are ultimately merged into one network community. This process yields 9 different network community partitions.

Step 4: Traversing through the values of modularity corresponding to each network community partition and select the partition with the maximum modularity value as the optimal partition. When the network community is divided into two communities {Allan-Tesla, 老薛-Tesla, Tesla, Musk} and {CNTV, 中国汽车新闻, 北京日报, 微博汽车, 胡锡进}, the modularity achieves the maximum value. This result represents the optimal partition of the network community, as illustrated in Fig. 9.

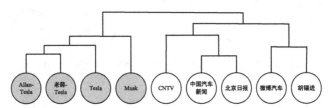

Fig. 9. The optimal partition of network communities

The above steps briefly illustrate the basic process of network community partitioning. By employing various community detection algorithms, different user interest communities are determined and stored as quintuple knowledge in the MDATA cognitive model knowledge base, providing a data computation foundation for the discovery of subsequent public opinion topics.

2.3 Knowledge Utilization Method of MDATA Cognitive Model for Complex Correlation of Public Opinion Topics

The communities and users are relatively stable, while topics, as the objects of network dissemination, have massive and explosively growing characteristics. Public opinion topics have complex relationships with communities and groups. In order to rapidly and accurately discover potential public opinion topics, we have proposed the community dissemination trend analysis technique based on the MDATA cognitive model knowledge utilization method.

In the task of network public opinion analysis, the community dissemination trend analysis technique based on the MDATA cognitive model can utilize the knowledge inference method of the MDATA cognitive model to infer whether topics will broadcast within communities. By employing knowledge inference methods to predict the implicit associations between topics and their respective communities. it forecasts the dissemination trends of topics within communities. This technique primarily leverages existing public opinion knowledge, such as embedded representations of user profiling and community structures, and utilizes the MDATA cognitive model knowledge utilization method to predict the potential associations between users and topics within quintuples.

As shown in Fig. 10, the topic of 'Starship Explosion' has already broadcast within Community 1 (dark nodes) and has influenced key nodes in Community 2 (CNTV). In public opinion assessment, there's a desire to understand whether the 'Starship Explosion' event will propagate and proliferate within Community 2, given that Community 2 comprises accounts and media outlets. If the event broadcasts, it is likely to elicit more user responses, thereby transforming it into a public opinion event. This question can be reframed as whether the topic of 'Starship Explosion' will affect the retweeting and dissemination behavior of users within Community 2, essentially calculating the dissemination probability of the topic.

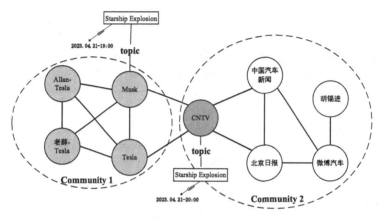

Fig. 10. Broadcasting the topic 'Starship Explosion'

To comprehensively and efficiently model the above problem, it is necessary to transform it into a relational inference problem, namely <北京日报, ?, Starship Explosion, Time, Space>. The inference steps for predicting whether '北京日报' will be involved in the dissemination of the 'Starship Explosion' topic are as follows.

Step 1: Looking up the stored knowledge base to retrieve the embedded vectors of quintuples related to user profiling in Community 1 and Community 2, along with the network structures of both communities.
Step 2: Utilizing graph neural networks to learn the interest preferences of users (CNTV) who have already participated in topic dissemination between communities, as well as the influence between users (edge weights), as depicted in Fig. 11.
Step 3: Employing graph neural networks to calculate the influence level of neighboring nodes of the user '北京日报' (including infected and uninfected users) on the user '北京日报', obtaining a vector representation of the user '北京日报' interest preferences.
Step 4: Extracting the vector representation of the topic entity 'Starship Explosion', and after training with a supervised deep learning algorithm, compute the cosine similarity between the two vectors, using the similarity value as the score for the user's retweet probability.
Step 5: If the probability score exceeds a threshold, then '北京日报' may broadcast the 'Starship Explosion' topic, thereby obtaining the complete quintuple <北京日报,

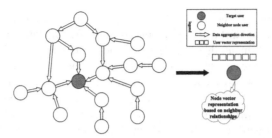

Fig. 11. Shows the relationship between neural network nodes

retweet, Starship Explosion, Time, Space>. Subsequently, iterate to calculate the dissemination likelihood of all nodes in Community 2, based on which the dissemination probability of the 'Starship Explosion' topic in Community 2 can be inferred, determining the trend of public opinion dissemination in the target community.

2.4 Complexity Analysis

Definition: In a public opinion event, let N_1 be the number of topics, N_2 be the number of social network user nodes, N_3 be the number of user attribute elements, and N_4/s be the number of social network user posts per second.

2.4.1 Time Complexity Analysis of Conventional Approaches

For each social network user post data in one second, analyze its relationship with topics, users, and user attributes based on its features to determine and identify the number of effective topics: $T_{a1} = f(N_4,N_3,N_2,N_1) = O(N_4 * N_3 * N_2 * N_1)$. Example: Direct association calculation. For data in a time interval t, analyze the relationships and find all topic spread paths (if the length of the topic spread path is m, then $t \geq m$): $T_{a2} = O((T_{a1})^t)$. The computation time grows exponentially with time t.

2.4.2 Time Complexity Analysis Based on MDATA Approach, Divided into Two Parts

(1) Pre-computation Time

Building the Knowledge Graph. $T_{b1} = g_1(N_3,N_2,N_1) = O(N_3 * N_2 * N_1)$. Building the association relationships between user numbers, user attributes, and topics. **Building the Query Graph for Topic spread Paths**. Assuming there are K topics and the maximum length of each topic spread path is m, $T_{b2} = g_2(N_3, N_2, N_1, m) = O(N_1^m + N_2 + N_3 + m)$. In the worst case, for all N1 topics, the complexity is $O(N1m)$. After the association, add the association relationships between users (such as the propagation relationships between users in the propagation of a topic) to the query graph, and add the time sequence m. Generally, there is no need to add user attribute nodes, but they can be included in the complexity (There may be some special cases involved, but it does not affect the complexity calculation.) For K topics, the time is: $T_{b3} = K \, T_{b2} = O(KN_1^m + N_2 + N_3 + m)$.

(2) Real-time Computation Time

Comprising three parts: determining if a post is related to a topic, building the data graph, and performing subgraph matching. **Determining if a Post is Related to a Topic.** After building the knowledge graph in 1.1, it is only necessary to associate it with user attributes. Then, based on the obtained results, query the corresponding user and event topic content, i.e., $T_{c1} = h_1(N_4, N_3, N_2, N_1) = O(N_4 * N_3 + N_2 + N_1)$. **Building the Data Graph for t Time Data.** After building the knowledge graph in 1.1, only the time and space information (adding 2 nodes) for each topic will be added. Therefore, the number of nodes in the main graph (excluding time and space nodes) does not exceed N_1 (note: generally, only a certain topic is used for calculation, if the entire large graph is considered, it also does not exceed $N_1 + N_2 + N_3$). The number of time and space nodes added per second does not exceed $2N1$. Therefore, the time complexity for building the data graph is: $T_{c2} = h_2(N_3,N_2,N_1,t) = O(N_1 + N_2 + N_3 + 2t * N_1)$. **Subgraph Matching.** The size of the query graph corresponding to each topic spread path does not exceed 3m (propagator, time node, receiver). Let L_1 be the number of nodes in the data graph, $L_1 = O(t * N_1)$, and L_2 be the number of nodes in the query graph, $L_2 = O(m)$. Therefore, the worst-case time for subgraph matching is $T_{c3} = h_3(L_1,L_2,K) = O(K * L_1^{L2}) = O(K * (t * N_1)^m)$. The time complexity of real-time computation is $T_c = t T_{c1} + T_{c2} + T_{c3} = O(K * (t * N_1)^m)$. Where m is a constant (e.g., the maximum length of the spread path is 10), and K is a constant. This time complexity grows poly nominally with t, transforming an infeasible real-time computation problem into a polynomial-time problem.

3 Network Public Opinion Analysis System Based on MDATA Cognitive Model – Eagle Strike System

The previous section mainly introduced the key technologies used in network public opinion analysis with the MDATA cognitive model. This section will introduce how the 'Eagle Strike' network public opinion analysis system based on the MDATA cognitive model achieves the monitoring of public opinion information on mainstream Weibo platforms at home and abroad (such as Sina Weibo, Tencent Weibo, NetEase Weibo, Sohu Weibo, Twitter), and conducts monitoring and early warning for key figures and other custom events in the field of network public opinion analysis. In the aspect of big data analysis in social networks, the 'Eagle Strike' system provides Weibo public opinion monitoring and analysis services, which can conduct in-depth analysis from multiple perspectives such as speech tendencies, social relationships, event correlation relationships, and event development trends. Based on the monitoring and information analysis results, the 'Eagle Strike' system can accomplish tasks such as scheduled posting and intelligent responses.

3.1 Architecture and Functions of the Eagle Strike System

The goal of the 'Eagle Strike' system is to manage, analyze, and mine terabytes (TB) or even petabytes (PB) of Weibo data, providing real-time alerts for sudden network public opinion events and guiding them according to established strategies. The system is divided into four layers, from low to high: scalable distributed computing environment/cloud platform, massive information storage and processing platform, system functional modules, and application of Weibo public opinion event monitoring system, as shown in Fig. 12. Each layer adheres to the specifications of distributed information processing systems, giving the 'Eagle Strike' system significant advantages in terms of availability, security, scalability, and other aspects.

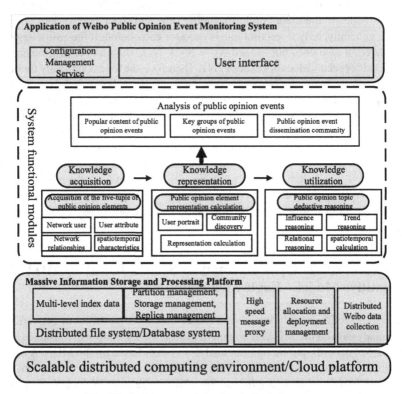

Fig. 12. Architecture of the 'Eagle Strike' system

The 'Eagle Strike' system integrates internet information collection technology and intelligent information processing technology. It achieves real-time collection and preprocessing of information from mainstream Weibo platforms at home and abroad, utilizes natural language processing and intelligent information analysis technology to conduct real-time sentiment learning for network users and blog posts. It also establishes a real-time MDATA cognitive model knowledge base and stores and indexes the knowledge to serve the association analysis of MDATA cognitive model knowledge utilization methods. The system essentially meets the needs of monitoring, early warning, analysis, and interaction on Weibo at home and abroad, and provides practical functions such as mobile phone text message alerts and email reminders for public opinion monitoring. The system is able to meet the comprehensive, accurate, timely, associative, continuous, and customizable requirements of Weibo platform public opinion monitoring, ensuring timely and accurate grasp of the dynamics of public opinion on Weibo platforms.

(1) Knowledge acquisition module

The knowledge acquisition module supports community analysis of user data for monitored individuals on Weibo platforms. It establishes network user preferences through knowledge acquisition, visually presents interaction frequencies, and filters influential users based on interaction rates. Simultaneously, it conducts preference knowledge acquisition for all key users of interest and supports discovery and expansion of key users. Once user preference obtaining is completed, users with similar spatiotemporal attributes and their associated relationships are stored in the knowledge base as quintuples, forming a more macroscopic user network relationship. Additionally, the 'Eagle Strike' system analyzes the relationships of key bloggers to store the interaction processes of user communities, providing a basis for group discovery and community analysis in public opinion events.

(2) Knowledge representation module

The knowledge representation module primarily learns and represents user profiling and network communities, and stores them in a database after establishing spatiotemporal indices. After creating effective user profiling, the module calculates for different users within network communities and implements relevant applications under representation learning. This includes the ability to provide real-time and effective characterization of the subjects of public opinion events through analysis of key monitored communities, laying the groundwork for the analysis of the dissemination of public opinion events.

(3) Knowledge utilization module

The knowledge utilization module is able to collect relevant remarks in real-time based on the user's input micro-topic, thereby achieving monitoring of the micro-topic. This module analyzes the real-time collected data and utilizes MDATA cognitive model knowledge to locate associations within the user community where the topic is being discussed. It also supports the analysis of the dissemination path of posts on the Weibo platform to determine the specific post's dissemination frequency. The module analyzes influential individuals and related dissemination chain layers at the level of impact, meeting the fundamental requirements for the analysis of public information dissemination.

3.2 Typical Application and Effect of Network Public Opinion Monitoring of Eagle Strike System

Next, this section takes the 'Starship Explosion' incident as an example and uses the 'Eagle Strike' system's functional modules to illustrate how public opinion monitoring and analysis are implemented. Firstly, the 'Eagle Strike' system uses user attention information as keywords and user input tags as key keywords for monitoring public opinion events. When the target topic is entered, the 'Eagle Strike' system homepage will display 3 columns of results, namely real-time post monitoring, event public opinion analysis, and analysis results. The analysis column for the event contains various operators/algorithms implemented under the MDATA cognitive model to complete the monitoring and surveillance tasks of public opinion events. The analysis results column in the figure can directly show the trend of event dissemination: regarding the 'Starship Explosion', after the starship exploded on April 20, 2023, there was a peak in public opinion dissemination around April 21. Then, based on the hot time to narrow down the monitoring range, combined with the trend analysis results, it can be concluded that the dissemination of the event peaked at 8 p.m. on April 20, as shown in Fig. 13.

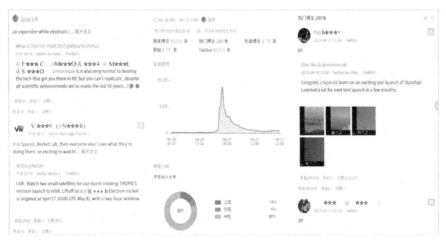

Fig. 13. Monitoring of 'Starship Explosion' by the 'Eagle Strike' system

(1) Community analysis

Faced with massive amounts of public opinion event data, the 'Eagle Strike' system is capable of rapidly and effectively conducting community analysis on a large scale within the context of monitored events. This is presented to users through the Community Circle module's view, as shown in Fig. 14. Utilizing community discovery technology, the system showcases the interconnected relationships among active users based on the real-time dynamics of communities behind public opinion events. This provides an intuitive entry point for group analysis.

(2) User profiling

The key figure analysis module focuses on exploring and analyzing the key character in the community structure who are concerned about the event. As shown in Fig. 15, for the relevant event, the system displays the key groups influencing the dissemination of public opinion events from three dimensions: activity, influence, and number of followers. It analyzes user groups with different levels of influence according to different indicators and continuously adds users of interest to community analysis, providing more accurate group information through feedback on community groups.

Based on the existing group analysis, the 'Eagle Strike' system is capable of displaying the emotional distribution of groups in a time series to illustrate the emotional

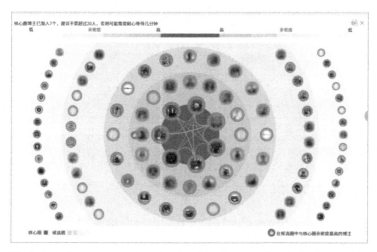

Fig. 14. 'Eagle Strike' system detection visualization of community circles for starship explosion events

(a) Key user monitoring module   (b) Key blog monitoring module

Fig. 15. Key character analysis module of the 'Eagle Strike' system

dynamics of groups towards the target event, simultaneously providing feedback on the public opinion trend of the target event. The emotion analysis reflected in Fig. 16 portrays the overall emotional distribution of the group towards the event, revealing a neutral sentiment trend (84%) for the 'Starship Explosion' event. However, the balanced process of positive and negative emotions leads to a significant polarization among emotionally charged users. When combined with the trend of dissemination, this indicates that the event has been in a rapidly broadcasting trend for a considerable period of time.

Fig. 16. Emotional analysis of public opinion events

(3) Public opinion topic analysis

The 'Eagle Strike' system is capable of real-time blog monitoring, continuously pushing blog content relevant to the theme and providing intuitive semantic situational results for events. In response to the focused information, we conducted an analysis of the dissemination structure of key posts and statements made by Elon Musk following the Starship explosion, discerning the dissemination paths and key nodes of critical blogs, as shown in Fig. 17. The analysis revealed a two-tiered dissemination structure primarily centered around the key node username 'alertatoal'. We also analyzed popular blog posts and hot words related to the event, with the results depicted in Fig. 18.

The above showcases some of the functions of the 'Eagle Strike' system for public opinion monitoring. With comprehensive support from MDATA's cognitive model and spatiotemporal correlation technology, the system can swiftly mine communities involved in the outbreak and dissemination of events from vast real-time internet and social media data. It can identify key disseminating groups and their relevant attributes within these communities, such as discovering influential users and topics of influence. For topics of public opinion events, the system can rapidly analyze key disseminating blog posts, dissemination paths, and the spatiotemporal trends of topics. Following an analytical process encompassing knowledge acquisition, representation, and correlation utilization, the system conducts monitoring and assessment of public opinion events. This approach addresses the challenges of low effective information value density, rapid evolution of public opinion topics, and the need for quick real-time responses in network public opinion analysis. It provides users with reliable data visualization support for swiftly and comprehensively grasping public opinion information and making decisions.

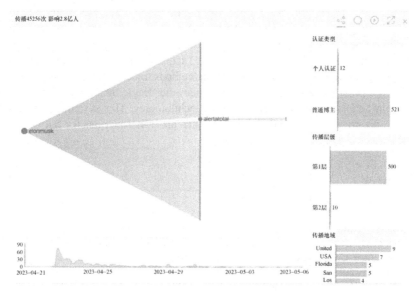

Fig. 17. Analysis of the communication structure of public opinion content

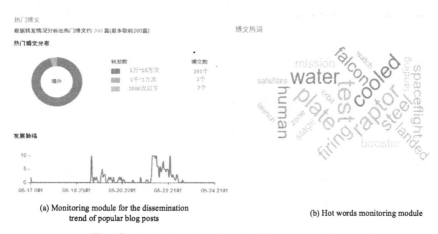

(a) Monitoring module for the dissemination trend of popular blog posts

(b) Hot words monitoring module

Fig. 18. Analysis results of popular blog posts and hot words

4   Summary

This chapter primarily explores the application of the MDATA cognitive model in network public opinion analysis. It begins with a detailed introduction to the concepts and techniques of network public opinion analysis, covering important concepts such as dissemination patterns and lifecycle, and summarizing the application of network space data and artificial intelligence methods in network public opinion analysis. Next, starting from the three-dimensional perspective involved in the study of network public opinion events, it analyzes the characteristics of network public opinion analysis research and the challenges it faces, proposing a network public opinion analysis method based on the MDATA cognitive model. Using the 'Starship explosion' event as an example, the chapter introduces knowledge representation methods that support the spatiotemporal evolution of network public opinion, knowledge acquisition methods tailored to massive community groups, and knowledge utilization methods for complex associations of public opinion topics. Finally, the chapter introduces the 'Eagle Strike' system, a network public opinion analysis system based on the technologies. This system provides early discovery, accurate mining, and correct guidance analysis functions for public opinion events.

References

1. Fang, B., Xu, J., Li, J.: Online Social Network Analysis. Publishing House of Electronics Industry, Beijing (2014)
2. Zhou, H.M., Zeng, D., Zhang, C.L.: Finding leaders from opinion networks. In: 2009 IEEE International Conference on Intelligence and Security Informatics, pp. 266–268. IEEE, Piscataway (2009)
3. Li, F., Du, T.C.: Who is talking? An ontology-based opinion leader identification framework for word-of-mouth marketing in online social blogs. Decis. Support. Syst. 51, 190–197 (2011)
4. Bodendorf, F., Kaiser, C.: Detecting opinion leaders and trends in online socialnetworks. In: Proceedings of the 2nd ACM Workshop on Social Web Search and Mining, pp. 65–68. ACM, New York (2009)
5. Cho, Y.S., Hwang, J.S., Lee, D.: Identification of effective opinion leaders in the diffusion of technological innovation: a social network approach. Technol. Forecast. Soc. Chang. 79(1), 97–106 (2012)
6. Zhai, Z.W., Xu, H., Jia, P.F.: Identifying opinion leaders in BBS. In: 2008 IEEE/WIC/ACM International Conference on Web Intelligence and Intelligent Agent Technology, pp. 398–401. IEEE, Piscataway (2008)
7. Miao, Q.L., Zhang, S., Meng, Y., et al.: Domain-sensitive opinion leader mining fromonline review communities. In: Proceedings of the 22nd International Conference on World Wide Web, pp. 187–188. ACM, New York (2013)
8. Duan, J.J., Zeng, J.P., Luo, B.H.: Identification of opinion leaders based on userclustering and sentiment analysis. In: 2014 IEEE/WIC/ACM International Joint Conferences on Web Intelligence (WI) and Intelligent Agent Technologies (IAT), pp. 377–383. IEEE, Piscataway (2014)
9. Li, Y.Y., Ma, S.Q., Zhang, Y.H., et al.: An improved mix framework for opinion leader identification in online learning communities. Knowl.-Based Syst. 43, 43–51 (2013)
10. Pang, B., Lee, L., Vaithyanathan, S.: Thumbs up? Sentiment classification usingmachine learning techniques. In: Proceedings of the Conference on Empirical Methods in Natural Language Processing, pp. 79–86. ACM, New York (2002)
11. Dave, K., Lawrence, S., Pennock, D.M.: Mining the peanut gallery: opinion extraction and semantic classification of product reviews.In: Proceedings of the 12th International Conference on World Wide Web, pp. 519–528. ACM, New York (2003)

12. Turney, P.D.: Thumbs up or thumbs down?Semantic orientation applied to unsupervised classification of reviews. In: Proceedings of the 40th Annual Meeting of the Association for Computational Linguistics, pp. 417–424. ACM, New York (2002)

13. Nies, T.D., Taxidou, I., Dimou, A., et al.: Towards multi-level provenance reconstruction of information diffusion on social media. In: Proceedings of the 24th ACM International on Conference on Information and Knowledge Management, pp. 1823–1826. ACM, New York (2015)

14. Riveni, M., Baeth, M.J., Aktas, M.S., et al.: Provenance in social computing: a case study. In: 2017 13th International Conference on Semantics, Knowledge and Grids (SKG), pp. 77–84. IEEE, Piscataway (2017)

15. Souza, C., Júnior, J.R., Prazeres, C.: An ontological model and services for capturing and tracking provenance in decentralized social networks.In: Proceedings of the Brazilian Symposium on Multimedia and the Web, pp. 221–228. ACM, New York (2021)

16. Newman, M.E.J.: Modularity and community structure in networks. Proc. Natl. Acad. Sci. **103**(23), 8577–8582 (2006)

Application of the MDATA Cognitive Model in Cybersecurity Evaluation

Weihong Han[1($\boxtimes$)] and Yan Jia[2]

[1] Pengcheng Laboratory, Shenzhen 518066, China
hanwh@pcl.ac.cn
[2] National University of Defense Technology, Changsha 410073, China
jiayanjy@vip.sina.com

Cybersecurity evaluation is an important application direction of cybersecurity and one of the important means and methods for cybersecurity assurance. The cybersecurity evaluation based on the MDATA cognitive model has characteristics such as comprehensiveness, accuracy, quantifiability, and evaluation throughout the entire lifecycle. This chapter mainly introduces the application of the MDATA cognitive model in cybersecurity evaluation.

The structure of this chapter is as follows. Section 1 introduces the definitions, methods, and characteristics of existing cybersecurity evaluation technologies, including classified protection of information system, risk assessment, and scenario-based security evaluation. Section 2 analyzes the main challenges facing current cybersecurity evaluation technologies. Section 3 focuses on addressing these challenges by elaborating on the information system security evaluation technology based on the MDATA cognitive model, including the overall approach and method, test construction process, and quantitative assessment method. Section 4 analyzes and introduces the security evaluation process based on the MDATA cognitive model through an evaluation example. Section 5 summarizes this chapter.

1 Current Research Status of Cybersecurity Evaluation Technology

Cybersecurity evaluation refers to the process of assessing the security status of information systems or their components according to certain standard specifications. This is achieved through a series of technical and managerial methods, testing, evaluating, and certifying the security of information systems, and providing a comprehensive judgment of the corresponding security situation [1].

Cybersecurity evaluation is an important safeguard for the security quality of information technology products and the safe operation of information systems. Regularly conducting cybersecurity evaluation of information systems helps relevant professionals to systematically understand the security of the information systems they manage; it helps responsible parties to identify and remedy deficiencies and prevent problems before they occur; and it facilitates supervision, inspection, and management by public security and governments. As an important and fundamental part of cybersecurity, cybersecurity evaluation not only protects the security of network assets but also has

© The Author(s), under exclusive license to Springer Nature Singapore Pte Ltd. 2025
Y. Jia et al. (Eds.): *MDATA Cognitive Model: Theory and Applications*, LNCS 15470, pp. 208–229, 2025.
https://doi.org/10.1007/978-981-96-3528-3_8

significant implications for ensuring the safe and stable operation of critical national infrastructure and key industry information systems.

Currently, there are three main types of cybersecurity evaluation technologies: classified protection of information system, risk assessment for information system, and scenario-based cyberspace security evaluation. In the following sections, we will introduce the definitions, methods, and processes of these cybersecurity evaluation technologies.

1.1 Classified Protection of Information System

The classified protection of information system should be determined based on the importance of the information system to national security, economic construction, and social life, as well as the degree of harm to national security, social order, public interest, and the legitimate rights and interests of citizens, legal persons, and other organizations caused by the destruction of the information system [2]. The "Information security technology Baseline for classified protection of cybersecurity" (GB/T 22239-2019) divides the security protection level of information systems from low to high into 5 levels [2].

The specific classified protection evaluation work is mainly carried out by third-party organizations with relevant evaluation qualifications [2]. The security to be protected includes both business information security and system service security. The objects affected and the extent of damage may vary. Therefore, the classified protection is determined based on both business information security and system service security. The security protection level of the graded object reflected from the perspective of business information security is called the business information security protection level, and the security protection level of the graded object reflected from the perspective of system service security is called the system service security protection level. The specific process of classified protection includes the following steps [3]:

First, identify the objects affected when damage occurs: ① Identify the objects affected when business information is damaged; ② Identify the objects affected when system services are compromised.

Then, determine the degree of damage to the object: ① Assess the degree of damage to the object caused by the destruction of business information security based on different damaged objects; ② Assess the degree of damage to the object caused by the destruction of system service security based on different damaged objects.

Finally, determine the security protection level: ① Determine the business information security protection level; ② Determine the system service security protection level; ③ Determine the higher level between the business information security protection level and the system service security protection level as the security protection level of the graded object.

Taking the financial industry as an example, industry standards such as "Implementation guide for classified protection of information system of financial industry" [4], "Testing and evaluation guide for classified protection of information system of financial industry" [5], and "Testing and evaluation service security guide for classified protection of information security of financial industry" [6] provide detailed descriptions of the protection objects, basic requirements, technical framework, equipment management, operation and maintenance support, and data storage for classified protection of information system in the financial industry. These guidelines are developed based on the characteristics and actual needs of information systems in the financial industry.

Classified protection of information system has the following characteristics.

① It has been researched and developed for many years, and the related processes and standard specifications are relatively mature;
② There are a considerable number of third-party organizations with relevant evaluation qualifications that can provide evaluation services;
③ It focuses on compliance testing rather than real-world security evaluations, and may not respond promptly to new vulnerabilities and attacks;
④ It is mainly aimed at the evaluation before the information system goes online and is not yet covering the entire lifecycle of the information system.

1.2 Information System Risk Assessment

Information system risk assessment refers to determining the expected amount of loss to the entire system caused by the absence or destruction of each resource in computer systems and networks, and is an assessment of the size of threats, vulnerabilities, and the associated risks [7]. Information system risk assessment helps to understand the information security environment and status, and improve information security capabilities.

According to the national standard "Information Security Technology Risk Assessment Method for Information Security" (GB/T 20984-2022) [7], risk assessment includes the following stages.

Assessment preparation stage. This stage includes determining the objectives of risk assessment, defining the objects, scope, and boundaries of risk assessment, forming the assessment team, conducting preliminary research, establishing assessment criteria, and developing an assessment plan. At this stage, the risk assessment organization should develop a comprehensive risk assessment implementation plan and obtain support and approval from the top management of the organization.

Risk identification stage. This stage includes asset identification, threat identification, existing security measures identification, vulnerability identification, and risk analysis. Based on the identified results, the risk value is calculated.

Risk evaluation stage. In this stage, the risk level is determined according to the risk evaluation criteria. There are several methods for risk assessment, which can be summarized into three categories: quantitative risk assessment methods, qualitative risk assessment methods, and comprehensive assessment methods that combine qualitative and quantitative approaches.

Here is an example of a risk assessment case. Based on risk assessment theory, Zhan Xiong et al. [8] proposed a security risk assessment method based on the fuzzy analytic hierarchy process for assessing the security of the State Grid edge computing information system. The study divided the information system into device layer, data layer, network layer, application layer, and management layer, and provided security assessment items for each layer. For cybersecurity assessment, the study compared the importance of assessment items using the analytic hierarchy process and calculated the overall evaluation value of cybersecurity using a fuzzy comprehensive evaluation matrix. Based on the assessment results, the study constructed a threat model for the State Grid edge computing information system, analyzed the risks, and proposed security reinforcement measures.

The characteristics of information system risk assessment are as follows:

① It has been researched and developed for many years, and the related processes and standard specifications are relatively well-established;
② It is flexible and relatively simple to implement;
③ The main assessment method is inspection and verification, and there is no unified set of risk assessment evaluation indicators, so the results are greatly influenced by the subjectivity of the evaluators;
④ In practice, it mainly focuses on risk assessment during the operational phase of the information systems and has not yet covered the entire lifecycle of the information systems.

1.3 Scenario-Based Cybersecurity Evaluation

Scenario-based cybersecurity evaluation refers to a process where a specific organization recruits selected participants (also known as white hats) through targeted invitations, and these participants conduct penetration testing on the information systems under evaluation at a specified time and location, according to predefined protocols, to determine the security of the target systems.

This is a cybersecurity evaluation method targeting critical information systems, which could be implemented by scenario-based evaluation on real-world information systems, or scenario-based evaluation on cyber ranges. Additionally, we will introduce scenario-based evaluation based on the MITRE ATT&CK framework.

1.3.1 Scenario-based Cybersecurity Evaluation on Real-World Information Systems

Scenario-based cybersecurity evaluation on real-world information systems refer to a security evaluation method where the participants perform attacks and penetration tests on actively running real-world information systems, in order to discover and evaluate the security of those systems and applications. Such security evaluation on real-world information systems often require a sizable organization with relevant qualifications to recruit personnel for participation, and typically consume significant human and material resources.

For example, August 11–15, 2022, the "Yue Dun - 2022" Guangdong Digital Government Cybersecurity Attack and Defense Drill was held in Guangzhou. The theme was to consolidate the cybersecurity base and build a strong security line. This event was organized by the Guangdong provincial government [9]. Fifty top-tier domestic cybersecurity attack teams from organizations like Tencent, 360, QAX, Sangfor, and Sun Yat-sen University participated in this 5-day, "24/7, across-the-weekend" attack and defense drill on real-world information system. The teams conducted drills targeting 120 e-government systems across 50 provincial departments and 21 municipal governments in Guangdong province, comprehensively testing the province's digital government cybersecurity capabilities.

The key characteristics of scenario-based evaluation on real-world information systems are:

① The results are more comprehensive and realistic, allowing for real-time discovery of security issues.
② They may disrupt the actual systems and even lead to serious attack consequences.
③ The attack behaviors are not monitored, and the standardization of the process is not guaranteed.
④ They heavily depend on the skill level of the evaluation participants (invited white hats). In this case, we cannot guarantee the coverage of means of testing. Because fewer issues do not necessarily mean that an information system is more secure, it is difficult to quantify and evaluate the security of an information system through such testing.
⑤ They only evaluate information systems before they are put into production, lacking coverage of the entire system lifecycle.

1.3.2 Cybersecurity Evaluation Based on Cyber Ranges

In recent years, as cyber range technologies have matured and the corresponding systems have become more widespread, an increasing number of cybersecurity evaluations are conducted on these cyber ranges. Cybersecurity evaluation based on cyber ranges refer to a method where a simulated environment of the information systems to be evaluated is first constructed, and then the evaluation participants attack and penetrate the simulated environment to evaluate the security of the systems, applications, and other information products.

For example, on July 31, 2014, the XP Challenge organized by the Evaluation and Exercise Working Group of the Cyberspace Security Association of China (in formation) commenced as scheduled, with 213 pre-approved participants attacking the "targets" [10]. In the XP Challenge operations command center, multiple security products being attacked in real-time were displayed on the large screen, including 360 Security Guard (XP Armor), Baidu Antivirus, North Information Source Golden Armor Defense, KingSoft Anti-Virus (XP Protection Shield), and Tencent PC Manager (XP Exclusive Version) as the "targets" receiving attacks from the participants. By 12 PM on the same day, two security products had already been breached. The five companies temporarily increased bonus to encourage the participants to attack their latest upgraded products.

The key characteristics of cybersecurity evaluation based on cyber ranges are:

① Compared to evaluation on real-world information systems, evaluation on cyber ranges is more flexible in form. The controllable cyber range environment can greatly unleash the subjective initiative of the evaluators, thus effectively expanding the test boundaries and deeply exploring the actual vulnerabilities in the information systems.
② Penetration tests on cyber ranges do not cause damage or impact to the actual running systems, and the attack behaviors can be monitored, making the entire security evaluation more controllable.
③ The information systems deployed on cyber ranges can be synchronized with real-world information systems for upgrades, so this approach can cover the entire lifecycle of the information systems.

④ The performance of cybersecurity evaluation based on cyber ranges depends on how realistically the cyber range simulates the real network. Cyber ranges with low fidelity may fail to completely and accurately replicate all user behaviors when operating the systems, so the evaluation results may differ significantly from those based on real-world information systems, making it difficult to uncover all vulnerabilities.

⑤ The test results are heavily influenced by the subjective factors of the evaluators, and the coverage of the attack methods cannot be guaranteed.

1.3.3 Cybersecurity Evaluation Based on the ATT&CK Framework

ATT&CK is a comprehensive knowledge framework for cybersecurity, which aims to understand and categorize attacker behaviors by observing the actual stages of the attack lifecycle. As it has been widely adopted by vendors and enterprises, the ATT&CK framework has become a mainstream standard for modeling attacker behaviors. cybersecurity evaluation based on the ATT&CK framework refer to a method that uses ATT&CK to guide the evaluation participants in attacking and penetrating the information systems under evaluation, in order to discover and evaluate the security of the systems, applications, and other information products.

MITRE Corporation (Massachusetts Institute of Technology Research Establishment) conducts simulations of different attack groups and evaluates the security products of various vendors each year.

The key characteristics of cybersecurity evaluation based on the ATT&CK framework are:

① The comprehensiveness of the attack plans can be quantified by calculating the coverage rate of the test schemes against the ATT&CK knowledge base.
② It can quickly cover new vulnerabilities and attacks.
③ It can deeply explore the actual vulnerabilities in the information systems.
④ Tests are based on real-world information systems, the attack behaviors are not monitored, and the standardization of the process is not guaranteed.
⑤ The ATT&CK knowledge base is Western-dominated, and the detailed information on specific attack tactics and techniques is not readily available, lacking knowledge related to actual attack methods.

2 Challenges Faced by Cybersecurity Evaluation

Traditional cybersecurity evaluation methods have a rich historical foundation. Compliance systems represented by classified protection and graded protection have made important contributions to China's cybersecurity construction, greatly improving the lower limit of system security capabilities. However, from the perspective of actual users' needs, cybersecurity evaluation not only requires comprehensiveness and high accuracy but also needs to meet real-time evaluation and quantifiability and support the evaluation of the entire lifecycle of the information system under evaluation. Therefore, traditional cybersecurity evaluation methods also face the following challenges.

1. Cybersecurity evaluation needs to be comprehensive. The method of scenario-based cybersecurity evaluation heavily relies on the level of evaluators (invited white hat hackers). The more capable the evaluators are, the more security issues could be found, and vice versa. Under this evaluation method, fewer problems being discovered does not necessarily mean that the information system is more secure, so the comprehensiveness of the evaluation results cannot be guaranteed.
2. Cybersecurity evaluation needs to be accurate. Existing attack methods gradually show the characteristics of specialization, systematization, and scenario-orientation. Traditional cybersecurity evaluation methods usually rely on the experience of testing experts, and the accuracy and pertinence of the obtained test results often depend on the level of the experts, which leads to uneven testing effects among various institutions. If a knowledge base with scenario-specific characteristics can be used in the process of formulating the evaluation scheme, the accuracy and response speed of the generated test scheme will be improved.
3. Cybersecurity evaluation needs to support real-time evaluation. Traditional methods are usually based on known vulnerabilities and attack methods and are not sensitive to emerging new vulnerabilities and endless new attack techniques. Traditional cybersecurity evaluation methods use vulnerabilities publicly disclosed and recorded in the vulnerability database to test the security of the system. When new vulnerabilities are discovered or new attack methods emerge, traditional methods may not be able to identify and evaluate these vulnerabilities and threats in a timely manner.
4. Cybersecurity evaluation needs to support quantifiable results. The method of scenario-based cybersecurity evaluation heavily relies on the level of evaluators (invited white hat hackers). Therefore, under this testing method, we cannot determine the coverage of security testing methods and further cannot measure the level of information system security based on the number of problems found.
5. Cybersecurity evaluation needs to support entire lifecycle evaluation. Traditional cybersecurity evaluation is usually conducted on information systems in the post-production operation stage, without evaluating the security of information systems in other stages, making it difficult to achieve entire lifecycle evaluation. The "Information Security Technology Risk Assessment Method for Information Security" [7] released in 2022 introduced the concept of lifecycle, which proves the importance of entire lifecycle evaluation. However, in the current actual evaluation, security evaluation in the post-production operation stage is still the main focus.

3   Security Evaluation Process Based on the MDATA Cognitive Model

The overall framework of security evaluation based on the MDATA cognitive model is shown in Fig. 1. The cybersecurity evaluation process mainly consists of the following 4 steps.

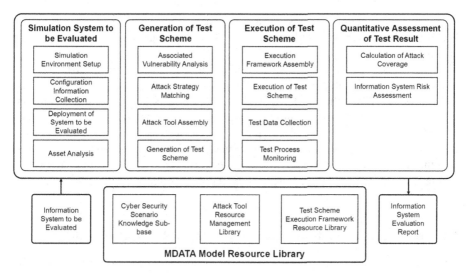

Fig. 1. Overall framework of cybersecurity evaluation based on the MDATA cognitive model

Step 1: Evaluation preparation based on the MDATA cognitive model. First, build a security evaluation simulation environment. Then, testers obtain global network topology, network configuration, asset list, security defense measures, and other information from the administrator of the information system to be evaluated, and deploy the information system to be evaluated in the simulation environment according to the obtained information. Finally, based on the multi-dimensional characteristics such as time, space, and semantics of the evaluated information system, deconstruct the cybersecurity specific scenario sub-knowledge base (such as education network scenario, enterprise network scenario, power network scenario, automobile network scenario, etc.) from the overall cybersecurity knowledge base to prepare for the construction of the test scheme in the next step.

Step 2: Test scheme construction based on the MDATA cognitive model. First, testers match the network topology, network configuration, asset list, security defense measures, and other information obtained in step 1 with the MDATA cognitive model in the cybersecurity scenario knowledge sub-base to discover possible vulnerabilities and weaknesses of the information system to be evaluated. Then, with the possible vulnerabilities and weaknesses of the information system to be evaluated, use the MDATA cognitive model to match knowledge in the cybersecurity scenario knowledge sub-base and provide available attack strategies. Finally, combine the attack tools associated with the attack strategies recommended by the MDATA cognitive model to provide all possible test schemes.

Step 3: Test scheme execution based on the MDATA cognitive model. First, the evaluators combine the MDATA cognitive model to provide all possible test schemes, as well as manually identify attack points that can be used to implement attacks to improve the test scheme. Second, the evaluators use the MDATA cognitive model and test scheme to perform associated matching on the framework resource management library to find the test execution framework related to the test scheme. Finally, the evaluators execute the test scheme containing all possible attack paths and check and record the test results. In addition, the evaluators should also rely on the cyber range to monitor the evaluation process and collect test process data.

Step 4: Quantitative assessment of evaluation results based on the MDATA cognitive model. First, evaluators calculate the coverage of attack tactics/techniques/sub-techniques involved in the attack test, and conduct a risk assessment of the information system in this test, including quantitative calculations of assets, weaknesses, and threats, as well as attack detection and blocking capabilities. Second, perform a comprehensive calculation on the attack coverage and information system risk assessment results, and quantitatively grade the information system's defense capabilities based on the calculation results. Finally, provide a complete test report containing the test process and the above analysis results.

3.1 Preparation for Evaluation Based on the MDATA Cognitive Model

Before starting the evaluation, the security evaluation team needs to clarify the basic information of the information system to be evaluated, the evaluation objectives, and the evaluation scope to provide sufficient guidance for the subsequent evaluation work.

After the security evaluation is initiated, the first step is to construct a simulation environment for the security evaluation and deploy the information system to be evaluated in the simulation environment according to the network topology. The construction of the security evaluation simulation environment is a very important step. Conducting security evaluations in a simulation environment can ensure that the tests will not have a negative impact on the production environment. Furthermore, the degree of simulation of the system under evaluation directly determines the quality of the security evaluation results. Therefore, the simulation platform must be able to provide flexible configurations for the internal programs of the target network nodes in various ways and provide multiple methods such as network device virtualization and virtual switch traffic mirroring to improve the fidelity of the target network. It should also provide unified resource management to support the construction of the target network.

The construction process of the cybersecurity scenario knowledge sub-base based on the MDATA cognitive model can be described as follows. First, we need to collect multi-dimensional features (time, space, and semantics) and scan the results of the objects to be scanned and detected. Then, we utilize the MDATA cognitive model in conjunction with the information to perform rough matching in the cybersecurity knowledge base. This knowledge base contains security knowledge for various scenarios (such as education, enterprise, power, and automotive industries, etc.) and security incidents involving attacks carried out by hacker organizations from different countries and regions, with different attack resource repositories, tactics, and techniques systems. The MDATA cognitive model constructs a cybersecurity scenario-specific knowledge sub-base using security knowledge and security incidents related to similar scenarios in the knowledge base. This can reduce the scope of subsequent knowledge matching, thereby improving the speed and accuracy of the matching response.

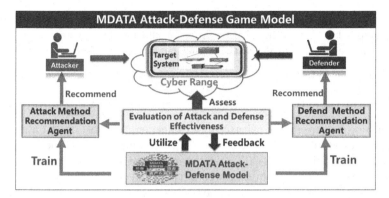

Fig. 2. MDATA Attack-Defense game model

Based on the MDATA attack-defense game model illustrated in Fig. 2, the process begins with utilizing the generated MDATA attack-defense model. This model integrates information about the target system gathered through various sensing mechanisms and contextual details about the current attack-defense scenario. The objective is to recommend optimal attack and defense strategies tailored to the specific conditions of the scenario.

The recommendations are implemented and their effectiveness is carefully evaluated to assess the impact of the chosen strategies. Based on this assessment, further recommendations are generated for subsequent attack and defense actions. These recommendations are then fed back into the MDATA attack-defense game model library, allowing for continuous refinement and adaptation to evolving scenarios and threats.

The specific workflow is as follows:

Step 1: Training and generating recommendation agents for attack-defense strategies. Using the MDATA framework, intelligent agents are trained to identify and propose effective methods for both attack and defense. These agents leverage historical data, learned patterns, and real-time inputs to provide context-aware recommendations.

Step 2: Attack recommendation agent. This agent is responsible for analyzing the current attack-defense dynamics and suggesting actionable attack methods to the attacking entity. The recommendations consider factors such as system vulnerabilities, attack paths, and resource allocation.

Step 3: Defense recommendation agent. Similarly, this agent focuses on the defender's perspective, offering strategies to mitigate or neutralize potential attacks. It takes into account the defender's current capabilities, the nature of the threat, and potential countermeasures.

Step 4: Iterative optimization based on attack-defense effectiveness. The implemented strategies are evaluated through rigorous testing and simulation to measure their success. The results of this evaluation are used to iteratively refine both the attack and defense recommendation processes. This continuous loop ensures that the MDATA model evolves to remain effective against emerging threats and changes in the operational environment.

This iterative and adaptive approach not only enhances the accuracy of the recommendations but also ensures that the MDATA attack-defense game model remains dynamic and responsive to the fast-changing landscape of cybersecurity threats and defenses.

3.2 Construction of the Test Schemes Based on the MDATA Cognitive Model

In conducting scenario-based cybersecurity evaluation, the most crucial aspect is the construction of a test scheme based on the MDATA cognitive model. The detailed steps are as follows: Utilizing the MDATA cognitive model and the sub-knowledge base of the cybersecurity scenario, the evaluator can collect potential vulnerabilities and weaknesses in the information system under evaluation, recommend usable attacks and associated attack tools, and combine the recommended attacks to generate corresponding tactical plans for system security assessment. Furthermore, the MDATA cognitive model will prune rules at each step to streamline the recommendation process, thereby reducing the recommendation space and preventing an exponential growth in the number of candidate test schemes. The recommendation process at each step is described below.

Firstly, the evaluator utilizes the MDATA cognitive model to conduct knowledge matching within the constructed cybersecurity scenario sub-knowledge base. This matching process is performed on the information gathered from the previous step, encompassing the target system's network topology, open ports with corresponding running services, and implemented security defense measures. By aligning the collected data with the sub-knowledge base, the model can recommend potential vulnerabilities and weaknesses that may exist in the information system under evaluation. Beyond promptly providing comprehensive details about potential vulnerabilities and weaknesses, such as types, CVE identifiers, severity levels, and attack vectors, thereby evaluating exploitability and impact magnitude of vulnerabilities and weaknesses, the MDATA cognitive model is also capable of laying the groundwork for threat modeling based on an in-depth analysis of these security flaws. At this stage, the model integrates practical experience to conduct a thorough review of the recommended vulnerabilities and weaknesses, identifying and eliminating any contradictory recommendations to ensure consistency and reliability of the results.

Secondly, for the vulnerabilities and weaknesses identified in the evaluated information system, the MDATA cognitive model is utilized to perform knowledge matching within the cybersecurity scenario sub-knowledge base, recommending potential attack vectors that could be leveraged. Concurrently, the model retrieves relevant attack tools from the attack tool resource library associated with these recommended vectors. These attack tools encompass various malicious software and exploitation utilities, such as backdoors, trojans, and brute-force cracking tools. At this juncture, the MDATA cognitive model will integrate practical experience to conduct a thorough review of the recommended attack vectors and tools, identifying and eliminating any contradictory recommendations to ensure consistency and reliability of the results.

Finally, the evaluators leverage the MDATA cognitive model, along with the recommended attack vectors and their associated attack tools, to orchestrate the combination of attack tools and generate test scheme proposals, resulting in a list of candidate test scenarios. Throughout this process, the model is integrated with practical experience to conduct a comprehensive review of the generated candidate test scenarios, identifying and eliminating any contradictory recommendations, thereby ensuring the consistency and reliability of the final test scheme output.

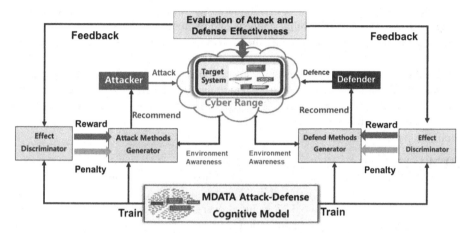

Fig. 3. Recommendation of attack and defense methods based on MDATA model

In the context of the MDATA attack-defense game model, as depicted in Fig. 3, the integration of Generative Adversarial Networks (GANs) and Reinforcement Learning (RL) techniques offers a robust framework for simulating and enhancing cybersecurity strategies. Based on MDATA training, attack and defense generators and discriminators are created to recommend attack and defense strategies. These methods are refined and adjusted continuously in real-world scenarios.

The MDATA model provides a structured approach to representing and analyzing complex cybersecurity scenarios. By incorporating GANs and RL, the MDATA model can simulate dynamic attack-defense interactions, allowing for the generation of realistic attack scenarios and the development of responsive defense strategies. This integration facilitates a continuous feedback loop, where the performance of defense mechanisms informs the refinement of attack simulations, and vice versa, leading to a more resilient cybersecurity posture.

In summary, the combination of GANs and RL within the MDATA attack-defense game model offers a sophisticated methodology for modeling, simulating, and enhancing cybersecurity strategies. This approach enables the proactive identification of vulnerabilities and the development of adaptive defenses, thereby strengthening the overall security framework.

3.3   Execution of the Test Schemes Based on the MDATA Cognitive Model

Upon the completion of test scheme construction, the evaluator will leverage the MDATA cognitive model and the test scheme execution framework resource library to recommend and adopt automated or semi-automated testing frameworks for executing the generated test scheme. However, due to the complexity of the attack environment, target environment, and the diverse nature of security issues associated with the test subject, fully automated execution of the test scheme is often challenging to achieve. The current approach typically involves a semi-automated method that combines automated execution with manual execution to carry out the generated test scheme encompassing all possible attack paths. The purpose of automated script execution is to leverage tools or scripts for automated vulnerability analysis and exploitation, while manual execution allows the testing personnel to ensure the correctness, coherence, and completeness of the attack paths throughout the testing process by orchestrating the test scheme, modularizing vulnerabilities, and monitoring the execution process. Additionally, the evaluator should utilize a simulated target environment to monitor the evaluation process and collect data from the testing procedures. The following are examples of typical penetration testing and vulnerability exploitation frameworks that security evaluators can employ to facilitate semi-automated execution.

(1) Metasploit

Metasploit is an open-source security vulnerability exploitation and testing tool that integrates common vulnerabilities and popular shellcode across various platforms. The latest version 6.3.13 includes over 2,300 exploitation methods for popular operating systems and application software vulnerabilities. As a security tool, Metasploit plays an indispensable role in security testing, and it can be leveraged along with existing payloads for automated testing.

(2) Immunity CANVAS

CANVAS framework, developed by Immunity Inc., is an automated vulnerability exploitation tool that includes hundreds of exploitation modules, covering a wide range of operating systems, devices, and services such as Windows, Linux, UNIX, network devices, application software, and middleware. It supports automated path testing methods like single-point, multi-point testing and provides detailed log recordings.

(3) Brutus

Brutus is a powerful Python-based vulnerability exploitation framework, which is capable of automating network-based vulnerability exploitation testing and web-based reconnaissance activities. The framework adopts a modular design approach, offering high scalability, and employs a multi-tasking and multi-processing architecture, ensuring exceptional performance.

(4) Shennina

Shennina is a powerful automated host penetration and vulnerability exploitation framework. It leverages artificial intelligence techniques to achieve full automation of security scanning, vulnerability scanning, and exploitation. Additionally, it employs intelligent cluster-based vulnerability exploitation and managed concurrent design, enabling high-performance execution. Shennina covers more than 40 tactics and techniques from the ATT&CK framework.

3.4 Quantitative Assessment of Evaluation Results Based on the MDATA Cognitive Model

Quantification refers to the process of converting a certain thing or concept into specific values or indicators, also known as quantitative analysis. Quantification helps us to describe and understand the security status of information systems more objectively and accurately. The system security evaluation based on the MDATA cognitive model evaluates the security status of information systems from two aspects: attack tactics and techniques coverage and information system risk assessment. The calculation methods for these two aspects are introduced below.

3.4.1 Attack Tactics and Techniques Coverage

Attack tactics and techniques coverage indicates the proportion of tactics and techniques used in simulated attacks within the entire cybersecurity knowledge base, reflecting the comprehensiveness of the simulated attack assessment. If the attack tactics and techniques coverage is below the threshold, it indicates that the selected tactics and techniques for the current assessment are limited and cannot assess the security status of the information system comprehensively and accurately, thus the assessment cannot proceed normally. If the attack tactics and techniques coverage is above the threshold, the assessment can proceed, and the attack tactics and techniques coverage can be used alongside other indicators to calculate the security status and defensive capabilities of the information system. The attack tactics and techniques coverage includes three aspects: tactics coverage, techniques coverage, and sub-techniques coverage. The evaluators and the personnel responsible for the system under test communicate and jointly determine the attack coverage threshold for the test. When the attack coverage is below the threshold, the test ends, or the attack is reconstructed; when the attack tactics and techniques coverage is greater than or equal to the threshold, the assessment continues. The specific calculation formulas for attack tactics and techniques coverage are shown in formulas (1) to (4).

$$\text{Tactics Coverage} = \text{Number of Tactics Used in Simulated Attack} \div \text{Total Number of Tactics} \quad (1)$$

$$\text{Techniques Coverage} = \text{Number of Techniques Used in Simulated Attack} \div \text{Total Number of Techniques} \quad (2)$$

$$\text{Sub} - \text{Techniques Coverage} = \text{Number of Sub} - \text{Techniques Used in Simulated Attack} \div \text{Total Number of Sub} - \text{Techniques} \quad (3)$$

$$
\begin{aligned}
\text{Attack Tactics and Techniques Coverage} = &\ \text{Tactics Coverage} \times \text{Tactics Coverage} \\
&\text{Weight} + \text{Techniques Coverage} \times \text{Techniques Coverage Weight} + \text{Sub} - \text{Techniques} \\
&\text{Coverage} \times \text{Sub} - \text{Techniques Coverage Weight}
\end{aligned}
\quad (4)
$$

The risk assessment of an information system quantifies the assets, threats, and weaknesses. Combined with the results of attack detection and attack blocking from the current assessment, the overall risk assessment result of the system is obtained.

3.4.2 Risk Assessment of Information System

Assets, threats, and weaknesses are the three elements of security risk management that can reflect the security status of an information system. Quantifying assets of an information system can clarify the value, importance, and relationships of assets. Quantifying threats of an information system can clarify the types of threats likely to occur, and their frequency. Quantifying weaknesses of an information system can identify various vulnerabilities, defects, and errors in the system. By quantifying assets, threats, and weaknesses, the risk value of each asset can be obtained, and thus the risk value of the entire information system can be determined. The security status of the information system can be measured by the ratio of the system's risk value to the attack tactics and techniques coverage. Next, we introduce the quantitative calculation methods for assets, threats, and weaknesses.

(1) Asset Quantification Method

Assets [2] are valuable information or resources to an organization and are the objects of security policy protection. Common assets include network devices, servers, applications, databases, and network services. Based on the scope of the assessment, an asset list is formed and asset values are assigned. The value of assets is manually input and agreed upon by both parties involved in the assessment. Asset values range from 1 to 5, with 5 levels in total, which can be referenced from the literature [2].

(2) Threat Quantification Method

Threats [2] are potential factors of undesired events that may result in harm to a system or organization. Threats can be internal or external, intentional or unintentional, technical or human. Common threats include phishing attacks, ransomware attacks, worm attacks, trojan attacks, distributed denial-of-service (DDoS) attacks, and social engineering attacks. Threat values ultimately reflect the likelihood of risk occurrence and range from 1 to 5, with 5 levels in total, which can be referenced from the literature [2].

(3) Weakness Quantification Method

Weaknesses [2] refer to the defects, vulnerabilities, or errors in the network environment that may be exploited by attackers. Weaknesses can be technical or non-technical, including software vulnerabilities, misconfigurations, human errors, etc. The evaluation of weakness values needs to consider two factors: one is the severity of the weakness, i.e., the extent of damage it would cause to the asset if exploited; the other is the exposure level of the weakness, which depends on the effectiveness of current control measures. If the controls are effective, the exposure level of the weakness will be relatively low. The weakness value ultimately reflects the consequences of risk occurrence. As shown in Table 1, based on the damage caused to the asset by the exploitation of the weakness, the weakness value ranges from 1 to 5, with 5 levels in total. The specific values can be referenced from the literature [2].

Table 1. Risk level assessment table

Risk Level		Risk Value
Very High Risk	VBI	Greater than 80
High Risk	HBI	Greater than 48 and less than or equal to 80
Medium Risk	MBI	Greater than 32 and less than or equal to 48
Low Risk	LBI	Less than or equal to 32

The risk value of an information system is the sum of the risk values of all assets within the system. The process involves calculating the risk value for each asset, followed by determining a weighted sum of the individual asset risk values. By referencing the predefined risk level definitions in Table 1, the current risk level and corresponding security status of the information system can be derived from the aggregate risk value. The risk levels of an information system are divided into four categories: Low (less than or equal to 32), Medium (greater than 32 and less than or equal to 48), High (greater than 48 and less than or equal to 80), and Very High (greater than 80). The specific calculation formulas are shown in formulas (5) and (6).

$$\text{Asset Risk Value} = \text{Asset Value} \times \text{Weakness Value} \times \text{Threat Value} \quad (5)$$

$$\text{Total Information System Risk Value} = \sum_{(i=1)}^{n} \text{The Risk Value of asset } i \quad (6)$$

3.4.3 Evolution and Improvement of MDATA Model

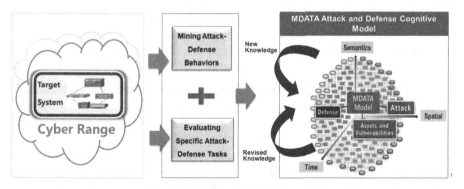

Fig. 4. Evolution of MDATA model

In the realm of cybersecurity, the continuous evolution and refinement of the MDATA attack-defense cognitive model are paramount as shown in Fig. 4. This progression is significantly enhanced through the mining of attack-defense behaviors within cyber ranges and the subsequent evaluation of specific attack-defense tasks.

(1) Mining Attack-Defense Behaviors in Cyber Ranges

Cyber ranges serve as controlled, simulated environments where cybersecurity professionals can engage in realistic attack and defense exercises. By analyzing the behaviors exhibited during these exercises, valuable insights can be gleaned regarding the tactics, techniques, and procedures (TTPs) employed by both attackers and defenders. This behavioral mining process involves collecting data on attack vectors, defense mechanisms, response times, and the effectiveness of various strategies. The insights derived from this analysis are crucial for identifying patterns and anomalies, which can inform the development of more robust security measures.

(2) Evaluating Specific Attack-Defense Tasks

Beyond behavioral analysis, it is essential to assess the outcomes of specific attack-defense tasks conducted within the cyber range. This evaluation focuses on the success rates of various attack methods, the resilience of defense strategies, and the overall effectiveness of the engagement. By systematically reviewing these outcomes, one can determine which tactics were most effective, which defenses were most resilient, and where vulnerabilities may exist. This evaluative process provides a quantitative basis for refining the MDATA model, ensuring that it accurately reflects the complexities of real-world cybersecurity scenarios.

(3) Continuous Improvement of the MDATA Model

Integrating the insights gained from mining attack-defense behaviors and evaluating specific tasks leads to the iterative enhancement of the MDATA model. This continuous improvement process involves expanding its knowledge base to encompass new attack vectors and defense mechanisms. By incorporating real-world data and experiences, the MDATA model becomes more adept at simulating complex attack-defense interactions, thereby providing a more accurate and effective tool for cybersecurity analysis and strategy development.

In summary, the dynamic interplay between mining attack-defense behaviors, evaluating specific tasks, and refining the MDATA model fosters a cycle of perpetual enhancement. This cycle not only strengthens the model's predictive capabilities but also contributes to the broader field of cybersecurity by providing a more nuanced understanding of attack-defense dynamics.

4   Example of the Peng Cheng Cyber Range Security Evaluation Based on the MDATA Cognitive Model

The Peng Cheng Cyber Range is a large-scale scientific facility for research, evaluation, and analysis of cyberspace security. The facility is based on software/hardware and network resources and simulates a specific Internet. It is used for exercise guidance, platform management, attack, defense, and five-party collaboration to support security talent training, attack and defense drills, cybersecurity product evaluation, and verification of new network technologies. The Peng Cheng Cyber Range has successfully implemented four application modes: "inside to inside", "inside to outside", "outside to inside", and "outside to outside". It provides strong support for talent training, attack and defense drills, network infrastructure security testing, information product security testing, and the "Operation Cyberguard" campaign. In the fields of autonomous vehicles, unmanned aerial vehicles (drones), rail transportation, defense fueling, and others, Pengcheng Laboratory actively conducts research based on the Peng Cheng Cyber Range, proposes security technology evaluation methods, establishes testing platforms, and playes a role in security assurance.

4.1 Evaluation Preparation Based on the MDATA Cognitive Model

We will use the university campus scenario shown in Fig. 5 to illustrate the process of constructing a security evaluation test based on the MDATA cognitive model. This scenario simulates a typical university network architecture, divided into three major zones: internet zone, branch campus zone, and university internal network zone. Internet zone includes routers and testing machines for security evaluation. University internal network zone consists of an external service zone, an isolation zone, and an internal network zone. The external service zone deploys applications that directly provide external services, the isolation zone deploys servers such as databases, and the internal network zone deploys internal services and applications for the school, such as the personnel management system and course selection system. The branch campus zone accesses the business systems via dedicated lines.

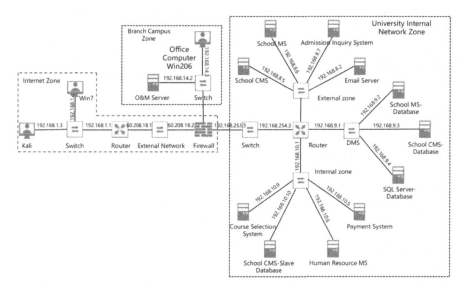

Fig. 5. Network topology of a university campus scenario.

The Internet area consists of routers, firewalls, and an external network, with two host machines, Kali (192.168.1.3) and Win7 (192.168.1.4), used as testing machines by the evaluators. Their gateway is the router in the Internet area. The Internet router has a target address translation policy that allows for port mapping of Kali and Win7, which is used for backdoor and session establishment during penetration process. The two host machines operated by the evaluators can also access the internal university network through ports opened by the firewall, allowing for penetration testing of the internal network.

4.2 Generation of Test Schemes Based on the MDATA Cognitive Model

To describe the security evaluation process based on the MDATA cognitive model concisely without losing completeness, we choose to describe the complete test process of an asset node SchoolCMS:192.168.8.5 of the current evaluation information system. Evaluators use the general scanning and detection tools (such as Nmap, DirBuster) and specific vulnerability scanning tools (such as OpenVAS, Nessus, etc.) recommended by the scenario sub-knowledge base to scan the open ports of target machine, as well as the services and valid URLs running on it. The results show that Nmap detected OpenSSH V5.5 running on port 22, LibSSH V0.8.1 running on port 23, and Apache Httpd V2.4.39 running on port 80. Port 53 is open but does not have any service information. In addition, the evaluators obtained that the target machine's operating system is Linux.

Evaluators use the MDATA cognitive model to match the collected asset information with the cybersecurity knowledge base and discover two potential penetration risks associated with the assets. The first is that the asset LibSSH V0.8.1 has the CVE-2018-10933 vulnerability, and the second is that OpenSSH may have weak password vulnerabilities. Relevant penetration attacks and associated attack tools are recommended for these two vulnerabilities and risks. The knowledge graph of the complete asset information collected, the recommended vulnerability information, and attack tool information for this node are shown in Fig. 6.

Vulnerability: The MDATA cognitive model, combined with the cybersecurity scenario knowledge base, provides the following five tuples:

<LibSSH V0.8.1, includes, CVE-2018-10933, 2018, NaN>.

This asset node has the CVE-2018-10933 vulnerability, which is a remote command-line authentication bypass vulnerability that allows bypassing SSH authentication by modifying the authentication status in the SSH request message, thereby allowing command-line operations on the target machine.

Test scheme 1: The MDATA cognitive model, combined with the cybersecurity scenario knowledge base, provides the following five tuples:

<CVE-2018-10933, exploit, msfvenom, NaN, NaN>;
<CVE-2018-10933, exploit, BurpSuite, NaN, NaN>;
<CVE-2018-10933, exploit, exp.py, NaN, NaN>.

This vulnerability can be exploited through a backdoor program, and three tools, msfvenom, BurpSuite and exp.py, are recommended for generating, uploading, and bypassing authentication to execute the backdoor. Msfvenom is a backdoor program generation tool that generates corresponding backdoor programs based on the target's operating system or service type, such as Linux backdoors, Windows backdoors, PHP backdoors. BurpSuite can upload constructed packets with paths for trojans or backdoors. The exp.py is a vulnerability exploitation script for the CVE-2018-10933 vulnerability.

Weakness: The MDATA cognitive model, combined with the cybersecurity scenario knowledge base, provides the following five tuples:

<OpenSSH, includes, weak password weakness, NaN, NaN>.

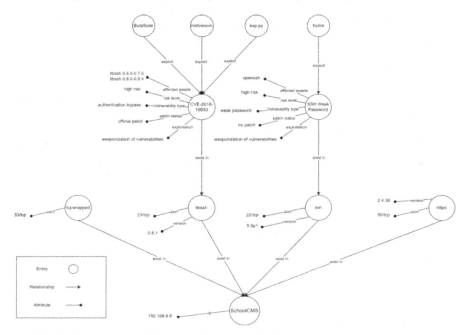

Fig. 6. Knowledge graph example of vulnerabilities and attack tools for the test node.

This asset node has weak password weaknesses, which may include simple passwords like "password", "admin123", "123456", etc.

Test scheme 2: The MDATA cognitive model, combined with the cybersecurity scenario knowledge base, provides the following five tuples:

<weak password weakness, exploit, Hydra, NaN, NaN>.

The above vulnerability can be exploited by password cracking tools, and Hydra is recommended to brute-force assets with weak passwords.

4.3   Execution of Test Schemes Based on the MDATA Cognitive Model

After executing the two test schemes mentioned above, through test scheme 1, we obtained administrator privileges using the generated and executed backdoor programs (Msfvenom, BurpSuite, exp.py). However, test scheme 2 did not successfully exploit the weakness. Furthermore, using tools such as Msfconsole, AntSword, Rdesktop, and combining them with administrator privileges, we performed file management, virtual terminal control, database management, and other operations on the target. We further discovered and controlled the master-slave database of SchoolCMS. With this, we have completed the penetration operation on the current target machine.

4.4 Quantitative Assessment of Evaluation Results Based on MDATA Cognitive Model

In this subsection, we introduce the process of quantitatively assessing the security state of an information system after testing is completed.

First, we introduce the calculation of attack tactics and techniques coverage (based on the ATT&CK framework V10 version). The ATT&CK framework V10 version has a total of 14 tactics, 188 techniques, and 379 sub-techniques. In the current scenario test, 14 tactics, 85 techniques, and 84 sub-techniques were simulated and constructed. The calculated attack tactics and techniques coverage is 81.11%, meaning the attack tactics and techniques coverage exceeds the agreed-upon threshold of 80%, meeting the evaluation requirements.

Table 2. Example of quantification of assets in a test path.

Asset Name	Asset Value	Threat Value	Weakness Value	Risk Value
SchoolCMS	2	5	4	40
SchoolCMS-database	2	3	2	12
SchoolCMS-slave database	2	2	3	12

To concisely yet completely describe the quantitative assessment process based on the MDATA cognitive model, we choose to describe the quantitative assessment process for a single test path within the current evaluation information system. For instance, as shown in Table 2, the attack objects involved in a certain path include SchoolCMS, SchoolCMS-database, and SchoolCMS-slave database, with asset values of 2, 2, 2, respectively. Based on the ATT&CK tactics used to attack these assets during the attack process, the corresponding threat values are 5, 3, 2. According to the attack results, the weakness values of these assets are 4, 2, 3, respectively. Therefore, the risk values for the assets SchoolCMS, SchoolCMS-database, and SchoolCMS-slave database are 40, 12, 12, respectively. Thus, the total risk value of the information system in this test path is 64.

5 Summary

This chapter introduced the application of the MDATA cognitive model in security evaluation. The information system cybersecurity evaluation method based on the MDATA cognitive model achieves comprehensive, accurate, real-time, and quantifiable security evaluation of information systems, and supports the evaluation of information systems throughout their entire lifecycle. Under the current new trends in security evaluation, the information system cybersecurity evaluation method based on the MDATA cognitive model, to a certain extent, solves new problems and new requirements that traditional methods cannot address. It provides a new perspective and approach to security evaluation.

References

1. Jianchun, J.: Information Security Engineer Tutorial, 2nd edn., p. 379. Tsinghua University Press, Beijing (2020)
2. Committee, N.I.S.S.T.: Information security technology Baseline for classified protection of cybersecurity: GB/T 22239–2019. China Standard Press, Beijing (2019)
3. Committee, N.I.S.S.T.: Information Security Technology - Classification Guide for Classified Protection of Cybersecurity: GB/T 22240–2020. China Standard Press, Beijing (2020)
4. People's Bank of China. Implementation guide for classified protection of information system of financial industry: JR/T 0071-2012. Beijing: People's Bank of China (2012)
5. People's Bank of China. Testing and evaluation guide for classified protection of information system of financial industry: JR/T 0072-2012. Beijing: People's Bank of China (2012)
6. People's Bank of China. Testing and evaluation service security guide for classified protection of information security of financial industry: JR/T 0073-2012 [S]. Beijing: People's Bank of China (2012)
7. Committee, N.I.S.S.T.: Information Security Technology Risk Assessment Method for Information Security: GB/T 20984–2022. China Standard Press, Beijing (2022)
8. Xiong, Z., Hao, G., Xiaoyun, H., et al.: Research on security risk assessment method of state grid edge computing information system. Comput. Sci. **46**(S2), 428–432 (2019)
9. Government Services and Data Management Bureau of Guangdong Province. "Yuedun-2022" Guangdong Province Digital Government Cyber Security Attack and Defense Drill was opened [EB/OL]. (2022-08-11)[2023-04-30].
10. Nan Ting. CyberSecurity Association of China Organizes XP System Security Attack and Defense Drill [EB/OL]. (2014-08-01) [2023-04-30].

Author Index

Printed in the United States
by Baker & Taylor Publisher Services